W9-BRU-333

DISCARD

'Taking you into the world never reached by today's journalism – cutting through the simplistic headlines of fear – this book is a brilliant description of what it's like to live within a modern insurgency. If you want to know what's really going on outside the Western pleasuredome, you should read this book.'

— Adam Curtis, writer–director of *Bitter Lake*
and *HyperNormalisation*

'Mary Harper knows more about, cares more about and writes better about Somalia than any other foreign correspondent I know. This book will become the defining account of Al Shabaab and its times.'

— Fergal Keane, former BBC South Africa correspondent

'Mary Harper has listened to Somalis' stories for decades, at considerable risk to life and limb. She captures the voices of those who join Al Shabaab, tolerate it, fear it, or would die fighting it. This unique book offers precious insights into the movement, and some slender hope for peace.'

— Michela Wrong, author of *Borderlines*

'This brave, nuanced and revelatory book chronicles the emotional and social impact of living in a state in the grip of terror. Mary Harper skilfully unravels the complex network of relationships that leads many Somalis to collaborate with Al Shabaab, and many foreigners to profit from its presence.'

— Lindsey Hilsum, International Editor, Channel 4 News

'A brilliant book. With brave energy and precision born of long experience, Harper vividly brings to life Al Shabaab fighters as I've come to know them over the past decade-and-a-half. This is a must-read for all those interested in the contemporary history of the Horn of Africa.'

— Mohammed Adow, Senior International Correspondent,
Al Jazeera English

'Mary Harper has written the essential book on Al Shabaab. With the gift of simplicity—allowing Somalis from all walks of life to speak for themselves— she has accomplished the remarkable task of allowing the reader to understand Africa's most resilient jihadist group.'

— Alex de Waal, Executive Director, World Peace Foundation,
and Research Professor, Fletcher School of Law and Diplomacy,
Tufts University

'Mary Harper has brilliantly pieced together something rare: an exhaustive account of human suffering that we've all collectively failed to notice. She has captured all angles of the conflict, from the fighters' zero-sum arithmetic to the very human stories of those living in Al Shabaab's wide zone of influence.'

— Hussein Sheikh Ali, Chairman, Hiraal Institute, and former national security advisor to the Somali government

'One of the most detailed examinations of Al Shabaab, and a great book about Somalia. Harper has drawn on her long experience reporting on the region to explain the political and social context allowing Al Shabaab to survive, with great sensitivity to the culture and resilience of the Somali people.'

— Richard Barrett, Director, The Global Strategy Network, and former Director of Global Counter-Terrorism Operations, British SIS

'Mary Harper has written an astonishingly good book—not about Al Shabaab, but about the Somalis who have lived under the militant group's control for more than a decade, and who know Al Shabaab not only as terrorists, but as brothers, neighbours and friends.'

— Bronwyn Bruton, Deputy Director, Atlantic Council Africa Center

'A massively insightful and rounded perspective of Al Shabaab's workings, thinking and governance, put into perspective by the experiences of those living under Al Shabaab. Mary Harper's journalistic professionalism, her humanity and deep understanding of Somalia make a major contribution to understanding Al Shabaab's growth and evolution.'

— Mark Bowden, former UN Resident and Humanitarian Coordinator for Somalia

'Only Mary Harper could have written such a vivid and insightful account of the perils and opportunities of daily life under Al Shabaab. This brilliant book allows the reader to understand the resilience of Al Shabaab as a political and military force through the voices of Somalis themselves.'

— Sara Pantuliano, Acting Executive Director, Overseas Development Institute

'Everything you wanted to know about Al Shabaab but were afraid to ask. This splendid book draws unique insight from Harper's years of reporting from and on Somalia, benefiting from her sharp journalistic eye and engaging writing. Essential reading for understanding this highly nimble, adaptable and resilient violent Islamist movement.'

— Alex Vines OBE, Head of the Africa Programme, Chatham House

'No one knows the Horn of Africa—and Somalia—like Mary Harper. No one else could have written such an intimate account of Al Shabaab. Her very human stories bring an important and untold chapter of the region's recent past—and present—to life.'

— Seth Kaplan, Professorial Lecturer, Paul H. Nitze School of
Advanced International Studies, Johns Hopkins University,
and Senior Adviser for the Institute for Integrated Transitions

'A must-read. Harper tells the story of Somalis and Al Shabaab like no one else before her—taking the reader on a gripping, deftly mapped journey to unmask this secretive, violent group by revealing its complex, and often surprising, human impact.'

— Judith Gardner, co-editor of *Somalia—The Untold Story: The War
Through the Eyes of Somali Women*

'Mary Harper has written an important and disturbing book on Somalia's Al Shabaab. Drawing on her personal encounters with Somalis, she describes our complicity in sustaining one of the world's most enduring violent insurgencies.'

— Mark Bradbury, Rift Valley Institute, and author of *Becoming Somaliland*

'Mary Harper has found a unique, compassionate way to tell the complex story of Al Shabaab. Much has been written about the organisation, but rarely do we hear of the human cost of its atrocities, from those most affected. It is their voices that are raised up by this book.'

— Idil Osman, journalist, and Senior Teaching Fellow, Department of
Development Studies, SOAS University of London

'Mary Harper combines long personal experience, analysis, compassion and journalistic craft in this compelling volume—an accessible "must-read" for anyone trying to understand the phenomenon of Al Shabaab.'

— Michael Keating, Executive Director, European Institute of Peace, and
former UN Special Representative of the Secretary-General to Somalia

EVERYTHING YOU HAVE TOLD ME IS TRUE

MARY HARPER

Everything You Have Told Me Is True

Is True

The Many Faces of Al Shabaab

HURST & COMPANY, LONDON

First published in the United Kingdom in 2019 by
C. Hurst & Co. (Publishers) Ltd.,
41 Great Russell Street, London, WC1B 3PL
© Mary Harper, 2019
All rights reserved.
Printed in India

The right of Mary Harper to be identified as the author of
this publication is asserted by her in accordance with the
Copyright, Designs and Patents Act, 1988.

Distributed in the United States, Canada and Latin America by
Oxford University Press, 198 Madison Avenue, New York, NY 10016,
United States of America.

A Cataloguing-in-Publication data record for this book
is available from the British Library.

ISBN: 9781787381247

This book is printed using paper from registered sustainable
and managed sources.

www.hurstpublishers.com

CONTENTS

LIST OF ILLUSTRATIONS

1. Beach to the south of Mogadishu. Photo by Mary Harper.
2. Ruins in central Mogadishu. Photo by Mary Harper.
3. Ruins of the old Italian cathedral, Mogadishu. Photo by Mary Harper.
4. Boys and girls await food handouts from Al Shabaab during the 2011 famine. Photo courtesy of Al Shabaab.
5. Children with their handouts from Al Shabaab during the 2011 famine. Photo courtesy of Al Shabaab.
6. Private security guard at an internally displaced people's camp, Mogadishu. Photo by Mary Harper.
7. Crazy wires in Hargeisa, Somaliland. Photo by Mary Harper.
8. A newly refurbished shop in Mogadishu. Photo by Mary Harper.
9. Bakara market, Mogadishu. Photo by Mary Harper.
10. An internally displaced people's camp, Mogadishu. Photo by Mary Harper.
11. A Koranic school in an internally displaced people's camp, Mogadishu. Photo by Mary Harper.
12. Dr Habeb with one of his patients in the Habeb Mental Hospital. Photo by Mary Harper.
13. Patients in the Habeb Mental Hospital. Photo by Mary Harper.
14. Making salt, south of Mogadishu. Photo by Mary Harper.
15. Former Al Shabaab office, Mogadishu. Photo by Mary Harper.
16. Old parliament building, Mogadishu. Photo by Mary Harper.

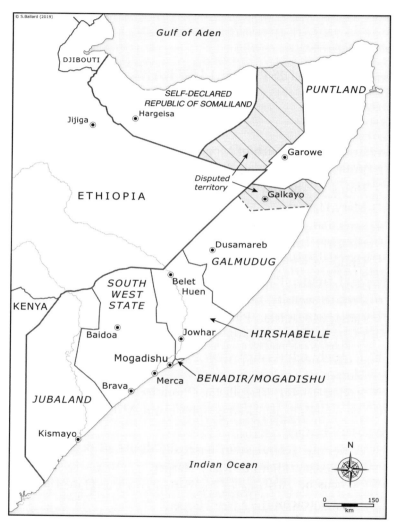

© S.Ballard (2019)

Gulf of Aden

DJIBOUTI

PUNTLAND

SELF-DECLARED
REPUBLIC OF SOMALILAND

Hargeisa

Jijiga

Garowe

Disputed
territory

Galkayo

ETHIOPIA

Dusamareb

GALMUDUG

SOUTH
WEST
STATE

Belet
Huen

KENYA

Baidoa

Jowhar

HIRSHABELLE

Mogadishu

BENADIR/MOGADISHU

Brava

Merca

JUBALAND

Kismayo

Indian Ocean

N

0   150
         km

Map of Somalia & surrounding region

ACKNOWLEDGEMENTS

This book is the result of years of reporting from and on Somalia. I have had hundreds of conversations with people, mainly Somalis, about what it is like to live in the shadow of a violent Islamist movement. I have also had dozens of discussions with members of Al Shabaab. These conversations form the building blocks of the book.

I would like to thank everybody who has spoken to me, some of whom have taken great risk by doing so. Many others, Somalis and non-Somalis, have helped me in other ways. I do not feel it is appropriate or safe to name the people who have contributed to the book. They know who they are and I want them to know how grateful I am. I would also like to pay tribute to the friends and acquaintances whose lives have been lost in Al Shabaab and other attacks.

Thanks too to my agent Rachel Conway at Georgina Capel Associates, to Michael Dwyer, Lara Weisweiller-Wu and Farhaana Arefin at Hurst, and to those who read through and perfected the manuscript. Thank you to the former editor of BBC Focus on Africa, Robin White, and his deputy, Elizabeth Ohene, for teaching me how to be a journalist. Most of all, I would like to thank my family for putting up with my absences, both when I travel to Somalia and other countries in the region, and when I bury myself in my writing.

INTRODUCTION

'You went into a shop on the ground floor of a multi-storey building. When you came out, you were holding a tube of Pringles potato crisps.' The voice on the telephone is a familiar one. It is one of my contacts in the violent Islamist group Al Shabaab. 'Then you walked to the bank next door, but it was shut. You knocked on the doors and tried to open them. You took some photos. Your bodyguards were not at all professional. They were wandering about, chatting amongst themselves with their guns slung around their shoulders, instead of keeping watch over you.'

The man, whose voice is soft and quietly assured, goes on to tell me that before visiting the shop and bank in downtown Baidoa, I had been to a school where the girls wore yellow uniforms.

Baidoa is a city in south-western Somalia. The innermost parts are protected by local forces, including a fierce militia known as the *darwish*; the outskirts by a ring of mainly Ethiopian troops serving as part of an African Union intervention force, AMISOM. Beyond that is open country and Al Shabaab, one of the most successful Islamist insurgent movements of the twenty-first century. Although there have been deadly internal disputes over the group's ultimate aims, including whether or not it should fight to establish a global caliphate, its senior members

1

are united in their desire to overthrow the Somali government and establish an Islamic state in the country based on sharia law. Al Shabaab has been in existence for many years and has shown a remarkable capacity for endurance. It emerged in the mid-2000s, at a time when a group of sharia courts, known as the Islamic Courts Union (ICU), briefly controlled much of southern and central Somalia. The courts rose to power in June 2006 after unexpectedly defeating a US-backed coalition of warlords known as the Alliance for the Restoration of Peace and Counter-Terrorism. The ICU was able to accomplish what no other central authority has been able to achieve before or since; it brought about relative peace and stability for the short six-month period it was in charge. But the alliance of sharia courts crumbled following an Ethiopian invasion in December 2006. Some in the ICU leadership fled Somalia, while other more hard-core elements, including members of its Al Shabaab military wing, survived by melting into the bush, regrouping and emerging as a far more extreme, uncompromising and violent force. Somalis at home and in the diaspora began to wake up to the existence of Al Shabaab. Some were attracted to this fierce, diehard little movement, with its relatively clear ideology and ambition to rid Somalia of the presence of its long-time foe, Ethiopia.

Although the US initially urged the then Ethiopian prime minister, Meles Zenawi, to exercise caution and to think long and hard about invading Somalia, it eventually gave its backing to the plan, conducting air strikes on suspected Islamist targets in southern Somalia in January 2007.[1] Some members of the US administration, including the then assistant secretary of state for African affairs, Jendayi Frazer, believed the ICU was closely linked to violent Islamist radicals, including members of Al Qaeda. 'The Council of Islamic Courts is now controlled by Al Qaeda cell individuals,' she said at the time. 'The top layer of the courts are extremist to the core. They are terrorists and they are in control.'[2]

Al Shabaab is highly nimble, adaptable and resilient. It has gone through several incarnations, from a tiny insurgent group to a movement which for a time controlled and governed much of Somalia, including most of the capital, Mogadishu, and many other major towns and cities, especially in the country's southern and central regions. These areas are often referred to as South Central Somalia, and exclude the semi-autonomous region of Puntland in the north-east and the self-declared Republic of Somaliland in the north-west. At its height, from around 2009 to 2010, Al Shabaab held sway over between 3 and 5 million people.[3] It is also present in other parts of East Africa and the Horn, especially Kenya. It has attracted recruits from all over the globe, who are prepared to go and fight in a country that for years topped the list of the world's most comprehensively failed states.[4]

But back to the man on the phone.

'Everything you have told me is true,' I say to him once he has completed his list of all the places I had visited in Baidoa. 'But how do you know all of this?' I feel sick to my stomach, because I try to be extremely discreet when I visit Somalia. I tell as few people as possible that I am coming to the country and switch off all my social media accounts when I am there. I change my local phone number regularly and use secure messaging apps whenever I can. Meetings are arranged at the last minute, with times and locations often changed again and again. I do not talk openly about my internal travel plans, only sharing them with my two trusted security advisers. How could Al Shabaab know all these details when my movements are so unpredictable and so few people know about them?

'We have been monitoring you wherever you go. We have people in the government, the security forces, NGOs, businesses and the media who tell us everything. They are our friends and they have been keeping their eyes on you.'

The man from Al Shabaab goes on to talk about which places I had visited in Mogadishu and which people I had met there. He gets it right every time. He talks about how a senior government official I had arranged to meet in what I believed to be a highly secure location had not shown up and how frustrating this must have been for me. This makes me wonder who in that so-called 'safe place' had been an Al Shabaab informant. Was he or she a member of the group's ruthlessly effective intelligence wing, the *Amniyaat*, or a more casual informer? It makes me think of a phrase I hear so often from Somalis: 'Al Shabaab is everywhere and you never know who is Al Shabaab.' It reminds me of the young boy from the coastal town of Brava, controlled for several years by the Islamists, who said, 'Al Shabaab do not fall from the sky. They know us and we know them. They are our cousins, brothers, aunts and uncles.'

Al Shabaab has my British phone number and whenever I return to London from Somalia, I almost invariably receive a call from a member of the group as I am collecting my luggage or am in the cab back home. I am asked about my trip, what the weather is like in the UK, and given a blow-by-blow account of what I got up to in Somalia, with a dose of Islamist propaganda thrown in along the way. The group usually beats my family and close friends when it comes to phoning to check if I have arrived home safely.

Al Shabaab is known to the outside world mainly through its acts of violence, especially the spectacular attacks on the Westgate shopping mall in Nairobi in September 2013 and on Garissa University College in eastern Kenya in April 2015, and the huge truck bombing in Mogadishu in October 2017, which killed between 500 and 1,000 people and is one of the worst terror attacks ever to have hit the African continent.[5] But less is known about its impact on individuals and families, and it is this aspect of Al Shabaab that the book aims to explore. This includes the impact on those who join it, those who live in areas it controls, and those whose lives are affected simply because they live in or come from a country where it has a presence. Much of this book involves personal testimony collected during my many visits to Somalia and the wider region. In order to protect people, some of whom have spoken to me at great personal risk, most names have been changed. As will become apparent, there are almost as many truths as there are individual stories, although some more general conclusions can be drawn. It is ironic that Al Shabaab has been able to describe to me so accurately what I do and whom I see when I visit Somalia while I have found it almost impossible to establish a single certifiable truth about the group.

Cooks, soldiers, car mechanics, cleaners, civil servants and street children can all be the eyes and ears of Al Shabaab. Some sympathise with the movement, while others are so terrified of it that they dare not refuse to carry out its demands. Some work on a 'pay as you go' basis, passing on information, throwing a grenade or planting an explosive device in exchange for a small sum.

Al Shabaab is not a black-and-white phenomenon. Of course there are those who embrace it entirely and those who reject and resist it. But there is a large grey area in between and plenty of blurred lines. Many people have multiple identities, one of which is some kind of association with Al Shabaab, sometimes voluntary, sometimes pragmatic, sometimes forced. Some are blissfully ignorant about the support they provide the group. Do people who buy sugar in Kenya, charcoal in Dubai or livestock in Saudi Arabia know that some of it has been taxed by Al Shabaab and used to fund its devastating attacks?[6]

Later on in the conversation with the Al Shabaab contact, he speaks about all the good work the movement has been doing to help people affected by drought, about how the group is far more efficient than what he describes as the 'apostates' in the

United Nations (UN) and the Somali federal government, who he says are destroying the local market by flooding it with donated goods. He is not happy when I put it to him that people fleeing drought in Al Shabaab areas told me that they had received no aid whatsoever from the Islamists, and that they looked frail and malnourished. 'They are lying. They say that to trick the aid agencies into giving them larger portions of food, donated by the crusaders.'

Then the tone of his voice changes. It becomes gentler, slightly wheedling. 'Have you been thinking about your religion, Mary? Have you been thinking about my suggestion?' He is referring to his attempts in earlier telephone conversations to persuade me to join the Muslim faith.

'You might think you have a lot of Somali friends, but they are not your real friends. Your true friends would save you from any problem, including that of hellfire, which is definitely where you will end up if you do not convert to Islam. I am very disappointed in your so-called Somali friends because they are not thinking about your life in the hereafter, when you will be sent directly to that fiery place.'

Most of my phone conversations with Al Shabaab are not about faith. They are about violence. Members of the group are usually quick to call, text or email to say Al Shabaab has carried out an attack on a hotel, a Kenyan town, a UN convoy, a military base or another target. Some of the more dramatic attacks hit the international headlines, such as the siege on a luxury hotel complex in Nairobi in January 2019, which left more than twenty people dead, and the double suicide attacks which killed more than seventy football fans watching the 2010 World Cup final in the Ugandan capital Kampala. Most attacks are smaller and barely make the news, even in the Somali media.

* * *

INTRODUCTION

I have been close to a number of Al Shabaab attacks. It is New Year's Day, 2014. I am having a meal with friends, eating delicious local lobster and drinking fresh watermelon juice.

'I bet nobody in the UK would believe you if you phoned and told them you were celebrating the New Year in Mogadishu, laughing and joking with friends, not a flak jacket or security guard in sight,' says Mustapha. He has recently returned home to Somalia to work with the government, after fleeing his war-torn country more than twenty years before and building a successful life in America.

Suddenly, an enormous blast thunders through the air. It is as if the sound has hit us physically. We flinch; our bodies stiffen, wide, frightened eyes darting rapidly from person to person.

'That was big,' says Mustapha, breaking the silence that has fallen amongst us. 'This is not our usual Mogadishu music.' This is the term Somalis use to describe the gunshots, grenade explosions, mortar fire and other blasts that have made up the background noise of their capital city in the past decades. Somalia has not had a strong, central government since the 1980s when rebel groups and clan militias rose up against the long-serving president, Siad Barre, who seized power in a coup in 1969. He was eventually ousted in January 1991.

By now, everyone is on the phone.
'It's the Jazeera Palace Hotel,' says Hussein, who helps with my security when I am in town, and has contacts everywhere.

The Jazeera Palace is just a few doors down from where we are. In many ways, it is more than a hotel as it serves as home and office to Somali politicians, businesspeople and foreign diplomats. Some have lived there for years.

Hotels play a big part in Somali culture and the Jazeera Palace is the place to be in Mogadishu. The tall white building, with its watchtowers and high perimeter walls, is one of the first things that strikes you as you drive into the city from Aden Adde International

Airport. It emits a sense of optimism and ambition, rising up from the crumbling low-level buildings which surround it, many bearing the scars of the series of conflicts that have hit a city once so beautiful it was called the White Pearl of the Indian Ocean.

Some of us run up onto the roof to get a better look. Flames burst out of the hotel; the charred, mangled remains of the suicide vehicle which was rammed into the perimeter wall lies amongst other destroyed cars. Ambulances and military vehicles race along the road beneath us, lights flashing, sirens shrieking.

A man wrenches me back with a rough twist of the arm. 'Don't be so stupid!' he shouts. 'Stray bullets.' Sure enough, there is a crack of gunfire, very close.

Shortly after the ambulances and security forces arrive at the hotel, there is another massive explosion. Al Shabaab often carries out double car bomb attacks, waiting for the emergency services, journalists and onlookers to gather at the scene before sending in another suicide driver in a second explosive-laden vehicle to ensure maximum casualties.

Then it sends in its foot soldiers to besiege the building and slaughter its occupants. The militants know that once they go inside they will never leave. In essence, they are on suicide missions, killing as many people as they can until they are shot dead by the security forces and, they believe, fast-tracked to paradise as martyrs. Al Shabaab says all fighters wear suicide vests during such attacks so they can transform themselves into a human weapon at any moment.

About fifteen minutes after the second blast at the Jazeera Palace, a senior security official arrives at our location with his entourage. He tells us he was the target of the attack.

We collect white plastic chairs and arrange them in a circle in the courtyard. The men sit there in stunned silence. At least ten people have been blown up at the hotel, including members of their team. But after a few minutes they start talking, discussing tactics for the fight back.

INTRODUCTION

A few hours after the attack I receive a call from a friend, Osman, who lives at the hotel.

'Please, come fetch me. Let's go to the beach.'

Even though the hotel is close by, I cannot walk there. The only way I can travel safely in Mogadishu is in a convoy, at least one vehicle packed with well-armed bodyguards, another with a driver, a few more guards and me. When I walk around in the city, I am encircled by guards, and all of us are nervous.

On the street outside the Jazeera Palace, electricians are busy repairing electrical wires brought down by the blasts, stringing them back up onto concrete posts. The mess of twisted vehicles has already gone, the bloodstains washed away and the body parts collected.

My bodyguards leap off the back of their pickup truck and form two parallel lines from my vehicle up to the entrance of the hotel. One of them opens the car door and shouts, 'Go, go, go—quickly.' As I move between the lines of men, the door to the hotel is opened by an invisible hand and I dart inside.

The Jazeera Palace's many shattered windows have already been boarded up and painted white. In the dining area, which took the force of the blasts, people are drinking cappuccinos and sweet, spiced Somali tea. Some are on their mobiles, calling friends and encouraging them to come to the hotel as a show of defiance.

'We will never give in to Al Shabaab,' says one man as he plunges his fork into a vast serving of meat and pasta. 'Let them come back tomorrow, next week, next month. We will wipe away the blood, we will patch up the damage. And we will do it quickly because we Somalis are very fast people. Al Shabaab will never conquer us.'

Osman appears. He points to the desk in the reception area that he and others had cowered behind during the attack. He apologises for not being able to hear me properly as his ears have been ringing with a terrible sound since the blasts occurred.

We drive to the beach, a half-kilometre stretch belonging to a mutual friend who, with characteristic optimism, plans to build a resort on the powder-soft, white sand. The guards stay well back, and soon we cannot see them at all. This beach is one of the only places in Mogadishu where I can be outside without armed protection.

As we wade through the warm turquoise of the Indian Ocean, Osman explains how he had organised for a special tent to be constructed on the beach so he could propose to the woman who is now his wife. He says he misses her desperately as, like so many other wealthy men in Somalia, he has sent her abroad to live in a safer place.

* * *

When I return to the UK, I speak admiringly of the resilience of the Somalis at the hotel, about how quick they were to recreate normality by repairing and repainting the building, by sipping their cappuccinos as if nothing had happened. Two female Somali friends tell me I am completely wrong to praise this behaviour. 'That is all that is the matter with Somalia and Somalis,' one says. 'Unless people pause and think about what has happened and how it has affected them and those around them, nothing will ever change. It is a sign of a society in trauma, of putting a tiny sticking plaster on a deep, open wound that nobody knows how to heal.'

The other friend agrees and describes how, the last time she was in Mogadishu, one of her aunts was killed in an Al Shabaab attack. Two of the aunt's children were forced by their relatives to dig their mother's grave without help from others and to fill it once her body had been placed inside. Above all, they were told not to cry.

I have a discussion about crying with a group of medical students in Mogadishu. Some have grown up or even been born abroad. They have come from Canada, Sweden, the UK, Tanzania and Kenya to study in Somalia because the quality of education is good, the fees are competitive and they want to learn about their culture. Others have never left the country. The two groups have sharply contrasting attitudes towards violence and how to cope with its regular presence in their lives.

A twenty-two-year-old who has lived in Mogadishu since birth describes how, since early childhood, he sometimes encountered dead bodies on the way to school. 'I adapted to the obstacles,' he says. 'I would make detours if there was active fighting nearby, but not if there were dead people. I would just walk past them, sometimes step right over them. Dead bodies would never make me late for school.'

A girl who was born and brought up in Sweden, and who has only recently arrived in Mogadishu, explains how she had sobbed openly when Al Shabaab attacked a building down the road from the university.

'My fellow students came to me and asked if one of my relatives had died in the explosion. When I told them I was crying because I was terrified and deeply sad that so many Somalis had just lost their lives, they mocked me and said there must be something wrong with me. People who have lived with this violence all their lives become changed. They don't feel anything. They keep telling me I have to become desensitised like they are. Even small children say none of this matters because everybody is going to die in the end anyway.'

I ask the students for their thoughts on what my Somali friends in the UK had said about how these displays of resilience are ultimately so damaging. Most of the young women agree that it is not healthy to mask emotions in the same way that bomb-shattered buildings are patched up so rapidly after an attack. The young men disagree, especially those who have never left Somalia. The twenty-two-year-old, who had been so blasé about dead bodies, says: 'We have just been studying psychology so now I know a little more about trauma and mental illness. But this is not the right time for us to grieve. We must fix the damage to our buildings and our streets, and we must move on. We must wait for peace to return to Somalia, whenever that may be, before we start examining our emotions.'

During my visits to Somalia, I have witnessed how living with intense violence affects people, often in profound, enduring and unexpected ways. Sometimes I will be the only person in the room who does not jump when a door bangs shut or a gust of wind slams an open window against a wall. A Somali psychiatrist who has lived in Canada for decades said he still panics every time he hears a plane overhead because it brings back memories of the Somali government's aerial bombardments of his hometown of Bur'ao during the civil war of the late 1980s. Confident Somali friends sitting in my living room in London have been reduced to wide-eyed, trembling wrecks at the sound of fireworks on Bonfire Night, arms wrapped tightly around their knees as they sit through the bangs and explosions that remind them of what they lived through back home.

People often refuse to answer calls from withheld or unfamiliar numbers, afraid that the caller will be a member of Al Shabaab phoning to issue a warning, a threat or an order to join the violent jihad. This even happens in the UK, where people who have fled Somalia because of threats from Al Shabaab are pursued with phone calls, emails and instant messages. After meeting me in Mogadishu or another part of South Central Somalia, a woman will tie a black niqab around her face, hiding all but her eyes. This is not because she believes in covering her face as an essential part of her religious practice, but because she wants to disguise herself as she leaves the building, afraid that Al Shabaab will want to punish her for speaking to a Westerner.

People in Mogadishu are often nervous of parked cars or vehicles that career down the road at speed. They are frightened of particular makes of cars or trucks. This fear is entirely rational as Al Shabaab often uses suicide car bombers, or 'vehicle-borne improvised explosive devices' (VBIEDs) as they are known in the jargon, and tends to favour certain vehicle models for such attacks. After the massive truck bombing in Mogadishu in 2017, social media was awash with comments about a new type of phobia that had developed in response to the make of lorry used in the attack. In one instance, a woman singlehandedly held up such a truck at gunpoint, demanding it be searched thoroughly to make sure it was not carrying explosives.

Some people feel anxious in traffic jams, fearful that they will be unable to make a swift exit in the event of an ambush, explosion or other attack. They are particularly nervous when they are stuck next to a stationary vehicle, afraid that it might explode at any time. When my car was trapped in a congested street in Mogadishu's main commercial district, Bakara Market, one of my bodyguards opened the window, pointed his gun upwards towards the cloudless blue sky and started firing live rounds of ammunition. When I asked what he was doing, he explained that this was the only way to get the other vehicles to move out of the way. 'Drivers pay attention to bullets, not horns,' he said. The only way to keep me safe, to avoid kidnapping or worse, was to keep moving, and to move quickly and unpredictably.

Another time, in the same market, I saw police beating a boy who looked about eight years old. He was carrying two large yellow plastic bags. I stopped to ask why these grown, armed men were hurting such a young child. They opened the bags. Inside was material they said was commonly used to put together home-made bombs.

On a visit to one of Mogadishu's many tent cities, which house the hundreds of thousands of people displaced by conflict and drought, a woman hurtled towards me, veil and robes flying behind her as she rushed through the sprawling collection of tightly packed, small, igloo-shaped structures made from sticks, plastic sheeting and scraps of ragged cloth lashed together with wire and string. One of my guards thrust out his arm, slamming it into her chest and pushing her roughly to one side. 'You never know what she might be hiding under her clothes,' he said. 'She might have a bomb strapped to her body.'

It turned out the woman wanted to tell me about how the people running the camp had beaten her up, and to show me the bruises and welts on her legs, arms and shoulders. They turned on her after she complained that they were stealing the food aid donated to the camp's inhabitants who had fled to Mogadishu from other even more dangerous parts of the country. My driver, who was doubling up as my translator, found it hard to keep up with the woman as she fired off her complaints in noisy, staccato Somali. She said the people in charge of the camp were selling the food for a handsome profit in Bakara Market. She also criticised these so-called 'gatekeepers' for charging high entrance fees to homeless newcomers desperate for a space in the camp, turning them away if they lacked sufficient funds. Then their only choice would be the streets, squatting in an abandoned, shell-shattered building or begging for shelter in a mosque.

It often seems as if the long years of conflict have permeated people's lives so deeply that their default position is to respond to everyday events in a violent or agitated way. Some women lull their babies to sleep with soft songs of brutality. These lullabies describe the different kinds of violence a mother will use to protect her child from people who, the songs say, have evil intentions lurking behind their sweet smiles.

Intense conflict had already been part of the fabric of Somalia for decades before Al Shabaab was formed. There was war with neighbouring Ethiopia in the 1970s, then years of clan warfare, warlordism, regional clashes and land disputes, some of which continue to this day. But Al Shabaab, which is formally affiliated with Al Qaeda, has brought something new to the country. It has fundamentally altered the way people live and has dragged Somalia and Somalis directly under the spotlight of the 'War on Terror' and all that comes with it.

Al Shabaab's links with other transnational violent Islamist movements, its attraction of foreign fighters, its aims to take the caliphate beyond Somalia's borders and threats to attack targets, including shopping centres in the US, UK and France, have introduced a global element to the conflict. Events in the country can no longer be brushed aside as internal Somali problems. They require an international response.

The West all but abandoned Somalia after a US-led humanitarian intervention went badly wrong in the early 1990s, ending in the infamous 'Black Hawk Down' incident in October 1993 when two American Black Hawk helicopters were shot down by clan militiamen in Mogadishu. Two UN peacekeepers and eighteen US servicemen were killed, their naked, mutilated bodies dragged through the streets by jeering crowds. It is estimated that between 300 and 1,500 Somalis died in the ensuing battles.[7]

The West has now returned, although at arm's length, this time with drones, airstrikes, special forces, and military advisers and trainers. As I write, a press release from US Africa Command has just dropped into my inbox. Like the many others I receive, it has informed me of the latest US airstrike on Somali soil, conducted 'in support of the federal government of Somalia' and which has, it says, eliminated Islamist targets. It says the US is aware that there are 'reports alleging civilian casualties resulting from this operation, and we take these reports seriously'. The press release says that 'US Africa Command will review any information it has about the incident' and that if this information 'is determined to be credible, USAFRICOM will determine the next appropriate step'. After these initial emails, it is rare for the US to release any further information about an incident or to divulge extra details on the phone.

A number of other foreign powers have also taken a keen interest in Somalia, including Turkey, Qatar and the United Arab Emirates. This has resulted in confused and often incoherent or openly conflicting strategies towards the country. At times this contributes towards the further fracturing of Somalia instead of helping to unite it into a functioning nation state.

Although Al Shabaab is a small organisation, whose membership numbers in the thousands, its existence has had unintended consequences for all Somalis, no matter who they are or where they live in the world. Being Somali comes with uncomfortable and, in almost all instances, unfair associations with the 'terror' brand. This can affect how Somalis are treated at school, whether they can get a bank account, where they can travel to and how they are treated at passport control.

However, there are also people who have benefited indirectly from Al Shabaab, just as there are those who have thrived during the decades of conflict in Somalia, profiting from lawlessness, weak government and a lack of regulations.

A whole industry has built up around Al Shabaab. Foreign and local security experts make a good living in Mogadishu, as do communications and counter-messaging specialists. Diaspora Somalis are employed by the security agencies to spy on their own communities in the US, the UK and elsewhere, and to keep their eyes and ears open for signs of radicalisation and possible plots to attack domestic targets. Highly paid consultants prepare briefing papers on 'Countering Violent Extremism' in Somalia, sometimes without ever setting foot in the country. Others make only a short stop at Mogadishu's heavily protected international airport, which is a world apart from the rest of the country.

Al Shabaab provides an ample source of stories for journalists like me. When there is not much news in Africa, I can be sure events in Somalia will provide me with a story. My job as an Africa specialist for the BBC has put me in the uncomfortable position of being a useful contact for Al Shabaab's media department. I feel dread when one of Al Shabaab's numbers lights up my phone screen, as it usually means news of yet another deadly attack.

The group uses its communications and propaganda machine both to spread the word to media organisations and to attract fighters, funders and sympathisers from across the globe, both Somali and non-Somali. The first suicide bombers from America, Denmark and Sweden were young men of Somali origin who blew themselves up in Somalia on behalf of Al Shabaab. They had been seduced away from their lives in the West by the movement's slick recruitment videos, jihadi rap songs and promises of paradise. Some also felt a strong sense of Somali nationalism following the Ethiopian invasion of December 2006.

There are many paradoxes surrounding Al Shabaab. The group has affected people's lives in different ways, mainly negatively, sometimes positively. It makes some people rich, others poor. Al Shabaab affects people's love lives and their businesses. It kills them, injures them, terrorises and scares them. But it also attracts people, some because they believe in its mission, others because it provides them with structure and laws. It is present and visible in people's lives in a way that government is not, especially in rural areas, and smaller towns and villages. For many, it is simply the best option available. In some ways, it has created the most effective system of governance Somalia has known since its collapse into chaos and conflict began in the late 1980s.

The intense focus on Al Shabaab by journalists, academics and analysts has masked other forms of violence that continue to rip Somalia apart. These include disputes over land, clan, business and politics. These conflicts are sometimes mixed in with those of Al Shabaab, or the small Islamic State (IS) affiliate based in north-eastern Somalia, but are often entirely separate. It would be wrong to attribute all or even the majority of violence in Somalia to Al Shabaab.

This book's aim is to shed some light on what has happened to Somalis, Somalia and the wider region since the advent of Al Shabaab. It will look at the human impact of Al Shabaab on Somalis and others who are touched by it. It will examine how they have suffered under its rule and influence, and the many and sometimes unexpected ways in which they have resisted it and sometimes benefited from its existence.

1

WHO AM I?

A head wrapped in the red-and-white or black-and-white checked cloth of the *kufiya* scarf, the body dressed in camouflage or khaki, the feet slipped into scruffy sandals. This is the standard dress of the Al Shabaab fighter. In his hands he will cradle a gun or a Koran.

If the militants are posing for a group photograph, there might be a bit of variety. Some carry larger weapons; others wear long, heavy necklaces of brass bullets. Once I saw a fighter wearing white disposable plastic gloves. But overall these men look like cardboard cut-outs, devoid of personality or individuality.

It would be easy to assume that they are all driven by the same mission—to establish a caliphate based on their draconian interpretation of Islam. But behind this mask of uniformity lie many different stories, probably as many as there are members of Al Shabaab.

Some people, especially those in senior positions, are unswerving ideologues. They are clear and uncompromising in their approach. Like Ali Dheere, the chief spokesman of Al Shabaab, they see the conflict and their mission in all-or-nothing, binary terms: 'The young Somali men who are dying are of two types. One is dying a worthless death in the path of the infidels. These are the ones who hurt our hearts. We feel very sorry for these young men who follow the infidels and die as non-believers and who suffer in humiliation and disgrace. However the one who dies while defending his country, his religion and his dignity, we believe Allah will be pleased with him.'[1]

A former leader of Al Shabaab, Adan Hashi Farah Ayro, who was killed in Somalia by a US Tomahawk cruise missile in May 2008, also believed it was a privilege to die for the cause. In a video released posthumously he said, 'Most of us in Al Shabaab feel that our morale and spirits will be lifted with each martyrdom in our ranks. It is a great honour to become a martyr. We can attain great success by seeking martyrdom and by shoving sand into the mouths of the infidels and their collaborating hypocrites.'

Al Shabaab did not emerge out of nowhere. Radical, violent Islamism has existed in Somalia for decades, although it has never before had the reach or influence it has under Al Shabaab. There are also conservative Islamist groups which do not espouse violence; some of them are still in existence and have influence within government. A number of Al Shabaab's leaders, some dead, some still living, have come up through the ranks of other extremist movements in Somalia, especially Al Itihad Al Islamiya, which established a small emirate in the country in the early 1990s. Like the Islamic Courts Union (ICU), Al Itihad was crushed by the Ethiopians. Some senior members of Al Shabaab have had overseas experience, training and fighting in the battle-fields of Afghanistan when it was the go-to destination for violent jihadis.

Others are motivated, at least initially, to join for reasons that have nothing to do with religion. For some, it has been national-ism, especially after the 2006 Ethiopian invasion of Somalia and, to a lesser extent, Kenya's military intervention in 2011. They believe Al Shabaab is the most effective fighting force available to liberate their country from what they perceive to be foreign enemies. It is one of the great ironies of modern Somali history that foreign forces, ostensibly intervening to rid the country of Islamist extremists, in some instances have ended up strengthening the very group they were trying to destroy. This is partly because their presence on Somali soil has angered Somalis both at home and in the diaspora, provoking some to join radical Islamist movements, especially the most local and relevant branch, Al Shabaab. Violent jihadis have exploited this sentiment. In 2007, the Somali Islamist leader Hassan Dahir Aweys said, 'I call on the Somali people to fight these forces which wanted to change the map of Somalia itself. In the offices of the provisional government, we found maps in which Ethiopia wiped out Somalia and annexed it to itself. It is common knowledge they have always wanted to do that.'[2]

About 70 per cent of Somalia's population is under the age of thirty. Whatever their motivations, there are plenty of young men in Somalia with few prospects and little to do. They are prime recruiting material for Al Shabaab. Some are uneducated, while others have been all the way through university, having studied at any one of the country's many educational institutions. Some schools and universities I have visited in Somalia are of extremely low quality. I have seen several cases of teachers who are unable to speak basic English teaching science, midwifery, sociology and politics in English-medium schools and universities. Sometimes, when I have visited these institutions, neither the teachers nor the students are able to answer or even understand my questions. Of course, many Somalis speak excellent English, including one of my main contacts in Al Shabaab. So smooth is his accent, so fluent his English, so solid his grasp of grammar and nuance, that I always assumed he had studied abroad. One day I asked him. 'Oh, I have never left Somalia. I learned it here. One reason my accent is so good and my vocabulary so wide is that for years I have paid close attention to the BBC. That is why I feel I almost know you, Mary. I have been listening to your BBC reports for years.'

Some people from marginalised groups, especially what are known as the 'minority clans', have viewed Al Shabaab as a way of gaining strength and weapons. They believe this could help them avenge the vicious mistreatment they received at the hands of more powerful groups during the years of clan warfare in the 1990s and 2000s. However, in many cases they have ended up serving as little more than cannon fodder for the Islamists, exploited by Al Shabaab just as they have been and continue to be exploited by the majority clans.

Others join for the money or are tempted to volunteer by promises that are never fulfilled. There are those who join for the adventure, attracted by the excitement promised in recruitment videos, or for a sense of belonging and a purpose. Some say Al Shabaab has recruited them forcibly from their homes, schools and places of work, or has threatened them and their families during visits and phone calls until they feel they have no choice but to sign up. Others are sent by their clans, who have been ordered by the Islamists to deliver a certain number of fighters and other recruits.

Even though Al Shabaab has been widely branded as a terrorist organisation, some of those who join it, or who take their families to live in areas it controls, are motivated by reasons that appear entirely logical and pragmatic. They are not looking for violence or a particular brand of Islam, but for predictability, structure, law and order in a country where government has for decades been all but invisible or a negative and destructive influence.

There are foreigners from neighbouring countries and further afield drawn to what was for a time one of the most appealing destinations for 'jihadi tourists'. Members of the Somali diaspora have also been attracted. Young disaffected Somali men have found more meaning in violent Islamism in their country of origin than in the street gangs of Minneapolis, Stockholm or London. More privileged and educated diaspora Somalis have also joined Al Shabaab, some as fighters, others in the group's media and communications department or elsewhere in the administration. A regular voice in Al Shabaab's English-language videos, for instance, has a distinctly London accent.

This chapter will describe some of the main reasons why people say they join Al Shabaab and provide testimonies from individuals about their motivations. Of course, many people join for a combination of reasons or are motivated by factors other than those outlined below.

The Ideologues

When one looks back over the history of Al Shabaab since it emerged in the mid-2000s, a small group of names crops up again and again. They include Hassan Dahir Aweys, Aden Hashi Farah Ayro, Ahmed Abdi Godane, Mukhtar Robow, Ahmed Dirie Abu Ubaidah and Ali Dheere, who is also known as Ali Mohamud Rageh. They tend to have long, violent jihadi pedigrees, and represent the inspirational leadership core of Al Shabaab. A number of them have or have had multi-million dollar US bounties on their heads and have featured on the FBI's Most Wanted lists. Some are now dead, mainly killed in American air strikes. Some have been captured and some have surrendered, while others remain active.

The group's former deputy leader Mukhtar Robow, who is sometimes known as Abu Mansour, had a $5 million US bounty on his head. He surrendered to the government in August 2017 after falling out with the leadership of Al Shabaab. He caused chaos in October 2018 when he announced he was running for the presidency of Somalia's South West regional state, one of the most powerful positions in the country. 'After receiving requests from the people of this region and their intellectuals, I have decided to run for the president of this state in the coming election,' he told hundreds of his supporters in the regional capital Baidoa. 'I have accepted the requests and, if God wills, we will win and peace will prevail.'[3] The federal government intervened, arresting Robow on the grounds that he was barred from running for political office due to his failure to formally repudiate Al Shabaab. A number of his supporters were killed in subsequent riots and many detained. When the then UN Secretary General's Special Representative to Somalia, Nicholas Haysom, questioned the federal authorities' aggressive conduct towards Robow and his supporters, he was declared persona non grata by the Somali government and expelled from the country after just a few months in the job.

Most of Al Shabaab's diehard ideologues will probably never give up their commitment to purist ideals of establishing a caliphate, although arguments about what form it should take have led to serious and sometimes violent divisions within the movement. Some believe the caliphate should be restricted within Somalia's current borders, while some think that it should comprise 'Greater Somalia', which would include the large Somali-speaking territories of Kenya, Ethiopia and Djibouti. Others want it to be something far bigger, stretching across East Africa, the Gulf and beyond. The former Al Shabaab leader Godane once said he wanted to take the jihad all the way to Alaska. In May 2009, he declared, 'We will fight and the wars will not end until Islamic sharia is implemented in all continents in the world and until Muslims liberate Jerusalem.'

Some of these men are charismatic, while others remain in the shadows. Godane was widely admired for his skills as an orator. As poetry, rhetoric and the correct and artful use of language are highly prized in Somalia, even people vehemently opposed to Al Shabaab would listen admiringly to the long, hypnotic audio messages sent from his hiding place. Although it was easy to find recordings of his voice on the internet, Godane remained all but invisible as a physical presence, even in photographs. This was not the case with Mukhtar Robow, who was for a time the public face of Al Shabaab, delivering firebrand speeches which were widely viewed online. Little is heard from or seen of the movement's current emir, Abu Ubaidah. As stated by the Mogadishu-based think tank the Hiraal Institute, 'his contrast with Godane was clear from the beginning: it took him almost two years to release an audio message, and only when it was absolutely necessary as the group was again facing mortal danger from within with the advent of Islamic State in Somalia.'[4]

Godane was one of the most effective of Al Shabaab's leaders. In their book *Inside Al-Shabaab*, the two Voice of America journalists Harun Maruf and Dan Joseph explain that:

> Al-Shabaab was never a ragtag rebel group, but the university-educated Godane, with his economics degree, installed a level of organization that set it apart from most militant groups of any stripe, and certainly apart from the thieving warlords and the corrupt or powerless government officials that Somalis were used to.[5]

* * *

Some of Al Shabaab's more junior members remain steadfast in their commitment to the cause of violent jihad. However, there is another group which initially joined for religious reasons but later became disillusioned.

I met one such person in a rehabilitation centre for former foot soldiers of Al Shabaab. He limped into the room, dressed in a shabby sarong, known locally as a *macawiis*, a faded camouflage T-shirt and old sandals. His hair was matted, his skin dull. He had the same dazed, dead-eyed expression as the other former fighters who milled around the compound outside, seemingly unable to hold conversations with each other.

It took a while for him to start talking.

'One day, a friend called me. He told me to come and fight for my religion. At that time, I had never seen a town or a city. I had spent my entire life as a nomad. All I knew were camels, sheep and goats. I thought fighting for one's religion would be the most beautiful and noble thing imaginable, so I went and joined Al Shabaab.'

The man sat awkwardly on a rickety chair. He would not make eye contact with me. I felt uncomfortable asking him questions. After some time he became more animated, his words flowing ever faster as if he wanted to spill everything out into the air between us.

'I performed two main roles for Al Shabaab. I was sent either on violent missions or to gather information undercover. I did this for about six years. Then, one day, the commanders told me I must kill an elderly man who they said was a spy. This man was so old that he was blind and deaf. He could not even walk. I asked myself which god could justify the killing of such a weak person? How could this old, disabled man have spied for anyone? I came to realise that no religion would allow such a person to be slaughtered like an animal.'

The man said he killed the old man because he was too frightened not to. But the next time he was given leave by Al Shabaab, he started walking and did not stop until he reached the town of Baidoa. There he had handed in his gun and surrendered.

'I walked for hundreds of kilometres. Look, look at my feet.'

The man took off his battered shoes and thrust his feet towards me. His soles were lacerated with wounds, some open, some beginning to heal.

'When I am finished here, I am going to have to disappear. I can never return to my community because they know what I have done. They know that I have killed. I also know Al Shabaab is looking for me because they have called me on the phone, threatening to kill me or members of my family because I am a deserter. They say I have stolen their weapon. I will try either to melt away in a big city like Mogadishu or, better still, make my way to Europe or the Gulf.'

The Nationalists

It would be too simplistic to argue that Ethiopia's invasion of Somalia in 2006 provoked so many people to join Al Shabaab that it was transformed from a tiny militant movement into a viable fighting force, ultimately establishing control over most parts of southern and central Somalia. But, as the Somalia expert Ken Menkhaus argues:

> The result was that most Somalis, even those who opposed Al Shabaab's radical Islamist ideology, believed that Al Shabaab's use of armed resistance to the Ethiopian occupation was entirely justified, and tended to view the group first and foremost as a liberation movement. To the extent that it was a 'jihad', it was understood as a defensive jihad, a variation on what Western scholars would call a 'just war'.[6]

There was also the fact that Al Shabaab was considered the best force available at the time to fight Ethiopia, which was seen by many Somalis as their oldest and most dangerous enemy. Somalia has had several wars with its vast western neighbour, the most devastating of which occurred in the 1970s. It long considered as part of its territory Ethiopia's large Ogaden region, which abuts Somalia and is populated mainly by ethnic Somalis. For its part, Ethiopia has regarded Somalia as troublesome, unpredictable and dangerous, and for decades has maintained an informal buffer zone between the two countries, with Ethiopian troops often stationed within Somali territory. When Ethiopia launched its large-scale air and ground invasion of Somalia in 2006, Somalis who wanted to resist had little choice, other than to join Al Shabaab. The transitional federal government was supported by Ethiopia and could not function independently; the warlords and their clan militias were severely weakened; and the ICU had fallen apart.

Some people may also have been attracted to Al Shabaab not because it espoused violent jihad and appeared to have potential as a fighting machine, but because it was associated with the ICU, which had brought some peace and stability to parts of the war-weary country during the few months it was in power.

I have a contact in Al Shabaab whose religious fervour is so strong that I always presumed that the group had appealed to him for reasons of faith. I found out how wrong I was when we spoke about why he had joined the group.

'I was born and raised in Mogadishu. I am a true son of the city. My earliest memory is the day a warlord's mortar crashed through the ceiling of my classroom, killing my best friend and injuring others. After that, I felt angry all the time.

'In 2006, the ICU came to power and, for the first time in my life, Mogadishu was quiet. I had grown up with nothing but clan warfare and brutal warlords. But a few short months after the ICU took over, the Ethiopians came. They removed the peace and butchered the people.'

He paused. The line went silent.

'I thought to myself, I am a man. I cannot just sit down and accept this. I had to make a choice and I chose Al Shabaab. It was the best option available to fight back against the Ethiopian invaders. More than ten years later, I have no regrets. Sometimes I sit down in a quiet place and think things over. I have concluded that Al Shabaab is a trustworthy, credible organisation. Al Shabaab is my saviour.'

So my contact's primary motivation was one of nationalism. He wanted to protect the sovereignty of his country and for him, there was simply no viable alternative to Al Shabaab.

I asked him about the people he had left behind when he crossed the line to join the Islamists.

'I have plenty of friends and family in the government of Somalia. I see them as apostates. They keep calling me on the phone and asking me to come back to live with them in Mogadishu. But I cannot live amongst mercenaries. I want to live in dignity. I want to live in freedom.'

I found it strange that during our conversation, he had not once mentioned religion. I asked whether faith had been a factor when he decided to join the group.

'It was not. I did not think about it at all. But it is helpful that Al Shabaab has a religious element because this means it has rules. Everything is clearer and easier because religion provides a ready-made rulebook.'

Marginalised Groups

Anyone familiar with Somali politics will be aware of the '4.5' formula, a quota system for how the country's clans should be distributed within the administration. The '4' represents the four majority or 'noble' clans, known as the Darod, Dir, Hawiye and Rahanweyn, which all divide and sub-divide into numerous smaller clans. The '0.5', like some kind of afterthought, represents the marginalised clans and groups. There are dozens of minority clans, sub-clans, sub-sub-clans and sub-sub-sub-clans in Somalia. In terms of their share of the population, they are believed to be proportionally underrepresented by the '0.5' they have been allocated. Some of these clans and sub-clans are associated with specific roles and professions, similar in some ways to castes in India.

The one factor that binds the minority clans together is the prejudice, isolation and cruelty they encounter from members of majority clans. During the civil war of the 1990s, they suffered disproportionate violence, rape and other abuse, partly because they did not have their own clan militias to protect them.

Some people in minority clans, or weaker majority clans, have been attracted to Al Shabaab because it provides access to weapons, therefore giving them some kind of power. I have spoken to a number of young men from these marginalised groups who say they joined Al Shabaab explicitly to seek revenge. I met a member of the Midgan clan in a rehabilitation centre for former fighters. The Midgan are associated with certain specific occupations such as hairdressing, ironwork, shoemaking, and male and female circumcision. As we sat in a small, dark room, he told me that his group is one of the most despised in Somalia.

'Children from majority clans used to hit me and spit at me on my way to school. They would move away from me in the classroom and refuse to sit next to me. When my mother sent me on errands to the shops, majority clan members would stop me in the street and steal the money. They treated me as if I were not human, as if I were some kind of dirty dog.

'During the civil war of the 1990s, members of powerful clans raped my mother and sisters. They killed my father. I was happy when Al Shabaab came because this was the best way to get armed and to get revenge. I am not a religious person and I was never interested in the religious aspects of Al Shabaab. I was just interested in their guns.

'Some time after I joined Al Shabaab, I came to realise that most of their leaders are from majority clans. Many of the youngsters who did the fighting were from minority clans or weaker majority clans and they usually died very quickly. But they were not frightened of dying because they have faced death every day of their lives. They have grown up with death all around them, so they were not afraid to carry out the most dangerous missions. Death was nothing for them.'

The man from the Midgan left the room and told me to wait inside. He came back with another man, this time from the leatherworkers' clan, known as the Yahar or Yibir. This man said he also wanted to tell me about how he came to be a member of Al Shabaab.

'In our region, we lived amongst the majority Hawiye clan. They did not treat us well. They called us gypsies and said we were on a different level from them because we made shoes, bags and other leather goods, and because we slaughtered animals. They told us we stank. When I was a boy, they would not let me play football with them. Sometimes they hit me with a stick.

'In early 2008, Al Shabaab came to our town. They talked to us about jihad and said we had to kill the Christians in AMISOM [the African Union Mission in Somalia] and anyone who supported the government, which they said was allied with the evil West. They made us close our shops and go to the mosque to listen to them for hours at a time. It was not good for business.

'One day about ten of them came to my house and said I must join the jihad. They took me to the centre of town where I found about 100 other men who had also been collected by Al Shabaab. Armed men surrounded the square. They spoke to us through loudspeakers for hours. Then they put up a big screen and made us watch a film about their work building bridges and irrigating farms. When it was finished they told us to go to their office in the town and to write down our names and our clans—in other words to sign up to join their fight. I felt power I had never felt before.'

Money

Soldiers in the Somali army and people who work for the Somali government often complain about poor, irregular or non-existent pay. Although Somalis are dynamic entrepreneurs, and seem to be able to magic business opportunities out of thin air, unemployment is a major problem in a country affected by so many years of conflict, instability and upheaval. About two thirds of Somalia's population is estimated to be unemployed; a significant majority of its people are under the age of thirty.[7] This is a dangerous mix for a country with an active, successful Islamist insurgency.

One thing that is not in short supply is young men with little to do. Another is guns; the country is awash with them. Put the two together and you have a business opportunity. A man with a gun can sell himself to the highest bidder, be it the army, a clan militia, a private security company, a wealthy businessperson or Al Shabaab.

When Al Shabaab controlled lucrative ports, cities and towns, it could afford to pay its fighters and other staff better wages than its competitors. According to the academic Roland Marchal, who specialises in Somalia, Al Shabaab fighters were paid between $60 and $200 a month, and they received this money regularly, on the same day every month.[8] At the time, Somali government soldiers received $100 a month if they were lucky. They were often not paid at all.

Some fighters are paid fixed amounts for carrying out specific tasks. The academic and Somalia expert Stig Jarle Hansen says:

> Al-Shabaab was thoroughly organised, consisting of squadrons of seven to eight men. Its militias were paid, US$20 for a hand grenade attack, US$30 for killing a soldier, US$100 for a road bomb or a mortar attack—this in a period when the TFG's [transitional federal government's] police and army failed to get any pay at all.[9]

However, a sixty-year-old former Al Shabaab fighter interviewed by UN independent monitors in Garowe prison in north-eastern Somalia complained that the group did not pay him properly: 'I was a fisherman in Harardhere. I joined Al Shabaab in 2014 for the benefit of my family. The pay depended on the work, normally just rice or pasta. At the end of each month we sometimes received some amount of money, not more than $30.'[10]

Marchal explains how the families of individuals who blow themselves up on behalf of the movement are compensated:

Even suicide bombers are rewarded economically. After they have prepared themselves, their family got money (the tentative figure is a couple of thousand dollars) and after they have performed this act, Al Shabaab members visit the family again to give their condolences and provide another sum of money.[11]

As Al Shabaab is far more than a fighting group, it needs administrative workers, communications experts, informants, judges, teachers, health workers and others to contribute to its governance system. It also needs drivers, porters, cleaners and cooks. An Al Shabaab official explained how some people work on a part-time basis: 'They have their own farms and businesses, but they are also mujahidin, or they contribute to our cause in other ways by working in our offices and ministries. They split the work so they earn money from their farms and businesses as well as from us.'

This 'part-time' aspect emphasises the many grey areas surrounding Al Shabaab, whereby people have multiple identities, some connected with the movement, some not. As one informant told researchers in the Bay and Bakol region, a person can be 'one day a special police officer and the next an Al Shabaab operative, then back to being a beneficiary of a vocational programme ... when facing unemployment carries out a small job for Al Shabaab.'[12]

There is also the question of what constitutes involvement or collusion with Al Shabaab. Many people living in government-controlled areas pay taxes and other fees to Al Shabaab as well as to the local authorities, terrified of the consequences of not doing so. Some prefer to use Al Shabaab's courts instead of the corrupt, slow and ineffective alternatives. They are prepared to travel out of government-controlled areas to seek the more efficient legal services provided by the Islamists. People living in towns and cities occupied by African Union troops and the Somali army know that it is worth keeping on the good side of Al Shabaab, as the militants usually march straight back in once AMISOM and the Somali military leave, killing those they accuse of acting as informants for the enemy.

Some people are paid for undercover operations, such as carrying out assassinations in areas outside Islamist control. One Somali friend described how members of Al Shabaab killed his brother in the heart of government-controlled Mogadishu after giving him an ultimatum to stop working for the federal authorities:

'One day, three young men in football shirts hung around in the street outside my brother's house. Nobody thought anything of it until my brother came home from work. The young men shot him in the head and ran away. That shows how Al Shabaab is everywhere amongst us. Who would have guessed that those boys loitering outside my brother's house had anything to do with the Islamists? But they were working as Al Shabaab's assassins. They killed my brother in plain daylight in an area said to be controlled by our so-called government.'

Ironically, some members of the Somali security forces, who are supposed to be fighting Al Shabaab, also work for the Islamists. Others have relatives in the group:

> The lines between the Transitional Federal Government and Al Shabaab forces were thin to begin with. Many of the TFG's troops had family members serving in the insurgency, and habitually used their mobile phones to forewarn Al Shabaab militias of troop movements and attacks. Al Shabaab forces were also able to gain access to most of Somalia's communication networks and to hack into AMISOM communications. At one stage, AMISOM commanders unwittingly contributed to Al Shabaab's knowledge by using an unencrypted Yahoo email account to transmit operational plans back and forth between Mogadishu and Nairobi.[13]

A member of Al Shabaab explained how informants and others working in the army are compensated:

'If someone stays in the army but also works for us, we will pay him even though we consider him to be an apostate. He might work as a spy or facilitate operations for us. If we offer the soldier $1,000 for carrying out an operation for Al Shabaab, we will pay $200 up-front and the remaining $800 when the job is done. We always keep our word as this encourages people in the army to do jobs for us again and again and again. But we still consider these people to be apostates, and if they are killed later on, that is their problem.'

When I suggested to the Al Shabaab official that some people's primary motivation for joining the movement is financial gain, he became angry, raising his voice and shouting down the telephone line.

'Nobody joins Al Shabaab for the money. Everybody joins voluntarily. We work for Allah and only Allah will reward us.'

After he had calmed down, he explained that people in Al Shabaab were paid, at least some of the time.

'Everyone in Al Shabaab gets money, but not necessarily regularly. The amount varies. Sometimes you get a lot, sometimes a little, sometimes nothing at all. It is the same for everyone in the movement, including our supreme leader.'

Money is also used by the 'other side' to obtain information about Al Shabaab. An intelligence officer in Mogadishu explained how people were paid more than the going rate for a gun if they reported an Al Shabaab weapons store. He said they received significantly higher sums if the information they provided resulted in the location and capture or killing of Al Shabaab members, especially senior officials.

Forced Recruits

Although Al Shabaab vigorously denies it recruits people by force or intimidation, the UN, human rights groups and the media have documented numerous examples of forced recruitment.[14] I have interviewed dozens of people, male and female, who have given me consistent accounts of how they, their relatives, their students, colleagues and friends have been taken by force. People have also described how Al Shabaab threatens and intimidates individuals and their families so they feel they have no choice but to join the group or carry out certain acts on its behalf. What is not clear is how many of those who join Al Shabaab do so because they are forced, in comparison with those who join by choice.

Some forced recruits end up fighting for the group, while others manage to escape. Al Shabaab is patient and persistent, at times contacting individuals repeatedly over a period of weeks or months. This slow-burn recruitment process follows a fairly typical pattern of phone calls from unidentified numbers, and visits, often by masked men, to the target's home and place of work. There are also accounts of Al Shabaab visiting children's schools and play areas.[15] One former Al Shabaab fighter described how the militants wore him down with threats:

'They phoned me and said, "We expect you to join the training. We are waiting for you." They telephoned again and again and said, "We know where you are and if you don't come over to our side, we will come to you and kill you like we killed your cousin." One time, they told me the colour of the shirt I was wearing, and they were right. They said it was green and, indeed, that was the day I wore my green shirt. They even told me which street I was walking down at a particular time on a particular day. It was as if they were my shadow. They always called using withheld numbers. One time they sent me money electronically to my mobile phone. They said the money was to buy my 'death clothes', the outfit I would wear to be buried in after they had killed me. That was the final straw, so I went and joined them.'

Other times, Al Shabaab simply grabs people from their schools, football pitches, homes, farms, market stalls or other places of work. Musa was abducted near the coastal town of Merca, which was under Islamist control for several years. He was taken in 2013 when he was nineteen years old.

'I come from a farming family. One day, I was working in the fields when a pick-up truck drove up with armed men inside. I could tell they were from Al Shabaab because of the way they were dressed. They wore long shirts and trousers which stopped above the ankles. Their faces were wrapped in scarves so only their eyes were visible. They jumped out, grabbed me and tied my hands behind my back. They threw me into the back of the vehicle. Four other young men were already in there, their hands also tied. They looked as terrified as I was. Al Shabaab drove us into the forest where they had a base. They dumped us there and left us tied up for the night.

'In the morning they woke us up very early and forced us to run around. If we got tired and stopped, they beat us. They hit me with sticks and the butts of their guns.'

Musa pulled up the sleeve of his T-shirt and showed me a round, shiny patch of skin. He said it was a scar from where a member of Al Shabaab had beat him with his gun.

'They forced us to dig trenches for them. When we weren't working they kept us in a metal container. It was hot and airless. It stank inside because we had to go to the toilet in a corner inside the container. One day, the camp was attacked by AMISOM and bombs from the sky and I managed to escape.'

UN monitors have also documented cases of forced recruitment, collecting testimonies from members of Al Shabaab detained in Garowe prison. They were captured after they carried out a seaborne assault in March 2016 on the small branch of Islamic State (IS) based in the semi-autonomous region of Puntland. Eighty per cent of the detainees came from the Rahanweyn which, although classified as a majority clan, is somewhat looked down upon by other 'noble' groups and has traditionally provided a significant percentage of Al Shabaab's rank and file soldiers. One man, Mohamoud, who was twenty-four years old, said he was captured by Al Shabaab in Merca and held for nineteen days.

'They offered me a choice,' he said. 'Be killed or work with us. They trained me how to use an AK-47 in their camp at Bulo Fulay. They used to blindfold us when we entered and left the camp. We received 15 days of training after which they loaded us onto trucks and took us to Harardhere.'[16]

In Harardhere, the men boarded boats and made their way north to Puntland where they planned to attack IS. 'On the boats everything went wrong. Some of us were vomiting. There were 80 to 100 of us, almost all children. Some of them were forcibly recruited, some abducted, some brainwashed.'[17]

Not all forced recruits have to fight for Al Shabaab. Some work as cleaners, porters, informants and clerical workers. Women and girls sometimes end up as jihadi brides. One man who worked as a nurse in a Mogadishu hospital explained how Al Shabaab had abducted him and forced him to treat their wounded fighters. 'They have informants everywhere,' he said, 'even in the hospital where I worked. Those spies told Al Shabaab about me, about how good I was at nursing trauma victims, so the Islamists came and abducted me from my home one evening. They told me they would kill me and everyone else in my family if I did not work for them.'

Al Shabaab also recruits people who work in or have access to government buildings, forcing them to serve as informants and facilitators. Ismail used to work for the country's largest telecommunications company, Hormuud:

'I was not the first person in the company to be threatened by Al Shabaab. One of my colleagues was contacted because he used to fix the antennae in the presidential compound, and had a pass that gave him access to the area. Al Shabaab told him that if he didn't help give them access to the compound they would kill him. He had no choice. He could either leave the country or help Al Shabaab. In the end he helped the jihadis. He was eventually caught by the Somali security services. Even though he explained that he had no choice but to work for Al Shabaab, that they had forced him to do so, he was executed by the government and held up as an example to others that they should never give in to the militants.'

Al Shabaab also tries to force people to recruit others on their behalf. One man in Mogadishu used to sell mobile phones for a living, but was now on the run:

'I was always polite to Al Shabaab. I obeyed them and made sure I paid my taxes on time. They continued to collect taxes from me even after they withdrew from Mogadishu in 2011. They warned me not to sell anything to soldiers or government employees, which was a difficult thing to do, especially with soldiers as they have guns and are not afraid to use them. After some time, Al Shabaab asked me to help them with recruitment and to spread their word. Lots of young people came to my shop so I think that's why they asked me to work for them, to help recruit the youth.

'Al Shabaab are not religious people. They do not care about Islam. They are violent men who want people to do as they say, to be obedient to them and to give them money. I knew that if I recruited for Al Shabaab I would be in their hands forever, and there would be no turning back. So I shut my shop, lost my livelihood, and am now trying to find a way out of this city. My relatives are trying to raise the funds to pay traffickers to take me to Saudi Arabia. I will start a new life there.'

I asked Al Shabaab about forced recruitment and intimidation, citing numerous examples of the stories I had heard personally, as well as those collected by the UN, human rights groups and the media.

'That is completely crazy. We do not force anyone to join. Everybody who joins Al Shabaab does so voluntarily. When we recruit someone we have to win his heart and mind. We do this by sending our sheikhs into communities, into towns and villages to talk to people there. When we recruit a fighter or a member of our police force, we give him a gun. When we recruit an administrator we give him a pen, a book and an office. But these people can leave at any time. We do not force them to stay.

'We have enough manpower. We do not need forced recruitment. You have to be very strong and very patient to be in Al Shabaab. We are not like the Ugandan Lord's Resistance Army; we are not like its leader Joseph Kony who took children from schools. We are not insurgents. We are a government.

'I don't blame people for saying they are forcibly recruited. They say this because they don't want to be in trouble with the Somali government or its apostate allies. Some people work for Al Shabaab for a few years, then leave and go to the government areas. They lie and say they have been forcibly recruited to avoid getting into trouble with the authorities. I don't blame them for doing that.'

The Foreigners

Al Shabaab is the first Somali Islamist organisation to have attracted significant numbers of foreigners into its ranks. As is the case with local recruits, the foreigners fall into several categories both in terms of their motivations and their identities.

The Internationals

During the 1990s, the combination of the general lawlessness in Somalia and the presence of a core of battle-hardened Islamists, some of whom had been members of Al Itihad Al Islamiya, which was crushed by the Ethiopians in 1996, attracted a number of foreign Al Qaeda operatives to the country. Some of the Somali extremists had trained with the Taliban in Afghanistan and met other international jihadis there. The best-known members of Al Qaeda who spent time in Somalia were three men accused of involvement in at least one major attack on African soil. These included the double truck bombings of the US embassies in Kenya and Tanzania in 1998 in which hundreds died and thousands were injured, and the 2002 hotel bombing and failed attack on an airliner on the Kenyan coast. They were the Comorian and Kenyan national Fazul Abdullah Mohammed, the Sudanese explosives expert Abu Talha al-Sudani, and Saleh Ali Saleh Nabhan, who was born on the Kenyan coast. All were on the FBI's list of Most Wanted Terrorists. Fazul Abdullah Mohammed had a $5 million bounty on his head.[18]

For a time, Somalia became one of the most popular destinations for foreign jihadis. Some were members of Al Qaeda's East African cell, while others came expressly to join Al Shabaab, which itself eventually became an affiliate of Al Qaeda. Al Shabaab also has a relationship with Al Qaeda in the Arabian Peninsula (AQAP), just across the sea in Yemen, with whom fighters, skills, information and weapons have been exchanged. The former Al Qaeda leader Osama bin Laden had Somalia on his radar from as early as July 2006 when the ICU was in control of much of the territory: 'We warn all the nations of the world not to agree to America's request to send international forces to Somalia. We swear to Allah that we will fight its soldiers on Somali soil.' In 2009, bin Laden released an eleven-minute audio message focusing entirely on Somalia. Entitled 'Fight on, champions of Somalia', the recording urged Somalis to overthrow their 'infidel' government and by doing so placed the country firmly on the map as a possible destination for would-be violent jihadis: 'You are the first line of defence for the Islamic world in its south-western part; and your patience and resolve support your brothers in Palestine, Iraq, Afghanistan, the Islamic Maghreb, Pakistan and the rest of the fields of jihad.'[19]

Among the most famous of Al Shabaab's international recruits was the Alabama-born Syrian American Omar Hammami, whose nom-de-guerre was Abu Mansoor Al Amriki. He became something of a poster boy for the movement, starring in recruitment videos and gaining a popular following as a jihadi rap artist. He was killed in an internal purge in 2013 after falling out with the leadership of Al Shabaab.

During what Hansen describes as the 'golden age' of Al Shabaab, from 2009 to 2010, the group attracted fighters from all over the world. One of Hansen's field researchers found a significant number of wounded foreign fighters in Mogadishu's hospitals following heavy fighting in June 2011. 'He found thirty-eight Western and Non-Arab Asians (including Chechens), 123 Africans including people from Kenya, Sudan, Tanzania, Zanzibar and Uganda and two men from South Africa, one American and two Arabs.'[20]

Some analysts suggest Al Shabaab has imported knowledge about explosives from AQAP:

> Al Shabaab has likely received episodic explosive fabrication training and material from AQAP, such as triggers and pressure sensors. In particular, the sophistication of the laptop explosive device used in the attack on Daallo Airlines last February [2016] and the size of some of Al Shabaab's vehicle explosive devices point to external infusions of capability, possibly from its Yemeni ally.[21]

An Al Shabaab official said the group welcomes recruits from all over the world as long as they are committed to the cause: 'We have no specific nationality. We are built by ideology and belief. We have fighters from every corner of the globe—Europeans, Americans, Asians, Africans, Kenyans and Somalis. We will accept anyone who is ready and fit.'

However, jihadi 'tourists', in search of adventure but with limited skills and experience, are of questionable use:

> These foreign fighters have little value and are actually a drain upon Al Shabaab's resources, because they have to be housed and trained

and they attract counter-terrorism attention, but offer little in return. In contrast, higher calibre foreign fighters can bring resources, tactical innovations, or promulgate alternative narratives that influence the movements they join.[22]

By the end of 2013, most senior international jihadis in Somalia, including the head of Al Qaeda's East African wing, Fazul Abdullah Mohammed, had been killed—either in military action by anti-Al Shabaab forces or in internal purges—or had left the country. Foreign fighters, including those from the Somali diaspora, started to drift away from Somalia, lured by what they saw as more attractive destinations, especially territory controlled by the IS group in Syria and Iraq.

Regional Recruits

Although many of its hardened and experienced international followers are no longer operational in Somalia, Al Shabaab has continued to attract fighters from the region and to strike beyond the country's borders. In recent years, many of its foreign adherents have come from Kenya, Tanzania and Uganda. Unlike some of the high-profile, influential international members, most of these regional recruits do not exercise much strategic influence. They mainly serve as foot soldiers and often spearhead attacks in Kenya.[23] Unless they are ethnic Somali nationals from those countries, they are of limited use in Somalia. They attract attention because of their non-Somali appearance and inability to speak the language. They tend to be concentrated in Al Shabaab's externally focused wing, Jaysh Ayman. During a graduation ceremony for Kenyan recruits in May 2017, Al Shabaab's spokesman urged them to become an 'army that will conquer Kenya'. The group has staged hundreds of attacks there, and has also hit Uganda, Djibouti and Tanzania. There have been Islamist attacks as far south as Mozambique by a group known locally as 'Al Shabaab' which has beheaded villagers and burned down hundreds of houses in the north of the country. The Mozambican militants say children should be educated in mosques, not schools, and that all taxation should be abolished. Despite its name it is not clear whether this group is in any way connected with Al Shabaab in Somalia.[24]

The 'East Africanisation' of Al Shabaab is evident in its publicity material, recruitment videos and online magazines, all of which are available in the Kiswahili language, which is widely spoken across East Africa. Many of those who feature in its Kiswahili videos are not Somali in appearance, and seem to come from other communities in East Africa. Al Shabaab says it has recruited Kikuyus, Luos and members of other Kenyan ethnic groups, including some who have converted from Christianity to Islam. About 11 per cent of Kenya's population is Muslim, mainly concentrated along the coast and in the east along the border with Somalia.[25] Al Shabaab says it has a ready-made army in the port city of Mombasa, where, like elsewhere in the country, Muslims feel economically and politically marginalised. They are angered by what they say is disproportionate harassment by the police and the shooting dead by the security forces of a number of radical Islamic clerics in the city.

According to Hansen, Kenya was important to Al Shabaab logistics from the start. 'Ethnic Somalis living in Kenya had functioned as a logistical hub, channelling funds and money into Somalia. However, from 2009 onwards, Al-Shabaab transcended ethnicity and non-Somalis were to become important.'[26] Hansen describes how Al Shabaab developed 'quite a substantial organisation within the country, and today perhaps as many as 10 per cent of its members are of Kenyan origin'.[27]

The Somali Diaspora

Somalia's nomadic and seafaring traditions, and the long years of war, have resulted in a significant proportion of its estimated population of 14 million living beyond its borders. Many live in neighbouring countries, others in the Gulf, Europe, the US, Canada, Australia and elsewhere. There are 900,000 registered Somali refugees living in the country's immediate neighbours,[28] which also host tens of thousands of undocumented Somalis, as well as having substantial Somali populations of their own. Together with the hundreds of thousands of Somalis living further afield, the global total of those living outside Somalia could be as high as 2 million, maybe even more. Many diaspora Somalis remain highly connected with their homeland, sending money to relatives, investing in businesses and regularly returning home, often for months at a time. In many cases, it might be more useful to think of diaspora Somalis as having one foot in Somalia, the other outside, so closely involved are they in the political, business and other affairs of their homeland.

Most members of the diaspora have a positive relationship with Somalia, sending home more than a billion dollars a year in lifeline support to friends and family members, and as funds to start and grow businesses.[29] Whilst remittances outstrip aid and are often key to people's survival, they can be problematic when in some cases they create dependency, with people relying on money sent by relatives abroad instead of trying to find work for themselves. For example, I visited a farm in Somaliland where a large family had a couple of poorly tended fields, with a few heads of livestock wandering about and trampling on the crops. When I asked why they did not try to control their animals or to better look after their crops, they said there was not much point in bothering with the farm because relatives abroad sent sufficient funds for the family to feed itself, educate the children and buy medicine when people fell sick.

Many Somalis have returned home permanently, some to safe areas, others braving the bombs and bullets to set up businesses or to work for non-governmental organisations, international bodies or the Somali federal and regional administrations. Others have established restaurants, banks, hotels and beauty parlours.

In 2012 a brave young man, Mohamed Mahamoud Sheik Ali, left a comfortable life in Dubai to set up Mogadishu's first dry-cleaners in more than two decades. Before Mohamed started his business, I was often surprised to see wealthy Somali business-men and high-ranking government officials board planes in Mogadishu with armfuls of dirty suits. I later discovered they were taking them abroad to be dry-cleaned as they had no way of cleaning them in-country. Once, at a summit held in Ethiopia's most luxurious hotel, I was astonished to see Somalia's top politicians marching down the plush carpeted corridors with armloads of freshly dry-cleaned suits.

Mohamed later branched into floristry, growing fresh flowers in the fertile lands of Afgoye, about 30 kilometres from Mogadishu, for sale in the capital. He brought in flowering trees from abroad and planned to green the city. Mohamed also set up a boys' orphanage and a support community for young people involved in start-ups. He became something of an inspirational figure, although he always remained modest and unassuming.

In August 2018, Mohamed was shot dead by two men in a busy part of Mogadishu. Although some speculated he had been killed by Al Shabaab, the group remained silent about his death, suggesting it was not involved. Like many other unsolved mur-ders in Somalia, there are several possible perpetrators, including not only Al Shabaab, but also politicians, business rivals, crimi-nals, or those involved in property disputes. In some cases, mur-der can be motivated by plain jealousy.

For Somalis returning home to work for the government, there are plenty of administrations to choose from. There is the federal government in Mogadishu, a number of regional administrations, and the government of the self-declared republic of Somaliland, which broke away from the rest of Somalia in 1991 but has not been recognised internationally. In some Somali administrations at least half the cabinet consists of people who have returned from abroad. This has led to resentment, with those who never left the country scorning the returnees. They accuse them of grabbing the top jobs and swanning around with their smart suits, laptops and foreign accents, with little understanding of complex clan politics and local culture. Unlike those who stayed behind, these individuals can use their foreign passports to leave Somalia at the slightest sign of trouble, or whenever they want a break from the unpredictable, insecure environment.

Members of the diaspora can also cause disruption within Somalia from their homes overseas. Many of the 760 or so Somali news websites are run from outside the country.[30] Somalis sitting in their living rooms in Dubai, Stockholm and Toronto can wreak havoc by publishing inflammatory articles that if written from inside the country could get them killed. Somalia is one of the most dangerous places in the world to work as a journalist, with at least sixty-four being killed between 1993 and 2017. 2012 was the most dangerous time, when at least twelve journalists were killed in a single year.[31] According to one report, fifteen journalists were killed between 1 January and 11 October 2012. None of the perpetrators were caught.[32]

Other members of the diaspora have gone to fight for Al Shabaab. Indeed, the majority of Al Shabaab's recruits from the West are Somalis. Although it is impossible to know the true figure, it is estimated that hundreds—possibly as many as 1,000—members of the Somali diaspora have joined the group, although numbers reportedly declined during the heyday of IS in Syria and Iraq.[33] It is not yet clear whether the declining fortunes of IS will put Somalia back in the spotlight as an attractive destination for violent jihadis, both Somali and non-Somali.

Some members of the diaspora have conducted suicide attacks in Somalia. At least twelve Somalis from the UK, Canada,

Denmark, Germany, Norway, the Netherlands and the US are known to have done so.[34] In 2009, a young Somali from Denmark blew himself up at a graduation ceremony in Mogadishu where the first set of medical students in years were qualifying as doctors. More than twenty government ministers, journalists, teachers, graduates and members of their families were killed, together with the suicide bomber. This incident was a turning point in terms of public support for the Islamists. The first anti-Al Shabaab march took place in Mogadishu after the bombing, with hundreds openly shouting 'Down with Al Shabaab' and setting fire to the group's black flag.

One study found that the majority of diaspora Somalis who left home to join Al Shabaab, 'were young, male, of the "1.5 genera-tion" (those who were born to first-generation parents or who immigrated to a host country at a young age), relatively well edu-cated, and radicalised in their country of birth or host country'.[35] The researcher found that, counter to prevailing narratives, many were well-adjusted, integrated into their communities and not alienated or isolated. Several had attended college or university.[36]

Some members of the diaspora work in Al Shabaab's publicity department, making recruitment videos in a style that appeals to those living abroad. They bring in useful skills, including foreign languages and a sophisticated knowledge of IT and social media.

According to Menkhaus, diaspora recruits are both advanta-geous and problematic for Al Shabaab:

> It is clear that the diaspora are not of much value as rank and file militia for the shabaab or any other fighting force in Somalia. Somalia is already saturated with experienced teenage gunmen and has no need to import more. In fact, evidence from the ICU in 2006 suggests that Somali diaspora as well as foreign fighters were as much a liability as an asset to the ICU. They were unfamiliar with the countryside, often spoke the Somali language poorly, were more likely to become sick, and required a fair amount of oversight.

But the diaspora are useful to shabaab and other armed groups in Somalia in other ways. Their familiarity with computers and the internet is a valuable communication skill. Their familiarity with the English language is helpful for translation. And ... a young diaspora recruit is, upon arrival in Somalia, entirely cut off socially and therefore in theory easier to isolate, indoctrinate, and control for the purpose of executing suicide bombings. ... From this perspective, a young diaspora member who heeds the call by a recruiter to 'join the cause' of fighting to protect his nation and religion is not so much a terrorist as a pawn, exploited by the real terrorists, those who are unwilling themselves to die for the cause but who are happy to manipulate a vulnerable and isolated youth to blow himself up.[37]

Forced Returns

Although they have not gained as much media attention as those who volunteer from abroad to fight in Somalia, there are other groups in the diaspora who are vulnerable to recruitment by Al Shabaab. These are people who are returned to Somalia against their will, either because their asylum applications have been refused or because their parents send them back as they are no longer able to cope with them. Some have brought shame upon their families by committing crimes, joining gangs, taking drugs, drinking alcohol, falling pregnant, or becoming too Westernised.

In the US, UK and other parts of Europe, it is becoming harder for Somalis to gain asylum or any other form of leave to remain in the country. The argument is that, for most categories of people, Somalia no longer poses a grave risk to life or livelihood.[38] There is also pressure on the approximately 300,000 Somali refugees in the vast Dadaab camps in eastern Kenya to go home. Between 2014 and 2017, more than 72,000 Somali refugees were taken from Dadaab to Somalia, some of whom were born in the camps and had never set foot in the country. They received little support on return, many saying they felt abandoned by the Somali government and international organisations. A report by the Mogadishu-based think tank Heritage Institute for Policy Studies argued that the Kenyan government should integrate into local society those who had been born in Kenya, had family links there or had adjusted to the Kenyan system. This it said 'would be preferable to shipping them to Somalia, potentially creating contingents of angry Kiswahili-speaking, Kenya-savvy potential recruits for Al Shabaab'.[39]

Somalis who have lived overseas since early childhood and fall into a life of crime are also at risk of being forcibly returned to Somalia. In the UK, those who receive prison sentences of twelve months or more are subject to automatic deportation to a country about which they might have almost no knowledge or experience, where they often have no close family or friends and whose language they cannot speak. According to one Somali who came to the UK when he was a toddler and, at the age of nineteen, was served with a deportation order after committing multiple crimes: 'It will be no different to sending any other British black guy over there.'

The US under Donald Trump has been particularly enthusiastic about the forcible return of Somalis, especially those who have committed crimes. In the first year of his administration, several planeloads of Somalis were sent to Somalia. In one notorious case, ninety-two Somalis were flown out of the US on 7 December 2017, only to return to the US the following day after a layover in Senegal because the relief crew had been unable to get sufficient rest. They wore handcuffs secured to their waists, their feet shackled together, for more than forty-eight hours. As they were not allowed access to the toilets, they had to urinate into bottles or on themselves. According to a lawsuit filed on behalf of the men, Immigration and Customs Enforcement agents wrapped some of them in full body restraints, kicking and beating others.[40] Sixty-one of the deportees had criminal convictions, including for homicide and rape. Somalis have reacted with horror to the idea that people 'who learned to be criminals abroad' are being put on planes and dumped on Somali soil. They fear they will bring new forms of criminality and anti-social behaviour to Somalia.

I have interviewed Somalis who have already been forcibly sent back to Somalia. One man, who ended up living in a camp for the displaced in Mogadishu, said people he suspected were from Al Shabaab came to him at night. They searched him and said they knew he had recently come from the West, accusing him of spying for the Americans and the Somali government. Another man, deported from the UK after living there for more than twenty-five years, lived in a squatter camp and said he had no money and no prospect of finding work. He told me he relied on the charity of a trader who occasionally brought him the half-rotten vegetables he was unable to sell in the market. He asked me to help him find a job in Mogadishu, to put him in touch with my contacts, but I was reluctant to do so as he had a string of convictions, including for sexual assault and grievous bodily harm.

Another man, Adan, who had served years in prison in the UK for attempted rape, drugs offences and serious violence, also asked me to recommend him to contacts who might be able to give him a job. He promised he was a reformed character and had no interest in returning to a life of crime. He came from the despised Midgan minority clan and said he believed he would have died in Mogadishu had it not been for the kindness of a man he met on the plane, who allowed him to stay at his home in exchange for doing odd jobs. Adan, who had been born in a village in southern Somalia, had come with his family to the UK as a toddler in the 1990s, fleeing civil war. He had no experience of Mogadishu, spoke poor Somali and had no known family in the country. He sometimes earned $1 a day by coaching young football players, but seemed at a loss as to how he would earn enough money to live independently.

'I have met a beautiful young lady from my clan and I want to marry her,' Adan said. 'But in order to marry her, I need to show her family I can support her. I need to rent a room for us to live in. Mary, please can you send me $300, which will enable me to rent a room for six months? Then I can marry, and have someone to cook and clean for me. I can have a companion and start a family. I learned some construction skills, like plastering, when I was in prison. I believe once I am settled with my wife, I will be able to get a job in construction as there is a real building boom here in Mogadishu, and a lack of skills. Lots of skilled construction workers have to be brought in from abroad.'

Some young men who have been served with deportation orders have told me they will actively seek out Al Shabaab on return to Somalia. Abdihafid's family fled with him to the UK during the civil war of the 1990s. Abdihafid was eighteen months old. He became involved in gangs from an early age and has a string of convictions. He is addicted to crack cocaine and alcohol and has been thrown out of the family home, so he couch surfs in the houses of friends, or sometimes sleeps rough on the streets. The courts have rejected all of his appeals, and he is destined for Mogadishu.

'The only people who will look after me in Somalia are Al Shabaab. When I get there I will not stop searching until I find them. They will provide my living and my food. They will give me a woman from their group of ready-made wives, and they will give me a gun. If I am forced to go to Somalia, I will have no choice but to join them. What kind of British government is this that sends me back from the country I have grown up in, that is all I know, to lead such a life in Somalia?'

I met another young man in a similar position to that of Abdihafid on a bright summer's day in London. He was staying in a scruffy northern suburb, where straggly plants were trying to squeeze their way through cracks in the pavement, cars parked haphazardly along the road.

The house I was visiting was one of the largest on the street. There was a blocked drain by the front door. A grey stinking pool of water had collected on the pathway. I stepped over it and rang the bell. It was broken so I knocked. A small boy with a closely shaved head and still dressed in his pyjamas let me in, then quickly darted into the darkness inside. All the curtains in the house were drawn.

A television blared in the living room, tuned to a Somali satellite channel. Five children tore around the room, leaping on and off the sofa where a woman sat breastfeeding. Through the darkness, I made out a baby's cot in the corner.

I asked for the young man, Ali, whom I had come to visit. Eventually he came down the stairs. Low-slung jeans hung on his wiry body. His eyes were red and there were shiny bald spots on his head where his hair had fallen out.

He explained that the woman was a distant cousin from Mogadishu. She and the children had recently come to London to join her husband, who had been granted asylum. She was depressed and wanted to go home, even though she had been living in a squatter camp in a particularly dangerous part of Mogadishu. She spoke no English.

I asked if perhaps, on this beautiful day, the children wanted to go outside to play in the large garden. Ali explained that the woman was used to keeping her children indoors in order to protect them from mortars and shrapnel. He said she had not yet acclimatised to the peace of London.

'I have reached the end of the road,' he said. He told me that he had come to the UK in the early 1990s, when he was two years old, after war broke out in Somalia. In his teens he had fallen into a life of crime, which led to fifty-seven convictions. When he received a sentence of more than twelve months in prison, he was sent a letter telling him he was subject to automatic deportation. He had appealed and appealed but this had led nowhere, so he was going to be sent to Somalia, a country he had not set foot in for more than two and a half decades. He would get off the plane in Mogadishu, a city he had never visited as he had been born near the Kenyan border and fled to Nairobi with his family before coming to the UK. He had heard about me through a relative and wanted to ask me about life in Mogadishu, and to know whether I could help him find work there.

'Do they have fish and chips in Mogadishu? Do they have McDonalds or Burger King? What will I do without burgers?'

I tried to calm him, telling him about the delicious fresh fish, camel meat, pasta and watermelon. But I felt bad, as I was painting a rosy picture of a broken place.

'The only people who will feed me in Somalia are Al Shabaab,' he said. 'That is the only solution. I have no family there, I don't know anybody. I cannot speak Somali. I am from a minority clan. Al Shabaab will give me food, money, a gun and a wife.'

I wanted some water and went into the kitchen. There I found the woman feeding her children cold mashed beans. The room was large and had a table and chairs, but she was serving them on torn pieces of cardboard laid out on the broken lino of the floor. The children squatted on their haunches, scooping up the food with their hands.

I went back to the living room to speak to Ali.

'I am scared to stay in the UK too. The last time they put me in a Category A prison even though I had only done a Category C crime. I met people convicted of terror-related crimes and they told me to do certain things for them once I got out of jail. They said they would get me if I didn't.

'I am staying with my relatives for a few days. Then they will give me the money to go back to my accommodation in Hull. I live with four other asylum seekers—they are from Zimbabwe, Iran, Iraq and Afghanistan. I don't speak their languages and I don't share their culture. I spend all day in my room watching videos on my phone. Sometimes I watch videos from Al Shabaab. They give me some strength.'

Shortly after I visited Ali, he disappeared. His relatives told me they had no idea where he was, but that he had probably vanished into the no-man's land of the British black economy, dodging police and other officials, and doing anything he could to avoid being sent to Somalia.

* * *

Another vulnerable group are those sent to Somalia not by the state but by their families. These are people who have become involved in crime, drugs or other such activities. Some parents feel so ashamed of their wayward children that they send them to Somalia to render them invisible and, they believe, to restore the rest of the family's reputation as an upstanding part of the Somali community. Others send them in order to get them away from bad 'Western' influences and to try to inculcate in them proper Somali values. They are known as *dhaqan celis* in Somali, which means 'rehabilitation', referring to the fact that they have been sent to their homeland to be rehabilitated as honourable, decent Somalis.

I met some *dhaqan celis* boys at a mental hospital in Mogadishu.

Somalia has one of the highest rates of mental illness in the world. According to the World Health Organization, one in three people in the country suffers from some form of psychological problem.[41] This is perhaps not surprising given the three decades of conflict and the breakdown of institutions. Mental illness is taboo in Somalia, with people chained up for years, or even put into cages with hyenas, as this is believed to cure them. One man who has dedicated his life to helping the mentally ill and to free them from their chains is 'Dr Habeb'.

'That must be it,' I said, pointing at a yellow wall painted with a picture of a large blue human brain. 'The Habeb Mental Hospital.'

Inside was a room crammed with metal beds. The spare patches of floor were covered with dark, yellow foam mattresses that were crumbling at the edges. There, stretched out, sometimes one, sometimes two, sometimes three to a mattress, were men. It was the middle of the day but they were all lying down. Some were asleep; others stared at me with dead eyes. They did not seem fully alive.

The heavy stillness was broken when a man rushed in, dressed in a white coat. It had obviously seen better days, but was clean and freshly pressed. His eyes sparkled. He gesticulated energetically. His voice was strained and high-pitched.

This was 'Dr Habeb', who is actually a nurse with three months of mental health training. He founded and now runs the hospital. In Somali, *habeb* means 'a voice which seems to be running out,' and that is just what his voice sounded like, as if there were not much left of it.

'There are 132 patients in here. Most of them are suffering from Post Traumatic Stress Disorder. Many have schizophrenia. Their families bring them here years too late. They all come here with their legs and arms in chains, because that is what Somalis do with mental patients. Here we have a "no chains" policy. Nobody in my hospital is chained.'

The men on the beds and the mattresses on the floor did not react. I asked Dr Habeb why they were all lying down.

'Because this morning I gave them psychotropic drugs. They are all happy now. Up until two years ago the World Health Organization gave us drugs. But then it stopped for lack of funds. Now I buy them in the local market. Sometimes they are out of date but what can I do?'

Suddenly Habeb started to weep. His voice went even higher. It cracked and broke. Tears poured down his face. His nose was streaming.

WHO AM I?

'Where is the United Nations? Where is the Somali president, the prime minister, the parliament? They all say "Habeb is a good person", "Habeb is a hero". But I don't need words. I need action.'

I gave Dr Habeb my handkerchief and we walked outside. The sun was warm and bright. There was the odd burst of gunfire, not far away. Dr Habeb told me how in the past few years, at least 300 mental patients had been shot dead by the security forces in Mogadishu. They do not know that it is not safe to walk around at night and that you should stop at checkpoints. So they get shot.

In a covered area, a bit like a barn for animals, I found dozens more male patients. Some of them were relatively alert. A group of young men approached me. They spoke English, in a variety of accents. They explained how they had fled Somalia with their families when war first broke out in the 1990s. They listed the places they had moved to, including Ottawa, Copenhagen, Minnesota, Cardiff and London. I found it odd that so many Somalis from the diaspora were living in a mental hospital in Mogadishu. The boys told me they had been sent to Somalia by their families after getting into trouble at home.

One young man in a bright orange T-shirt said he came from the Netherlands. He explained how he got into trouble, smoking cannabis, skipping school and getting into fights.

'My mother brought me to Somalia two years ago. She told me she would collect me last summer, but she never came. Maybe she will come next summer. I was living with distant relatives here in Mogadishu but I did not fit in. I had trouble adjusting to life in this city. I was terrified by the gunfire and other explosions and, I cannot lie to you, I missed smoking weed. My relatives brought me here, to the Habeb hospital.'

Another young man asked if I came from London. When I said I did, he asked me to write down a phone number so that I could call his family and tell them he wanted to come home. When I called the number on my return to the UK and passed on his message, the person who answered the phone cut me off. When I tried to ring back, my calls were not answered.

Dr Habeb explained that by medicating these boys, he was helping them with their mental illnesses. By keeping them in his hospital he was protecting them from Al Shabaab and other armed groups who might want to recruit, intimidate or harass them.

For its part, Al Shabaab says it welcomes people from the diaspora who want to come to live in the areas it controls, as long as they abide by its rules.

'Some people from the UK and the US are living in areas under our control. They have farms and houses. We phone people in the West to invite them to come to our areas to make investments and do business. We tell them that we will be responsible for their security. We interview them first to make sure they are not planning to spread Western culture and Western lifestyle, for example by opening a cinema. We call the Somalis in South Africa and elsewhere, who are being massacred and persecuted by the locals, and tell them to come back.'

I have met Somalis in Britain who tell me they have farms and other business ventures in Al Shabaab areas. Some say`they make good profits and that neither they nor the people working for them have problems with the Islamists as long as they pay their taxes and keep to the rules. Most of these diaspora Somalis feel no sympathy whatsoever for Al Shabaab's mission, but seem happy to pay fees to the militants as long as they continue to make money. Once again, this reveals the many grey areas surrounding Al Shabaab and those who operate in areas it controls.

As this chapter has shown, Al Shabaab is made up of many different types of people, who have joined for a multitude of reasons. A bit like Somalia itself, the movement consists of a patchwork of different groups and individuals, who sometimes act in unison and sometimes behave in a more fractured and disjointed way. Many people say they are in Al Shabaab against their will, while some join for reasons that have nothing to do with religion. Others believed they knew what they were signing up for, only to discover the group represents something entirely different.

Despite the fractured nature of the group and its competing ideologies, it has proved remarkably resilient, especially in the Somali context, where political movements and armed groups so frequently break apart or realign with former adversaries, only to split away from them a short time afterwards. The differing motivations for joining the group, the existence of foreign fighters, and Al Shabaab's supple nature and ability to quickly adapt to changing circumstances make it all the more difficult to try to defeat it militarily, negotiate with its leaders or coax its members to defect. In some ways, Al Shabaab is like water running down a hill, sometimes acting as a large, united force, at other times dividing into multiple rivulets, taking unpredictable paths and sometimes meeting dead ends.

The fact that so many people have a loose association with the movement, flitting in and out of the group or performing certain duties on its behalf, makes it almost impossible to define Al Shabaab. It is simultaneously everywhere and nowhere, maintaining a shadowy presence or influence throughout and beyond Somalia.

2

WOMEN AND CHILDREN

I sat with a group of men in a hot, stuffy living room. They were all wearing sarongs and were sprawled across a low, cushioned lounging area built around the perimeter of the room. They shouted and gesticulated, voices notching up to ever higher pitches as time progressed, arms waving ever more wildly.

In front of each man was the equipment that would see him through the afternoon and at least half the night. There were large bunches of leaves and an assortment of plastic bottles filled with water and luridly coloured soft drinks in improbable shades of red, orange, green and yellow. There were thermoses of tea, dainty china cups, small towels to wipe the sweating brow and a plastic waste bin to throw the stalks into once the most succulent of the leaves had been picked or nibbled off. One side of each man's cheek bulged as if afflicted by a large tumour, packed with a big lump of mashed, chewed up leaves. When the men spoke, small, wet, green specks flew into the air. The smell was of newly cut vegetation, almost like a freshly mown lawn or a trimmed hedge.

This was a qat-chewing session, where business deals, cease-fires and political agreements are made, broken and made again.

The leaf acts as a stimulant. Its overuse can exacerbate mental health problems and badly damage people's teeth, turning them to dark brown stubs. In 2014 qat was classified as a Class C drug in the UK. It has also been banned in the US and a number of other European countries, causing great frustration to many in the Somali community but relief for family members who felt they had lost their husbands, brothers and uncles to the drug. Although some Somali women chew qat, they do so in private. The vast majority of chewers are men. A Somali friend from Bristol emigrated to Ethiopia soon after the UK qat ban was imposed, so desperate was he to keep on chewing. Another moved to Somaliland from Liverpool for the same reason.

Others find ever more desperate ways of accessing the drug, including smuggling dried qat leaves into the UK, immersing them in water and chewing the resulting brown mush or drinking it like tea. Qat is readily available in this form in London. It took me about five minutes to track down an illegal qat seller in a north-western suburb. He was a Moroccan who sold small plastic bags of the dried leaves for £5.00 each from a small, dark room at the back of his café. Qat-loving Somali friends in the UK have told me they sometimes manage to buy fresh leaves, which they say are smuggled in by Eastern Europeans who hide the qat amongst lettuce, spinach and other green vegetables.

I am usually the only woman present at qat-chewing gatherings, where I feel my identity as a foreigner and a journalist somehow cancels out my status as a female. While there are exceptions, women in Somalia tend to have less of a voice in public space, with older men often dominating the political, religious and economic spheres. Sometimes, when I am sitting in a mixed group of people in Somalia, a man will only greet the other men and ignore the women, acting as if he cannot see them, as if they are completely invisible.

A more liberal-minded friend was present at this 'green bar' or 'green pub' as he likes to call the qat-chewing sessions. He lit a golden, translucent lump of resin in a pretty charcoal burner carved from pale soft stone. It bubbled slightly, the white smoke rising up and filling the room with the aroma of pure frankincense. This precious perfume is tapped from trees grown in Puntland and Somaliland.

'You know, in our country, women get a very bad deal,' he said. 'We have a saying about the Somali social hierarchy which states that men come first, then camels, then boys, then other livestock, then women, and last of all, at the bottom of the pile, are the girls. When a boy is born, we celebrate by slaughtering at least two animals. When it is a girl, we might slaughter one, or none at all.'

I left the men to their chewing and went deep into Mogadishu to speak to some women who had agreed to talk to me about their experiences with Al Shabaab.

Despite their being pounded by nearly three decades worth of weapons fire, it is still possible to trace the city's history through its buildings. The narrow, snaking streets of Hamar Weyne on the seafront are among the most ancient and have a distinctly Arab feel. There is the crumbling white grandeur of the Italian colonial period, some structures no more than elegant skeletons; others, like an ornate water fountain, still miraculously intact although long run dry. There are the stark, straight lines of the 1970s socialist era, and daring new buildings, painted pale shades of blue, yellow and pink. Some of these freshly painted modern structures already bear the scars of recent attacks. Turkey, which from 2011 has had a strong influence in parts of Somalia, especially the capital, has announced its presence by building a huge Ottoman-style mosque. Its exquisite, intricate crimson, blue and gold decorations were painted by specialist artisans flown over from Istanbul.

In amongst the ruin and decaying former splendour are Mogadishu's tent cities. Here people live in the flimsiest of constructions, made from bent wood covered with a patchwork of tattered cloth and plastic. Occasionally, there will be a tin shack. Some people have lived like this for almost thirty years, fleeing violence and drought in other parts of the country or a former home in Mogadishu destroyed by shellfire. Many are members of minority clans.

It is in one of these camps that I met Maryan. We bent down low to enter her shelter. She spread a cloth on the bare earth for us to sit on. To one side was a baby flat on her back on the soil. She was sound asleep.

'Rats sometimes scurry through my home,' said Maryan with a wry smile. 'But rats are good news because it means there are no snakes here, which are far more deadly. I know the snakes are here when there are no rats. This is because the snakes usually eat them all.'

Maryan started to talk about the day Al Shabaab changed her life.

'I used to have a small teashop. I had a couple of tables and a few plastic chairs. My stall was on the roadside, very close to a military base in the town of Belet Huen. Most of my clients were soldiers. I would sell them tea, very sweet. It was popular and I made enough money to get by. One day, I received a phone call from a withheld number. A man said I was serving tea to infidels and that I must stop or I would be killed. I was terrified. I did not know what to do because I have no husband, and it was only by selling tea to soldiers that I could feed my children.

'I continued to sell the tea, and I continued to receive the death threats. One day, the man on the phone said I must actively help Al Shabaab. He said I must carry some explosives for them and hide them under my tea stall so the militants could blow up the soldiers who came to drink there. I became angry and said there was no way I would work for Al Shabaab, and that they should just go ahead and kill me if they wanted to.'

Maryan then decided to give up her tea stall and move with her children to Mogadishu. She now survives on food handouts from Turkish charities. At night she is afraid as her cloth shelter has no door to lock. She has heard of rapes in the camp, sometimes by men in military uniform. Al Shabaab has stopped calling her, but she suspects they know where she is as she is sure they have informants working for them in the camp. She is terrified the militants will want to punish her for refusing to plant explosives under her tea stall and for running away from Belet Huen. She explained that it is impossible to hide in Somalia, that people can always work out precisely who you are by asking you to reveal your clan, sub-clan, sub-sub-clan and sub-sub-sub-clan. In a sense, a person's clan identity is like a passport that also serves as a kind of address book or telephone directory. Somalia has a powerfully oral culture and information is stored in people's heads, not on pieces of paper or digital devices. I am often astonished by how quickly Somalis can track down people I am trying to trace, even if they have never met them and know nobody in the area they live.

* * *

It would be wrong to class all women as passive victims in the conflict. Over the decades, they have taken active roles in financing war, mobilising fighters, nursing the wounded, looting, gathering intelligence, providing logistical support, and even occasionally taking up arms themselves.

According to a study on the role of Somali women in conflict and peacemaking, 'Women's role in the mobilisation of militiamen is also under-reported. They often deploy songs and poetry, and techniques of humiliation and emasculation, to goad young men into fighting or to holding their nerve.' Somali men have told me how women have humiliated them with crude, mocking songs, some about how they are nothing but a weak breed of semi-males with female genitalia, as a way of shaming them into going out to fight. This is especially common during periods of clan conflict, when women feel as passionately as men do about protecting their group's interests and fighting for its supremacy. Indeed, at times, they are considered to be the main instigators of clan conflict due to the energy they put into encouraging men to take up arms. As one elder cited in the study said, women 'have a big role in heating the conflict.'

The study, which focused on the southern city of Kismayo and surrounding areas, found that a small number of women also served as fighters and killers. The researchers looked mainly at the roles played by women during periods of clan conflict, rather than during the Al Shabaab insurgency. As well as documenting women's role in violence, it discussed their equally important function as 'vital peacebuilders'.

Some of the women spoke about how they took up arms to protect themselves and others. A woman who sold clothes described how she organised a clan militia to look after her stock as well as that of fellow traders. She explained how she worked as a guard, sleeping amongst the militiamen as they guarded the property at night.

Interviewees described how during periods of clan conflict some women put on military uniform, took up arms and actively joined in the fighting. 'I shaved my hair and wore a hat. No one noticed I was a woman ... I wore a sweater, a jacket, trousers, boots and my gun. And that is how I walked around with the militias.' Another woman, 'Khadija', said, 'I used to have my own AK ... I was part of the fighting. I got involved even before some of the men did. When male fighters were on the street defending, I ran there and arrived before other men ... We are not so few women who took up the gun ... Women participated in the war, and the same rules (as for men) applied to them, too ... Some women used guns; others slashers or big knives ...

Everyone participated. No one is clean. Even if you didn't support by carrying guns or helping during the fighting, you were supporting in your heart.'

While some women fought alongside men, others operated alone as snipers and assassins. Some specialised in 'finishing off' the injured 'by cutting them with machetes'. One respondent described seeing women 'putting detergent (soap powder) into wounded men's mouths, cutting them with knives and finishing them off. It happened everywhere ... There could be 30–50 women involved.'[1]

Unlike the Nigerian Islamist group Boko Haram, which regularly uses women and girls, even toddlers, as bombers, strapping explosives to their bodies and sending them into crowded places, Al Shabaab rarely deploys women to carry out acts of violence. With the exception of a few female suicide bombers, women generally perform other roles for the group, such as serving as intelligence gatherers, couriers, fundraisers, brides, cooks and cleaners, or carrying and hiding equipment. While some women support Al Shabaab's ideology, others are forced to work for the group against their will.

A young Somali man who had come to live in Mogadishu from Toronto spoke about the day in June 2011 when his cousin killed her uncle, the interior minister Abdishakur Sheikh Hassan. They had been sitting in the minister's house watching television together as they often did during the long, dull days that stretched ahead of them. Al Shabaab's presence in the city and its ferocious, unpredictable battles with the African Union Mission in Somalia (AMISOM) and the Somali forces made it too dangerous to walk the streets or go to the beach. The young man decided to go upstairs, and his cousin came with him.

'As usual, I gestured for her to go first up the stairs, but this time she refused. She insisted firmly that I go up before her, which I thought was strange but no big deal. I went to my room, and she went on down the corridor. Some minutes later there was a terrific blast. My room shook.'

The young woman had gone into her uncle's bedroom, where he was resting. She had detonated a suicide vest packed with explosives so powerful that her head was blasted from her body. The reason that she had not wanted to go up the stairs first was now clear. She did not want her cousin to see what she was wearing under her dress.

Women have also been accused of working as informants for Al Shabaab. In one instance, in October 2016, the district commissioner of the southern town of Baardheere, Abdullahi Noor Hassan, accused wives of Al Shabaab militants of working as spies for the movement. He threatened to arrest them if they did not leave the area: 'Al Shabaab wives and their children must leave the town within seven days or we will take legal action against them. The fighters get all their information from their wives during the night. The women tell them which routes to take and which targets to attack. After thorough investigations we have come to the conclusion that the insecurity in Baardheere is due to the presence of Al Shabaab wives here. We have ordered them to leave town peacefully and to go live with their husbands in areas under the Islamists' control.'[2]

Al Shabaab has made it clear that women should not take on leadership roles within the movement. As one Al Shabaab official said, 'Women are important members of our community. They are our sisters, our mothers and our wives. Their job is to raise the next generation according to the principles of Al Shabaab, which are the purest Islamic principles of all. They can work as traders, teachers, doctors and nurses, but their main job is to look after our homes and our children. Their role is to make the leaders, not to become leaders themselves. Only men can be governors, and religious and military leaders. Only men can fight on the battlefield. I think you know the phrase, "behind every great man there is a great woman". That is a woman's role—to be behind the man.'

According to a report on women and Al Shabaab, women who marry into the group enjoy an enhanced status in the areas under Islamist control. The researcher, who spoke to women who were or had been married to members of Al Shabaab, found that, 'on the whole, their circumstances were considerably better than those experienced by most women in Somalia'. The researcher found that wives of Al Shabaab fighters led a 'privileged existence' compared with other civilians living under the group's rule. They were actively encouraged to run businesses, including food stores and clothes shops. Some worked in the construction industry and in vehicle maintenance. The women said they were allowed access to smart phones and to travel freely. The militants' wives were perceived as fulfilling two important functions: producing and bringing up the next generation of fighters and inculcating their children with Al Shabaab's beliefs.

Some of the women interviewed for the study said they would carry out suicide attacks if necessary. One told the researcher she 'operated as an internal security agent within Al Shabaab–controlled areas. She was occasionally armed with a pistol during security purges, should she need to act immediately against "spies".'[3]

While many women have suffered unspeakable horrors at the hands of Al Shabaab, some, including those living overseas, have contributed to its success. Court documents from the US reveal how women in the highly connected Somali diaspora raised funds for the group. Muna Osman Jama from Virginia and Hinda Osman Dhirane from Washington State were sentenced to twelve and eleven years respectively for providing material support to Al Shabaab. They were also found guilty of organising what was referred to as the 'Group of Fifteen', which included Somali women from the US, Canada, the UK, Sweden, the

Netherlands, Egypt, Kenya and Somalia. This group would hold regular virtual meetings in an internet chat room to raise money to help pay for the Islamists' operations in the Golis Mountains in northern Somalia and two Al Shabaab safe houses in Kenya. One of the properties was used to store weapons and prepare for attacks, the other to treat Al Shabaab fighters who had been wounded in battle. The court documents said the two women had close connections with the leadership of Al Shabaab. They were also recorded laughing on the telephone while the Westgate Mall attack was underway in Nairobi and giggling about the carnage of the Boston Marathon bombing.

* * *

Back in the tent city, Maryan said she had friends who, like her, had been forced to stop working because of threats from Al Shabaab. She took my hand in hers, which was dry and cracked, pulling me through the labyrinth of dwellings. Outside each hut were little grey circles of ash and burned charcoal. Sometimes a metal pot lay on its side in the sand. These were the minuscule outdoor kitchens where the cooking was done. The air smelled of human excrement and unwashed bodies.

We stopped outside a windowless tin shed. As my eyes adjusted to the gloom inside, I could see it was filled with children—boys on one side, girls on the other. It was a koranic school or madrassa. Some of the children clutched long wooden tablets, dipping thin sticks into black liquid as they wrote out koranic verses in Arabic script. A young man in a grubby white vest, worn sarong and flip flops sat in front of the children, reciting religious texts in a dull and expressionless way. I asked the children what they were learning. They did not respond. The man grabbed a girl with one hand, raising a stick with the other as if to beat her. She muttered something incomprehensible. 'This place is a dumping ground for children,' Maryan said. 'Parents bring them here in the morning, go to work or to look for work, and fetch them in the evening. It is not a place for learning. It is a holding centre. The children learn nothing except fear and koranic verses. They are being primed for Al Shabaab.'

Maryan's friends were sitting in the shade under a couple of corrugated zinc sheets propped up with sticks. 'I used to be a health worker, vaccinating children against polio,' said Halima. 'One day I received a call from a man who said he worked for the pure Islamic movement known as Al Shabaab. He accused me of poisoning the children with the vaccine. He said Al Shabaab would kill all of us health workers, one by one. He said they would slit our throats. So I gave up my job.'

Another woman, Fatima, dressed in an orange robe with a blue veil, lost her entire family to Al Shabaab. The militants came to her home in the farmlands of Afgoye, the area near Mogadishu which supplies the city with fresh fruit and vegetables. They abducted her husband and two sons as fighters, her daughter as a wife. 'They did not take me because I was pregnant, but they said they would come for me after I delivered the baby so I too could become one of their wives. I never saw my husband and children again. I lost the baby I was carrying and I fled to Mogadishu. I heard that members of a majority clan have taken over our farm, which was our only livelihood. How will I ever get it back, as a single, destitute woman from a minority group?'

The women called over a girl, who, like Fatima, was a member of a minority clan. She said she was sixteen years old.

'Last year, Al Shabaab came to my house near Brava. They took my two sisters and me. They blindfolded us, threw us into the back of a pick-up truck and drove for what seemed like hours. They kept us locked up in a small room with some other girls. Al Shabaab uses women for sex. They say they are going to marry the girls, but this does not always happen. They also make women do domestic work—cooking, cleaning and laundry.

Sometimes they force them to carry weapons, even bombs. Al Shabaab treats women as slaves. They might not deliberately kill us with bullets, but they kill us in other ways.'

The girl explained how she managed to escape when the Al Shabaab base came under attack and those who could ran away. She did not say what Al Shabaab did to her personally, but her eyes told many stories.

Later on, in the same camp, a man who used to live in an area of southern Somalia controlled by Al Shabaab described how girls between the ages of about fourteen and eighteen were kept at the militants' base, but in a different area from where the male fighters stayed.

'Sometimes we would see them doing the cooking or washing dishes and clothes in the river. Sometimes we would hear them screaming. We knew these were the girls who had been forcibly taken by Al Shabaab to become their wives. Some men join Al Shabaab because it promises them money. Others, especially younger men, are attracted by the lure of marriage. And it is true. Al Shabaab finds beautiful young girls for them to marry. They abduct girls as young as nine years old and prepare them for marriage.'

Despite the numerous accounts of the abduction and forced marriage of women and girls, examples of which have been documented by the media and human rights groups,[4] Al Shabaab vigorously denies it takes them by force.

'Reports that we force women into marriage are absolutely false. The media and Human Rights Watch are merely spreading propaganda. There are no human rights groups in the areas we control so how do they know what we do? Their sources are lying to them or they are lying to themselves.

'Marrying girls by force is unacceptable in our religion. According to the *hadith* [traditions of Prophet Mohamed], the girl must accept and we must have the permission of her family, especially her father. If this does not happen, the marriage is invalid.'

As our discussion continued, the Al Shabaab official became quite excited. He started to spout out a long list of rules, and became angry when interrupted. He manically chanted the sentences in a staccato voice. It was as if he had learned them by rote.

'Here are some of our rules. If a boy and a girl run away and get married without permission, we do not accept this. The boy and the girl should be punished, as should the person who marries them. We destroy the houses where these kinds of fake marriages take place.

'If you have sex and you are not married, this is fornication. The punishment is 100 lashes. If you have sex [with someone] while you are married to someone else, you are stoned to death, as this is adultery. If a man rapes a married woman, he is stoned to death. If the woman is not married, the rapist is lashed 100 times or made to pay some money. He should also marry the woman. If he does not do so, he will be expelled from the area for one year. But in our areas, rape is very, very rare, unlike in the places controlled by the infidel government, where it happens all the time.'

Rape and other forms of sexual violence are common in many parts of Somalia. Women can expect little protection from the Somali security forces and AMISOM, who themselves have been accused of carrying out acts of sexual violence.[5] There have been shocking cases of women being arrested and jailed for reporting that they have been raped. In February 2013, a woman who accused the security forces of gang rape was sentenced to a year in prison. The judge in the case said her crimes were those of 'offending state institutions' and making a 'false accusation'.[6] A journalist who interviewed her about the case was also sent to jail and has since been granted asylum in the United Kingdom.

Many women lose their menfolk to Al Shabaab, either through death or forced recruitment. In 2017, the third consecutive year drought had come to Somalia, I visited a camp on the outskirts of Baidoa. People were fleeing in their thousands from drought-hit rural areas, most of which were controlled by the jihadis. There were the same dome-shaped structures as there were in Mogadishu, but here they were smaller and all were covered in new, bright orange plastic. The people who had arrived most recently had no shelters and were living under acacia trees.

There were no able-bodied men in the camp, just women, children and the odd elderly man. I asked one woman where the men were. She started shouting at me, accusing me of being yet another aid worker come to do yet another assessment, to ask endless irritating questions and then leave, never to return. 'What we need is food, water, medicine and shelter, not questions!' she bellowed. When I told her I was a journalist, she grew even more furious, accusing me of never having done anything good for anybody. Then she stormed off into the dusty distance.

Another woman agreed to speak to me. She explained that the men had stayed behind to look after whatever livestock had survived the drought, and to guard any land they might have. 'But we have heard that Al Shabaab is now harvesting the boys and men we left behind on our parched land, offering them a few dollars and a meal. Against their will, our children, brothers and husbands have become Al Shabaab's new army.'

Some of the women who had lived for years under Al Shabaab contradicted what the militants had told me about women being allowed to work. It is impossible to know who to believe in such instances. Perhaps some branches of Al Shabaab do allow women to work in certain roles outside the home, while others do not. Perhaps the truth is not always told.

A group of women from an Al Shabaab–controlled village not far from Baidoa said they were not allowed to work outside the home, that men and women were banned from mixing in public, and that women were forbidden from going out alone. They complained about having to wear thick, heavy robes with a full niqab covering their face whenever they went out, being forced to stay indoors at certain times, both during the day and at night, and being ordered to pray.

They explained how life in the village had become much quieter under Al Shabaab. There were fewer people in the streets. Shops no longer played music, a small video parlour had been shut down and musical ring tones on mobile phones were banned. People had stopped trusting each other, as nobody knew who was working as an Al Shabaab informant. One day, a van with loudspeakers drove around the village ordering everyone to go to the main square to watch the execution of a man who had been found guilty by an Al Shabaab court of spying for the government. The women said they were told to take their babies and toddlers and to collect their older children from school, so that all of them could watch the execution. One woman asked how anybody could expect her children to grow up as normal, civilised human beings after being forced to witness such violence.

* * *

Hundreds of thousands of Somali children have been born and brought up in areas controlled by Al Shabaab. Many have known no other influence in their lives. Propaganda videos show tiny children wearing black Al Shabaab bandanas and headscarves, brandishing brightly coloured plastic machine guns. Sometimes they appear as mini Al Shabaab fighters, dressed in khaki or camouflage with a *kufiya* scarf wrapped around their head. They perform military drills, march in straight lines along the beach and participate in koranic recitation competitions.

Although Al Shabaab has run madrassas for years, in April 2017 it introduced its own curriculum. Schools in Al Shabaab areas now offer a fully Islamist syllabus, much of it in Arabic. Subjects include science, mathematics, history, geography, Somali, Arabic, *hadith*, *fiqh* (Islamic jurisprudence), *tawheed* (Oneness of God) and *tajweed* (rules governing pronunciation during the recitation of the Koran). The group has tried to impose its curriculum in areas outside its control, including Kismayo and Mogadishu, but has had little success in doing so.

Like the Boko Haram Islamists in Nigeria, Al Shabaab has warned parents not to send their children to schools that teach a Western 'apostate' syllabus. In October 2018, the group warned educational bodies not to accept a new government policy which introduced a standard model of schooling across the country in an attempt to bring together a system that had been fractured and broken by thirty years of conflict and instability. Al Shabaab's chief spokesman, Ali Dheere, who is also the head of its Office of Education, said 'strong action' would be taken against any school that ignored the warning. He said the new curriculum did not comply with the sharia and accused the United Nations Educational, Scientific and Cultural Organisation (UNESCO) of propagating an 'incorrect' system which opposed Islam.

According to the Hiraal Institute, in 2016 the militants banned traditional Somali koranic schools, known as *dugsi*, replacing them with what they called 'Islamic Institutes'. Each clan is allocated a quota of children aged eight to fifteen, who are handed over to these establishments. Al Shabaab has published photos of boys graduating from the Islamic Institutes. During the ceremony, they sit on the floor, holding flags. They all wear black headscarves decorated with the white logo of Al Shabaab.

People who have defected from Al Shabaab describe how they are taught current affairs from a 'jihadi perspective'. They are told the Somali government is illegitimate and that joining Al Shabaab is an obligation. Once they reach the age of fifteen they are sent to military training camps. Defectors told researchers from the Hiraal Institute that the children who come through this system, and who have known nothing else, are 'among the most ideological and fanatical fighters they have encountered'.[7] They said that during the Ramadan offensive of 2017, Al Shabaab suffered such a severe shortage of manpower that it decided to deploy schoolchildren under the age of fifteen as frontline fighters.

There are many other reports of children living inside and outside Al Shabaab areas being forced to fight or otherwise work for the movement. According to the UN, as many as half of all Al Shabaab's forces are males under the age of eighteen.[8] In many cases, children are forcibly abducted, while in others they are lured with false promises. In 2016, UN monitors noted that child recruitment was on the increase, possibly because popular support for Al Shabaab was waning, and the group was becoming ever more desperate to fill its depleting ranks. 'From the patterns observed, Al Shabaab appears to be filling immediate operational needs to deploy large numbers of relatively untrained foot soldiers, but also to be implementing a longer-term strategy to build a cadre of loyal fighters indoctrinated from a young age.'[9]

Human Rights Watch found that in Bay region in mid-2017, Al Shabaab began an increasingly aggressive campaign to recruit children for indoctrination and military training. In September 2017 the militants threatened to attack elders, Koranic teachers and rural communities that refused to provide them with hundreds of children as young as eight. Local residents told Human Rights Watch that Al Shabaab took at least fifty boys and girls from two schools in Burhakaba district and moved them to Bulo Fulay, where it has religious schools and a major military training facility. Some of the children fled unaccompanied to areas outside Al Shabaab's control in order to escape recruitment.[10]

A contact in Al Shabaab said he had read the Human Rights Watch report. 'It is true that we oblige children to attend our schools. It is compulsory for them to go to school, just like it is in many other countries. We concentrate on Islamic teaching but we also teach them other basic subjects like maths, Somali, English and Arabic. They have to know how to read and write. But we only take children once we have secured the agreement of the clan elders. Al Shabaab and the community run the schools together. The community pays for the books, which we have written specially for our curriculum, and we provide the teachers. Once the children have completed their studies they can go for other duties.'

People living in Al Shabaab territory say communities have resorted to ever more desperate techniques to avoid children being recruited by the militants. They say some clans have 'bought' children from poorer groups to take the place of their own. They gave an example from one Al Shabaab–controlled town in central Somalia where the Islamists ordered residents to provide them with forty children. Families raised $1,000 each to 'buy' thirteen children from southern Somalia to send to Al Shabaab in the place of their own.[11]

According to the UN, it is not only Al Shabaab that recruits children, but also the Somali military and other groups. In 2015, the UN documented the recruitment and use of 903 children by armed groups. Al Shabaab took 555 of them; the remaining 348 were recruited by the Somali army and other armed groups. During the first three months of 2016, the UN found that 472 children had been recruited and used as fighters, thirty of them girls. Of this number, 276 were attributed to Al Shabaab, the rest to other groups. In 2015, the UN verified 218 cases of the recruit- ment and use of children by the Somali National Army, up from 197 the previous year. It also found that children were used as spies by the National Intelligence and Security Agency (NISA).[12]

Local officials told UN monitors about a specific incident of child recruitment by Al Shabaab in southern Somalia:

In March 2016, the local community in two villages in Lower Shabelle rejected Al Shabaab's specific request to 'provide' children in the age range of eight to 15 years old and presented an older group of potential recruits for consideration. Al Shabaab did not accept the substitution, and abducted 60 to 70 small children from koranic schools in the area. Later rumours circulated that the children were intended to be used as suicide bombers to interrupt the 2016 political election.[13]

* * *

Some children in the tent city said they had direct experience of Al Shabaab. One was a tall, open-faced fifteen-year-old girl dressed from head to toe in black nylon robes. 'I came here recently from my village, where my family had a farm by a river. Al Shabaab lived in amongst us. They were part of our community. They were proud to say they were members of Al Shabaab. Some carried guns and wrapped their heads in scarves. Others wore ordinary clothes and looked like everybody else. They forced us to study our religion and made people shut their shops earlier than before. Sometimes they would fight with AMISOM and the Somali army for control of a bridge near our home.'

The girl continued speaking with a steady voice, her eyes fixed on some invisible point ahead of her. 'Al Shabaab would take women and girls away if they did not wear a proper hijab. They would take girls as their wives when they reached the age of fifteen or they would take them off to work as cleaners, housemaids, to help with the shopping and to spread religion. It was just what happened.

'One day some members of Al Shabaab stopped me in the road. One said, "*Mashallah*, you are a big girl now." I was not surprised by this. I knew my day would come. I went home and told my mother. She told me not to worry and made me stay inside our small house. Soon after that she prepared a small bag for me. Both of us tied on the full niqab so nobody could see our faces. My mother took me to a minibus and told me not to get off till I reached Mogadishu. I find it strange, big and noisy here ... I had never before left my village. At first I was astonished and terrified, but I am a Somali and I am strong. I can survive anywhere. One day I will go to school. Then I will go to college and train as a nurse.'

A bright-eyed, confident teenager, dressed in jeans and a fake leather jacket, said he used to live in an area controlled by the Islamists, and had recently managed to escape from Al Shabaab. When he was twelve years old, the local imam came to his school and invited him and some of his friends to the mosque.

'When we got to the mosque we found approximately thirty other boys inside, aged between about eleven and eighteen. There were a few men present, dressed in military uniform. They were from Al Shabaab and they told us to sit down. The imam and the other men started lecturing us about Al Shabaab and all the good it was doing for the community. They went on for hours and it was very boring. Then they showed us a film on a big screen about how Al Shabaab helps with farming, irrigation, fixing roads and building bridges. The film was quite long and very dull.'

After the presentation, the men asked the boys to join Al Shabaab. They handed out forms, which were written in Arabic. They told the boys to write their names down in clear letters, with their signatures beside them. The boys could not understand Arabic so did not know exactly what they were signing up for, but they were too frightened to ask questions or to refuse to sign the forms. They were then ordered to go home and return the following day to be assigned their duties.

'My parents were devastated when I told them what had happened. But they knew I had no choice but to obey, as the alternative was death, not just for me, but possibly for other members of the family too.' The boy explained how that night his parents convinced a truck driver passing through their village to take him to Mogadishu, where his mother's relatives met him and took him to the displaced persons' camp where they lived. He said Al Shabaab visited his family shortly after his departure, demanding they summon him home so that he could join the jihad. The boy said he was terrified the militants would take revenge on his family because of what he had done. During occasional phone conversations with his parents they told him Al Shabaab was still insisting he come back. The boy said he sometimes thought of returning home and joining the insurgency just so the rest of his family would be left alone.

Another boy, who came from a different area, also controlled by Al Shabaab, described a similar procedure.

'I did not want to join Al Shabaab. I do not agree with what they do. They kill people in the name of our religion, which is not right. Al Shabaab fighters have no mercy and they take people's lives for no reason. But I had no choice but to join them as it is well known that if you refuse, they will kill you. They will not kill you with guns. They will use knives.'

The boy explained how he and his friends were taken to an Al Shabaab camp and put into groups with other boys from different areas, all of them aged between about eleven and eighteen. They were given different duties, according to their ages. Older boys were given military roles, and younger ones assigned as porters, cleaners and message bearers.

'We young boys were put into a group and told our duty was to make sure people attended the mosque for each of the day's five prayers. We were told we must wake people up for the early morning prayer. We were each given twenty houses and told we were responsible for ensuring every member of those households prayed five times a day—and that nobody was allowed to give an excuse.

'I used to knock on the doors of the houses, greet the people inside and tell them it was nearly prayer time. I told the men they had to go to the mosque and the women to pray inside the house.

It was also my job to tell people I met on the street that it was prayer time and to go to the mosque. If people did not go to pray, we wrote their names down on a list and gave it to Al Shabaab.'

The boy explained that the first time people failed to attend prayers they would receive a warning from Al Shabaab. If they continued to stay away they would be punished, firstly with ten lashes of the whip. If they still refused to go, Al Shabaab would lock them up.

'As for us boys, we would also be punished if we failed to carry out our duties. If a boy did not have a good excuse, such as being ill, the first time he would be warned, the second time he would be whipped and the third time he would be killed.'

Another boy, in clothes so old and tattered it was impossible to know their original colour, spoke of the day he was assigned a different job from his usual task of washing uniforms.

'One night in July 2011, four names were called out in the mosque after evening prayers. My name was among those called. We were told to stay behind in the mosque for a meeting, which was held in a side room. Three members of Al Shabaab appeared. I had never seen them before. They lectured us for about an hour, telling us we were brave, pure young Muslims and that it was our responsibility to defend our religion. After the lecture, they told us we were lucky enough to have been selected for a suicide mission and that our reward would be to go to paradise. We were told that we would carry out the attack the following Friday.'

The boy explained how he had gone home and told his parents what had happened. The next day they had put him on a bus to Mogadishu where he was told to find a distant aunt, with whom he was now living in the tent city. He said he was afraid Al Shabaab would come looking for him. There was no point in telling the security services what had happened to him, he said, because they were likely to accuse him of being an Al Shabaab sympathiser because of his previous experience with the group.

WOMEN AND CHILDREN

Al Shabaab denies it uses children as fighters. But according to one Al Shabaab official, the group defines children and adults in a different way from Westerners. 'Let me clarify two things for you. First, the age we consider people to be children is totally different from you people in the West. You think that anyone under the age of eighteen is a child. In our religion, in our culture, anyone under the age of fifteen is a child. Anyone who is fifteen or over is an adult. That is the age you have to start to pray and to fast during Ramadan. Anyone who is fifteen or over can fight. The second thing I would like to tell you is that reports that we have fighters under the age of fifteen are false, unfounded and untrue. Never, ever would we allow people under the age of fifteen to fight.'

I asked the official about reports of forced recruitment. 'They are lies. We never do that. We never force them, even if they are fifteen years old. If a father comes to us and says his son, who is aged fifteen or over, does not want to fight but wants to continue with his education, work on the farm or otherwise, we have no problem with that. That's fine by us. You can't force anyone to fight for you because one day they will throw their gun aside and flee. Anyway, we have more than enough men who are happy and willing to fight for us. The only thing we do is go to the villages and give inspiring speeches to encourage people to fight for Al Shabaab.'

Whatever the truth about the extent of child recruitment by Al Shabaab, it is clear that a whole generation of children in Somalia is growing up either in areas controlled by the group, or in places where it has some kind of influence. They are being educated in Al Shabaab schools, attending Al Shabaab events and being parented by active members of the group. The Somali governments, both federal and regional, are too weak and under-resourced to provide robust and attractive alternatives for these children. Even if the group is eventually defeated as a fighting force, it will be an enormous challenge to win back the hearts and minds of the hundreds of thousands of children who have grown up knowing nothing other than Al Shabaab.

3

MODUS OPERANDI

Imagine you are looking at Somalia from space. The territory has been divided into a series of different colours, depending on who controls which part. The self-declared republic of Somaliland in the north-west would be one colour, except for the disputed eastern regions. The semi-autonomous region of Puntland in the north-east would be made up of a few different shades, with one colour reserved for the Somali branch of Islamic State (IS). The rest would be a madly swirling kaleidoscope, colours and shapes constantly changing and shifting. According to the UN, there were more than forty armed groups in Somalia at the end of 2017,[1] the amount of territory controlled by each one ceaselessly ebbing and flowing.

A dominant colour in southern and central Somalia would be the one assigned to Al Shabaab. Although the group has been pushed out of major towns and cities, it holds sway over vast areas of countryside, including villages and smaller towns. Whenever foreign or Somali troops withdraw from a town, Al Shabaab moves back in, usually within a few hours. It does this just to show it can, as it tends to leave again after a short period, often after executing those it accuses of collaborating with the enemy. Al Shabaab's enduring presence in the outskirts of urban areas was highlighted in 2018 when it occupied the town of Afgoye three times between July and September.[2] Afgoye is just 30 kilometres from Mogadishu.

At the height of its power, Al Shabaab was the most effective force in the country. Journalists Harun Maruf and Dan Joseph argue that at its most dominant, the group had:

> shoved aside the official government to become the country's true ruler, similar to the Taliban in Afghanistan, Hezbollah in Lebanon, or ISIS in parts of Syria and Iraq. In territorial terms, Shabaab had indeed reached a new peak. By mid-2009, the Shabaab–Hizbul Islam alliance controlled about 80 per cent of Somalia south of the Puntland region. The remainder was ruled not by government but by the militia group Ahlu Sunna Wal Jama'a or local clans.[3]

For most people, what goes on in Al Shabaab territory remains a mystery. While it remains out of bounds for most foreigners, including me, some Somali journalists and researchers have managed to come and go. These people take immense risks. Foreign reporters sometimes take advantage of them, flying into Somalia for a few days to do pieces to camera in front of shell-shattered buildings—preferably with the sound of gunshots or other explosions in the background—and using or sometimes misusing the information supplied by the Somali journalist. They return to their comfortable hotels in Nairobi, Istanbul or Addis Ababa with war stories and glory, but with little thought of the consequences for the Somalis they leave behind, perhaps especially the local journalist or fixer without whom it would have been impossible to do their work.

I have been invited by Al Shabaab to visit and have been promised that my security would be guaranteed, but as I do not know how I would cross safely into and out of its territory, I have declined the invitations.

In order to try to build a picture of how the group operates and how it affects those who live under its rule, I have had to rely on telephone conversations with active members of Al Shabaab, and face-to-face interviews with former members of the group, people who live or have lived in areas it controls, and those who visit from time to time. Also, Al Shabaab produces videos and informs me each time it makes a new one. Some are gory, blow-by-blow accounts of attacks, with Al Shabaab cameramen embedded with the fighters, filming assassinations of officials in Mogadishu, the mass slaughter of villagers on the Kenyan coast and other blood-soaked scenes from the battlefield. Some are more mundane portrayals of village life, while others show the somewhat surreal entertainment the group provides during religious festivals.

If one were to believe Al Shabaab's videos of daily life in the areas it controls, it would be easy to fall under the impression that people live in some kind of rural idyll. Bountiful markets brim with fresh local produce. New irrigation systems water the land. Bridges are built, roads repaired and floods controlled, with Al Shabaab emphasising how it brings true development to Somalia, unlike the hollow government, which is stuck behind high-security walls in Mogadishu and is unable to do anything to improve people's lives.

In June 2018, Al Shabaab enhanced its green credentials by banning single-use plastic bags, saying they were bad for the environment and posed 'a serious threat to humans and animals alike'. It did not elaborate on how the ban would be enforced or what kind of punishments would be meted out to those who continued to use them. Somalia is littered with cheap, flimsy plastic bags. They pile up in the sand, clog waterways and catch in thorn trees and bushes, sometimes giving the landscape a light blue haze as they flutter in the hot breeze. They find their way into the stomachs of goats, sheep, cattle and camels, making them sick or even killing them.

The ban provoked much mockery on social media, with people comparing lists of things banned by Al Shabaab, such as cinemas, music, satellite dishes, smartphones, plastic bags and humanitarian agencies, with those it permitted, such as bombings, assassinations and the killing of civilians. Some described it as 'surreal' and 'weird' that Al Shabaab could express concern about human welfare when it had carried out so many brutal acts. One asked how the group could 'kill 500 people with a single truck bomb in 2017' yet find the time or inclination to ban single-use plastic bags. Another person said they could not understand how a movement that had no qualms about 'bombing people while they lie on the beach, work in government offices or shop in busy markets' could care about the environment.

In its film *Stone Stoves and the Development of Society after the Deception of the Agencies*, Al Shabaab shows in great detail how people make stoves out of soft stone. The video also focuses on the production of local food such as beans, maize, sesame and sorghum, contrasting them with the imported staples of rice and pasta. It speaks of how food aid has destroyed the local market, and criticises Somalia's dependency on food imports. The film extols the benefits of local fruit juice over imported soft drinks, which it says are full of harmful chemicals.

For their part, the Somali government and its international partners also present an unrealistic picture of life in the country. They produce glossy images and videos of relaxed, happy boys playing football on the beach, people eating ice cream in outdoor cafés, and cars driving at night under solar-powered street lights, all under the slogans of 'Somalia Rising' and 'Mogadishu Rising'. These give the impression that the country is some kind of tourist paradise rather than a broken conflict zone.

The information I have received about life under Al Shabaab is highly contradictory. At times Al Shabaab says one thing and people living in areas it controls say the opposite. Sometimes people living in one area controlled by the group say something different from those in another. Some women have described being brutalised and humiliated by the Islamists, while others have said they are treated with respect. This makes it virtually impossible to set out any hard-and-fast, universal truths about the reality of life in areas under Al Shabaab control. Rather, I have obtained a series of snapshots from people who are or have been active in the group, or those who live or have lived in areas under its control.

Violence

Al Shabaab is most visible when it perpetrates acts of violence. This can take spectacular form, such as the September 2013 siege of the luxury Westgate mall in the Kenyan capital, Nairobi, in which sixty-seven people died, or the slaughter of 148 people, mainly students, in April 2015 at a university in Kenya's eastern city of Garissa. There have been enormous truck bombs in Mogadishu, the worst of which exploded near a fuel tanker that then ignited, killing more than 500 people and injuring hundreds more. The incident, which took place on 14 October 2017, has become known as Somalia's 9/11. The lights of the Eiffel Tower in Paris were turned off in memory of those who died. The Somali government marked the first anniversary of the explosion by executing by firing squad a twenty-three-year-old man, Hassan Adan Isaq, who was convicted of masterminding the bombing. The judge, Hassan Ali Nur, said, 'He has killed hundreds as an Al Shabaab member and today he was rewarded with a painful death.'

Although the October truck bombing bore all the hallmarks of an Al Shabaab attack, the group remained uncharacteristically silent about the incident. Its usually ruthlessly efficient press office failed to issue any statements about the bombing. When I called an Al Shabaab official to ask about the attack, he was reluctant to speak. He said he was travelling and we would have to talk another time. This had never happened before, as Al Shabaab is usually more than happy to tell me about the acts of violence it has perpetrated or to deny the ones it says it has had nothing to do with. I said I needed just a few seconds of his time and a 'yes' or 'no' answer. I asked him again whether Al Shabaab could confirm it carried out the attack. 'I told you, I am travelling,' he said firmly. 'I cannot speak to you now.' I persisted, repeating my question. This time he said simply that he had heard about the bombing and that he would get back to me another time. Then the line went dead. He did not call me back.

It appears that Al Shabaab was embarrassed about the killing of so many civilians, and that they were not the intended target. The group repeatedly warns civilians to stay away from government buildings and military bases. It tells them to avoid restaurants, cafés and hotels frequented by government workers, the military and employees of international organisations, and not to associate with these people in any way. Al Shabaab insists it does not target civilians directly, and that it is entirely their fault if they ignore its warnings and get killed by venturing near government buildings, sewing uniforms for Somali soldiers, selling tea to civil servants or otherwise having a connection with the 'apostate' authorities.

I have had numerous conversations with Al Shabaab about the killing and injuring of civilians, all of which follow a twisted kind of logic. Al Shabaab says the civilians know perfectly well that they are supposed to avoid restaurants, hotels and other places frequented by government officials, and that they are not supposed to work for or otherwise have links with the 'apostates'.

On one particularly chilling occasion, I asked a member of Al Shabaab how the group could justify pulling Kenyan teachers out of a minibus and killing them one by one. 'Oh, that is easy to explain,' he said casually. 'The Kenyan government declared war on Al Shabaab when it invaded Somalia in October 2011. It is doing everything it can to destroy us. But who voted in that government? Who is ultimately responsible for its existence? It is the Kenyan people. As they are responsible for choosing that infidel government, it is actually the Kenyan people who declared war on us. Therefore every single one of them is a legitimate target. It is entirely logical.' When I said I could not understand this line of argument, the Al Shabaab official became highly irritated. He repeated again and again that, as Kenya was a democracy, its people were responsible for the government they had. It was perfectly reasonable to attack and kill them all, he said, regardless of whether they were civilians or not.

Although they often require significant planning and preparation, most Al Shabaab attacks are carried out by a small number of people. Just four men strolled casually through the marble corridors of the Westgate shopping centre, shooting people dead as they went. On 15 January 2019, five men stormed the luxury hotel complex on Nairobi's Riverside Drive, one blowing himself up as he entered the lobby.[4] In Somalia, hotels, government buildings and the African Union's AMISOM bases are usually attacked first by vehicles laden with explosives, then stormed by a small group of armed men on foot. They know they will never come out alive. As one senior Ugandan AMISOM commander said: 'The fact that certain death and the promise of paradise are part of the deal for these attackers makes it much harder for our troops to fight them. Even the best-trained AMISOM soldier has an instinct for self-preservation, whereas Al Shabaab militants seem to go towards their deaths joyously, with no fear whatsoever. This makes them terrifying battlefield adversaries.'

Most attacks by Al Shabaab do not make the headlines, even in Somalia. These are the routine incidents, including shootings, the planting of explosive devices in people's cars and the throwing of grenades. They are simply part of everyday life in some parts of Somalia. Most people I speak to who live in these areas have stories about how the violence has affected them personally. Then there are the friends who can no longer tell me their stories because they are dead, killed in a targeted assassination or during an attack on a building.

I have a Somali friend who went back to Mogadishu for a holiday after twenty years working as a security guard in London. He was walking through the car park of a restaurant after having lunch with friends when he saw a man collapse on the ground and begin to writhe around as if he were having a fit or a seizure. He rushed to help the man, as did several other people nearby. As they gathered around him, there was an enormous explosion. This was no sick man in need of assistance. He was a suicide bomber who only detonated his vest once he had drawn in enough people within striking distance. My friend survived as he was still some way away, but he was badly wounded by flying metal. He lifted up his shirt to show me the livid scars where the shrapnel had lacerated his chest and stomach. 'This is my Somali holiday souvenir,' he said. 'These scars and the flashbacks and the nightmares. I won't be going back there in a hurry.'

Another friend, who left the UK to work for the Somali government, has a long list of Al Shabaab stories and narrow escapes. In one incident he was sitting in a café in a busy Mogadishu street when a young man in a red shirt approached him. The man was sweating profusely and holding a laptop. He veered from table to table, attracting the attention of everybody in the place. Then there was a loud bang and a fizz, as smoke poured out of the laptop. This was an improvised explosive device gone wrong.

There was also the day the same friend came back from work to the hotel where he was living. His room was gone, blown up in an Al Shabaab attack. The desk where he normally sat had been reduced to a small pile of ashes and burnt, splintered wood.

The first time this friend was caught up in an attack was in October 2011, shortly after he arrived in Mogadishu. A truck bomb smashed into a government building where Somali students were registering to apply for scholarships to study in Turkey. Seventy people were killed. My friend was passing by when the explosion occurred. He was not injured but was badly shaken. His first instinct was to call his mother in the UK to tell her about what had happened and how terrifying it was. 'I have learned not to call my mother for comfort after attacks anymore,' he said. 'She is worried enough about my being here and I don't want to scare her even more. Also, after that first blast, I became more acclimatised and desensitised to the violence in this city. I am not sure that's a good thing.'

Journalists, ambulance drivers and members of the security services are more vulnerable than most to Al Shabaab attacks because it is their job to rush to the scene to help the injured and to bear witness. A journalist friend once sent me a photo of his car after its windscreen had been shattered by the force of an Al Shabaab explosion. On the roof of the vehicle was a severed arm and part of an upper torso. Another time, he was sitting in his favourite seaside restaurant when Al Shabaab militants came in quietly from the beach and took over the building. They went from room to room shooting as many customers as they could. My friend lay down amongst the bodies and played dead. He described how the Al Shabaab fighters went from person to person, kicking them to see if they moved, and shooting them if they did. He managed to stay still. When the militants moved on to a different room, my friend crawled to the door and started running for his life. As soon as he was outside, he heard AMISOM soldiers shouting that he was a suicide bomber and should be shot immediately. He stripped, ripping off his shirt to show he was not wearing a suicide vest. He heard people shouting out his name, and pleading with AMISOM not to shoot him as he was a well-known journalist, not an Islamist militant. My friend now has scars all over his face, especially around his eyes, from where shrapnel hit him during the attack.

When Al Shabaab called me to boast about the beachside restaurant attack, I lost my temper. I said my friend the journalist had always reported the news in a fair and balanced way. He correctly attributed attacks to Al Shabaab, and gave an accurate picture of what was going on in the country. My contact gave a chillingly cold response. 'We know this journalist and we respect him. But we have warned him to stay away from places frequented by the apostates. He knows full well that government officials sometimes eat at that restaurant. We have no regrets about what happened to him. We do not feel guilty. It is his fault for ignoring our advice.'

Although it no longer engages in conventional warfare, Al Shabaab remains one of Africa's deadliest terror groups. This is largely through its use of improvised explosive devices, many of which are put into vehicles and driven directly into buildings. Its use of such devices has increased over the years. In 2016, the UN recorded 395 attacks using improvised explosives, eleven times more than in 2010.[5] Between 1 January and 12 October 2018, 334 IED incidents and nineteen more complex attacks were recorded in the parts of Somalia where AMISOM operates, the majority of them targeting African Union troops and the Somali security forces.[6] Some 400 kilogrammes of military-grade and home-made explosives were used in the massive truck bombing in Mogadishu in October 2017.[7] The increased use and sophistication of such devices comes at a time when Al Shabaab has become more insular, with fewer foreign fighters in its ranks. It is debateable whether it has imported expertise from Al Qaeda in the Arabian Peninsula (AQAP) or whether its knowledge is home-grown. The equipment to make such devices is certainly available locally as Somalia is awash with arms and ammunition, and Al Shabaab regularly replenishes supplies during raids on AMISOM and Somali army bases. The group is also internet-savvy so will be able to access online guides of how to make instruments of destruction.

Al Shabaab says it has no problem planting devices and carrying out attacks wherever it chooses: 'We manage to drive cars past dozens of checkpoints in cities like Mogadishu. We have our way of doing things but I am not going to give you further details. The presidential palace is one of the most well-guarded places in Somalia but how many times have we blown up cars at its front and back gates? How many times have our men stormed the place and entered far inside? Of course, not all of our attacks succeed but I would say about 80 per cent of them succeed and 20 per cent fail.'

* * *

The most expensive hotels in Mogadishu are like fortresses, surrounded by a double layer of thick, high, concrete walls, some piled up with sandbags to absorb blasts. You must pass through a series of metal gates to enter them, plus have a patting down from a security guard, with all bags thoroughly searched and scanned. All of this with good reason, for every few months one of these hotels is attacked by Al Shabaab and sometimes besieged for hours.

Al Shabaab views some hotels as legitimate targets, and warns civilians to stay away from them. 'We consider five, six or seven hotels in Mogadishu as prime targets,' said one member. 'I forget the exact number ... Everybody knows which hotels I am talking about as they provide lodgings for members of the apostate government, certain members of the diaspora, foreigners and other infidels.'

The group employs a strange logic to justify attacks on hotels, in some instances describing them as military bases. A Somali television interview with Al Shabaab's spokesman, Ali Dheere, illustrates how this line of argument works. In the clearing of a heavily wooded area, Ali Dheere and the journalist sit opposite each other on green plastic chairs. Ali Dheere is dressed in camouflage and wears khaki boots. His head is wrapped in a black scarf, his beard streaked with grey. 'We have to ask ourselves, are these so-called hotels really hotels or are they army bases? Al Shabaab has never targeted ordinary hotels where Muslim civilians stay. The ones we attack are surrounded with huge concrete walls. They have security guards to protect them. This shows that they are not hotels because normal hotels where Muslim civilians stay do not have concrete barriers. We are fighting the infidels and we do not care what they call the places they live in. Whether they say it is an army base or a hotel, it all means the same to us. Therefore all the hotels that we attack are army bases. They serve as ministerial offices for the infidels and apostates. The finance ministry is operating from a hotel, the so-called transport ministry is operating from a hotel, and the ministry of education is operating from a hotel.

'We warn people day and night to stay away from these places. Not a single person who does not support the infidels goes to these hotels. One hundred per cent of the people who go to these hotels are connected with the leadership, the intelligence and security services. We do not deliberately kill our fellow Somali Muslims or any other Muslim. In fact, we prefer to let an infidel escape than to let a fellow Muslim die. We are very careful about the areas we target. It may take months to monitor a place before we carry out the attack.'[8]

It is indeed the case that some hotels in Somalia serve as the homes and offices of senior Somali politicians, foreign diplomats and other prime Al Shabaab targets. I have spent long evenings in such places, pacing up and down the courtyards with government ministers and other officials as they try to get some exercise and walk off the stress of living and working in Mogadishu. It is like being a caged animal. I have sipped coffee in hotel foyers that weeks later have been attacked by Al Shabaab, the friends I was drinking with blown up or shot dead in a siege. Even though these hotels are unable to protect themselves from Al Shabaab, they somehow succeed in creating a false sense of security for those inside. People noticeably relax once they enter hotels, despite the fact that they are key targets for the militants.

When I hear a hotel is under attack in Somalia, I dread the almost inevitable phone call that comes from Al Shabaab. On one such occasion, on 1 November 2015, I received a call to say that the Sahafi hotel was under attack.

'Our men are inside as I speak. They are really enjoying themselves. There is an apostate army officer in there, General Abdikarim Dhagabadan. We have been after him since August 2011 because he is the man who commanded the operation that forced us out of Mogadishu. Now we have him, that infidel creature.' At least twelve people were killed in the attack, including the general and two members of parliament. An acquaintance, the Sahafi's owner, Abdirashid Mohamed, also died. The attackers were said to be wearing Burundian army uniforms, perhaps seized during an Al Shabaab raid on an AMISOM base in the town of Leego in June of the same year.

On 9 November 2018, I was driving near my home in London. My phone rang and the call was routed to the car's hands-free system. A Somali number flashed onto my dashboard so I accepted the call and asked who was phoning.

'Have you forgotten my number, Mary?'

The voice was instantly recognisable. It was a member of Al Shabaab's communications department. 'Oh, it's you,' I said. 'I'm driving and your name didn't show up.'

'Please stop talking to me immediately. You must not phone while driving. You will have an accident or you will be arrested by a traffic cop.'

'It's fine,' I replied, somewhat taken aback by his stern, bossy tone. 'I have a hands-free system. Anyway, I'm nearly home now so let's keep talking while I park and go indoors so I can find a pen and something to write on.'

'I expect you know why I am calling. It's about the Sahafi.'

So, almost exactly three years later, the hotel was under attack again. I had a quick look at my Twitter feed, which was crammed with video clips showing a massive grey cloud of smoke rising up into the clear blue sky of Mogadishu.

'First we sent in two or three car bombs,' the man told me. 'Then our men stormed the place on foot. You know the drill.

'I would like to clarify something. Some of your fellow journalists think the real target of the attack was the Criminal Investigation Department, which is very near to the Sahafi. It was not. Our target was the hotel. As you are well aware, we consider establishments like the Sahafi to be non-civilian hotels. We consider them to be government buildings, not civilian buildings. People in these hotels look like civilians but they are not civilians. This is because members of government live and work there. Many government ministers do not have functioning ministry buildings. They do much of their work from hotels. Oh, and by the way, we were lucky enough to kill the new owner of the Sahafi. I think you know him, Abdifatah Abdirashid, the son of Abdirashid Mohamed.'

I did know Abdifatah, just as I had known his father, the hotel's previous owner whom Al Shabaab had killed in November 2015. I was surprised to hear about Abdifatah as, like many successful Somali businesspeople, he was mainly based in the Gulf. I learned later that he had come to Mogadishu for a short visit.

I asked the man from Al Shabaab about people like Abdifatah and the people who worked for him in the Sahafi as cleaners, cooks and waiters. They were civilians, not government employees.

'We consider people like Abdifatah and his father before him to be as bad as government people. By allowing members of government to live and visit their hotels, they transform themselves into legitimate targets. We have warned civilians to stay away from such hotels. So it is entirely the fault of the cleaners and other hotel employees if they get killed. They know that we consider as an enemy every person who visits or works at such hotels. We repeat this again and again. If you don't want to get killed, stay away from such places. Cleaners, guards, cooks and chefs. If they go there, it is their fault for getting killed. Basically, they go there just to die.'

It was time to end the call.

'Please take care, Mary, especially while driving. Bye bye. Have a lovely weekend.'

The following day, I received a WhatsApp message from a friend who works as a journalist in the Somali capital. It said 'Horrible blasts in Mogadishu yesterday' and was accompanied by a video. True to my friend's message, the scenes in the video were of unadulterated horror. Mangled remains of vehicles lay in piles on the street, next to the giant sandbags that formed the perimeter wall of the Sahafi. Bodies, some intact, others in pieces, were scattered around them on the ground, lying in large pools of dark blood. Members of the Somali security services wandered about, seemingly oblivious to the carnage around them. They walked in easy, loping style; there was no sense of urgency or panic. A few of them issued directions, but nobody seemed to be paying much attention. Some of the bodies strewn on the ground started to move. They pulled themselves up slowly with bewildered, dazed expressions on their faces, as if waking from a dream. Some sat up in their own blood; others rolled to one side and stayed there in the dust. Nobody went to help them.

In order to hit high-value targets like the owners of the Sahafi and General Dhagabadan, Al Shabaab needs informants inside the hotels to tell them who is visiting at any particular time. Sometimes the attackers are hotel employees. In one case, a woman, Luul Dahir, who worked as a receptionist in Mogadishu's Central Hotel went to work on 20 February 2015 with a suicide vest under her robe. She was the mother of six young children and had recently moved to Somalia from Holland, where she had lived since childhood. That day, a car bomb exploded at the hotel during Friday prayers as the deputy prime minister and other senior government officials were worshipping in its mosque. As survivors from the initial blast staggered around the courtyard, Luul Dahir appeared and blew herself up, significantly increasing the number of casualties. It was later discovered that her husband, Abdi Salan, had died taking part in a 2014 Al Shabaab attack on the presidential palace, known as Villa Somalia.

Somali friends have told me that when Al Shabaab struggles to find an opportunity to kill a target, it sometimes deliberately kills people close to the intended victim. The group knows it will then have the chance to attack the real target when he or she attends the dead person's funeral. This technique was used in August 2007. On the morning of August 11, a popular young talk show host from the Horn Afrik Media Company, Mahad Ahmed Elmi, was shot with four bullets to the head on his way to work. His boss, Ali Iman Sharmarke, who had lived in Canada for years before returning to Somalia to set up one of the country's most respected independent media houses, attended his funeral in the afternoon of the same day. On his way home from the burial, Sharmarke was killed when his car was blown up by a remote-controlled landmine.

* * *

It is not just people living in dangerous parts of Somalia who use hotels as their homes and offices. Hotels play a central part in Somali urban culture, whether in Mogadishu, Hargeisa, Galkayo or Garissa. Perhaps this is because movement and migration are integral to the Somali experience, from the traditional nomads with their camels, goats and other livestock to the seafarers of the nineteenth century; from the great exodus of the late 1980s and early 1990s, when conflict spread across the country, to today's highly-connected modern nomad, sealing business deals in the lobbies of five-star hotels in Dubai, London, Nairobi and Addis Ababa. I have witnessed multi-million-dollar agreements being struck in hotel bedrooms which have been converted into qat-chewing rooms for the day, the floor strewn with discarded leaves and stalks, marking the long hours of noisy deliberations.

It is always easy to tell when a senior Somali politician is in town. Not only are the reception areas of, for example, the Dorchester in London or the Sheraton in Addis Ababa filled with Somalis, but so are the streets outside. Hotel guests look on bewildered as they discover that all the sofas and chairs in the lobby have been taken by Somalis angling for a meeting with whichever president, prime minister or other top official is in town. People walking in the most upmarket parts of Washington and Dubai are astonished to see the pavements filled with noisy Somalis, jostling and shouting as they crowd the streets around the hotel hosting the dignitaries. Hotel lobbies in Garowe, Mogadishu and Nairobi's mainly Somali district of Eastleigh are dream spots for journalists like me. They provide a near-constant stream of government ministers, members of parliament, senior security officials and other interesting characters to pester with questions.

I write this in the lobby of the Maan-Soor hotel in Somaliland's capital, Hargeisa. It is early evening and I have already bumped into the ministers of finance and foreign affairs, a famous singer and a former Olympic athlete. I have had tea with the former head of intelligence, lunch with a business tycoon and fresh papaya juice with a television star. Last night I stayed in a hotel in the capital of Ethiopia's Somali region, Jijiga, which happened to be filled with the country's top military brass, people I would normally find it impossible to meet.

Some Somalis stay in hotels for years, with their families living far away in Europe, the US or the Gulf. A former foreign minister of Somaliland told me he had lived in a hotel in Eastleigh for more than ten years; one television presenter is a permanent resident of a hotel in Hargeisa; and, as already mentioned, hotels in Mogadishu serve as the homes of government ministers and other senior officials. These predominantly male groups band together to form substitute families, eating with each other, passing long evenings over spiced tea and cappuccinos, and speaking to their wives and children via WhatsApp, Skype, Signal and other messaging applications.

Governance

Whilst it is best known for its acts of violence, Al Shabaab is about far more than hotel attacks, truck bombings and mall sieges. Unlike some of the world's other violent Islamist movements, it has held large areas of territory for many years, including, for a time, most of the capital Mogadishu and other large towns and cities. The group has developed a form of Islamist governance that has been held up as an example by prominent Al Qaeda figures, including the now deceased Yemeni American cleric Anwar al-Awlaki.

An Al Shabaab official explained that the group has written guidelines on how power should be distributed. 'We have a document that only a few people are allowed to see. I myself have never seen it but I know it exists. It sets out the different roles and responsibilities for the emir, his deputies, regional governors and so on. It is a very useful document and far more effective than the chaotic nonsense of the so-called federal government.'

Al Shabaab is not only in the business of creating fear and violence. The academic Marchal argues that: 'Contrary to common belief, Al Shabaab not only secures the areas it controls, it also provides important public goods by managing public infrastructure, helping destitute people and addressing important issues for the population such as conflicts about family issues, inheritance and property titles.'[9]

Apart from the difficulties in maintaining its hold over territory seized from Al Shabaab, one of the main challenges facing the Somali government and its allies is to provide the population with the level of services they received under the Islamists. They have come to expect a degree of law, order and certainty, as well as rigid sets of rules to live under. They might not like the style of education offered by Al Shabaab, but at least there are functioning schools in many areas occupied by the group. They might not like paying numerous taxes and other fees, but the redistribution of at least some of this money helps support the destitute. People who live or have lived in areas controlled by Al Shabaab have told me the group is not corrupt, whereas successive governments in Somalia have become synonymous with venality. Every year, the anti-corruption group Transparency International ranks countries according to their perceived levels of corruption. Somalia has come top of the list for the past twelve years in a row, from 2007 to 2018. Before that, so intense was conflict in the country that it was impossible to gather data, meaning that Somalia did not appear on the index.[10]

During its heyday in the late 2000s, Al Shabaab ran a relatively efficient administration which managed both to make use of Somalia's powerful clan structures and to transcend them, at least to a degree. Although the group is fairly decentralised, it is headed by a well-organised bureaucracy, which has been described as 'certainly the most extensive and effective administrative structure that has existed in southern Somalia since the collapse of the Siad Barre regime in 1991'.[11] Unlike most Somali power bases, which tend to restrict their focus to certain regions or clans, Al Shabaab has a broad reach and ambition. Its only competitor in this regard is the Somali federal government, which so far has failed to fully control the capital Mogadishu, let alone the rest of the country.

I was given a telephone lecture about the group's governance structure by an Al Shabaab contact. He presented an image of a system running in parallel with that of the Somali federal government, which he described as a 'fake fantasy construct of the United Nations and its infidel Western backers'. He said, 'Al Shabaab has a supreme leader, whom we call the emir. We have an entire government with all the usual ministries. We have a head of the military, which we call the *Jabhat*, a head of the police, which we call the *Hisbah*, a head of the intelligence wing, which we call the *Amniyaat*, and a head of media. As well as gathering intelligence, the *Amniyaat* is also responsible for what we call special operations, such as assassinations and suicide bombings. The *Hisbah* are easily identified because they wear different uniforms and patrol the streets to keep people safe. Of course, we also have the all-important head of religious affairs. We have governors in every region, including in Mogadishu because we are still active there. We controlled most of the city from 2008 to 2011, but even after our fighters withdrew we maintained a military and administrative presence in the capital, as we do in several other places under government control. Al Shabaab's governor in Mogadishu, or should I call him the shadow governor, oversees our administration in the city. For example, he runs our taxation system there, whereby people pay us *zakat* and other taxes. We then redistribute to the poor, sick and needy the money we raise through *zakat*, which I suppose you Christians would call tithes.'

I spent time in a former Al Shabaab office during a visit to Bakara Market in Mogadishu. The district is a maze of streets, some specialising almost entirely in one particular item. On what people call 'Pharmacy Street', the shopfronts are painted with bright, bold, cartoon-like images of syringes, thermometers, medicine bottles, boxes of Viagra, and red and yellow pills. There is a 'Shoe Street', a 'Suitcase Street' and a 'Meat Street'. Another area sells big tin safes, painted blue and green and decorated with large pictures of US dollar bills. The faces of market traders peeked out from behind giant piles of watermelons, bananas, mangoes, limes, papayas and other fresh fruit. One street seems to be occupied almost entirely by wheelbarrows piled high with fresh loaves of bread. Another area, deep inside the market, sells used empty plastic bottles, tied up with string and dangled from the fronts of tiny kiosks. The earth and air turns black in the zone reserved for the sale of charcoal, the export of which has been banned by the UN. Another section offers large sacks of rice and other grains, with the logos of the UN World Food Programme, USAID and other donors stamped on their sides.

We walked to the local police headquarters, which, less than a year earlier, had been used as an office by Al Shabaab. The police chief was sitting at what looked like a child's old wooden school desk perched on the rough, uneven floor. The walls were painted a deep turquoise colour and all over them, scrawled in large black and blood-red Arabic script, were the familiar words 'Harakat Al Shabaab Al Mujahideen'. I began to imagine what it must have been like when Al Shabaab was running this place, its militants prowling around the dark rooms. I was only half-listening to the police chief as he told me how, shortly after Al Shabaab left the city, he had found the remains of beheaded bodies nearby.

Suddenly there was a burst of gunfire outside the small window, its pane of glass long gone. The police chief grabbed a gun from under the desk. His subordinates tensed and readied their weapons. The gunfire subsided. It was time to leave.

Not far from the police headquarters, we walked past a teenage boy on the pavement, rocking back and forth on the hind legs of a chair. His ashen face wore a dazed expression, his hair matted and wild, and his long, rough-skinned limbs stretched out straight in front of him. 'He used to be in Al Shabaab. Maybe he still works for them in one way or another,' one of the policemen said. 'He just sits there all day, gazing at nothing. I have never seen him speak.'

Despite no longer holding the city in its grip, the militants maintain an influence over people in Mogadishu. A member of Al Shabaab gave me an example of the group's continued ability to control life in the city. 'In March 2018, we banned people from playing football in three districts of Mogadishu where we still have a significant presence: Huriwa, Yaqshid and Karan. People immediately obeyed the ban. They stopped wasting their time playing this foolish game while dressed in inappropriate, revealing kit. That shows just how powerful we are.'

During the lecture I received on the phone about Al Shabaab's governance system I was told, 'Sometimes people in Mogadishu ask for one of our judges to try a case because our judiciary is efficient and effective. It gets things done, unlike the corrupt and spineless apostate judiciary of the infidel Somali federal government. We see the Somali judiciary as a legitimate target, and have already hit it hard. That was in April 2013 when we stormed the Supreme Court in Mogadishu and killed at least twenty people.'

Although most media coverage of Al Shabaab's justice system focuses on the stonings, beheadings and amputations, the reality involves far more than gruesome punishments. As Hansen argues, 'While many Western observers believe that Al-Shabaab's imposition of the sharia is widely resented by ordinary Somalis, its relatively successful law enforcement and justice system generated sympathy among locals who were used to predatory warlords or the ineffective and corrupt governance of the TFG [transitional federal government].'[12]

While Al Shabaab has lost significant public support through its acts of violence against civilians and the obstruction of humanitarian assistance during times of drought, some people say its justice system is the best available, particularly when it comes to solving financial and property disputes. I know a number of Somalis who abhor what Al Shabaab stands for but who use its courts because they are more efficient and reliable than the official judiciary. They say the Islamists do not allow powerful people to use their wealth and positions of influence to bully, buy or intimidate judges into ruling in their favour. Moreover, when Al Shabaab makes a ruling, those involved in the case are likely to obey, as they are terrified of the consequences of failing to do so. There have even been cases of judges in Mogadishu advising people to go and seek justice in Al Shabaab courts.[13] Marchal describes how residents of the capital travel to Al Shabaab courts in Lower Shabelle to deal with land, debt and business disputes.[14]

According to a study by the Somali researcher Hussein Yusuf Ali:

Al Shabaab's success is seen as a result of its ability to establish effective security and justice systems in the territories it controls, and to put in place mediation and conflict resolution mechanisms among warring clans, resulting in a drastic reduction of clan-based armed conflicts. Al Shabaab has also exported mobile courts to areas adjacent to government-controlled cities and towns for arbitration of commercial and land disputes. Rather than this being the benevolent provision of services on the part of Al Shabaab, getting closer to where the bulk of citizenry lives enables Al Shabaab to generate revenue.[15]

During telephone interviews with Al Shabaab, members of the group are always careful to explain that suspects have to go through a thorough legal process in the courts before they are found guilty and punished. The severity of the punishment depends on the nature of the crime: 'It obviously depends what the crime is. With qat, for example, we will give you time to stop chewing or selling it. If you don't stop, we will give you more time. If you still don't stop, the drug will be burned. If you hide the drug in your car, we will burn the qat and your car.

'We don't kill people for crimes like chewing qat or watching Western films. We kill them for fornicating. There are certain behaviours we insist on. If you are a woman, you have to wear a hijab. But you don't have to wear a niqab. If you are a man, you should have a beard but it is not a crime not to have one. You must be encouraged to have one, but not punished for not having one.'

Although several Somalia experts have focused on the positive role played by Al Shabaab courts, journalists Maruf and Joseph argue that they are far from perfect:

> When the group captured a town, it set up a local court consisting of one to three judges and a clerk that would hear both civil and criminal cases. Court rules allowed for neither juries nor lawyers, empowering judges to both collect evidence and issue verdicts. In theory, the system might have been fair if the accused had some basic rights. But in practice, defendants in criminal cases were at a severe disadvantage. The accused had to appear in person before the judge, while the accuser was given the option of either appearing or sending an agent. Not only were the defendants denied legal counsel, but they also faced judges who sometimes didn't bother to hear their side of the story.[16]

Interviews with people living in Al Shabaab territory suggest that, in some areas at least, the group is less tolerant of certain types of dress and behaviour. Men say they have been whipped for not having a beard and have had the bottoms of their trousers cut off in public if they are not short enough to show the ankles as is recommended in *hadith*. A teenager from northern Mogadishu told me members of Al Shabaab came to him and his friends and ordered them to cut their hair as it was too long, and styled in a 'Western' fashion; a man from the town of Jowhar said Al Shabaab shaved his head with a piece of broken glass. Some women have told me they are forced to wear the full niqab whenever they leave their homes, only their eyes peeking out from a slit in the cloth. People say they have been beaten with rifle butts and had their phones confiscated for using them to play Somali songs and Western music.

Some crimes, such as spying for the Somali government, AMISOM or Westerners, are punishable by death. 'If you are a spy, there is only one punishment,' said an Al Shabaab official. 'It is a one-way ticket to the day of judgement. There is only one option. You will be killed whether you are a man or a woman. Obviously we have to prove it first. We have a special court to try these crimes, with special judges. If you are found guilty, you will face the firing squad in a public place, never in a secret location. Everyone must witness the killing of the spy and hear the sound of the bullets—thwack, thwack, thwack. Spies must have three, four or five bullets in the head. We do not carry out beheadings for spies. But if we catch an apostate soldier or a member of AMISOM we can behead him.'

Although the Islamists are feared for imposing unforgiving rules and harsh punishments they are not perceived as corrupt, unlike government troops and members of other armed groups who have been accused of extorting bribes. During a journey from the Kenyan border to Mogadishu, one researcher's experiences were significantly different at checkpoints controlled by Al Shabaab to those at checkpoints manned by other groups:

> he was stopped at sixty-seven checkpoints, sixty-one of them controlled by Al-Shabaab. The militiamen manning all but one of the non-Al-Shabaab checkpoints demanded money from him and one of them even stole his mobile phone. Only one Al-Shabaab-controlled checkpoint demanded payment, but he noted that road construction work was going on at the post, so he presumed the money was being well spent.[17]

Another individual who regularly passes through Al Shabaab territory said he is given a receipt when he pays money at the first checkpoint. After that, he does not have to pay at any other Al Shabaab checkpoint as long as he produces the receipt.

Finance

During its heyday, Al Shabaab obtained much of its revenue from ports in southern Somalia, especially through the lucrative export of charcoal to the Gulf, worth tens of millions of dollars a year. It also obtained significant income from sugar, which is imported into Somalia and then distributed locally or transported south across the border into Kenya and beyond. Other imports were also taxed. The group is reported to have charged $500 for every small car imported into Somalia, and $1,000 for larger vehicles.[18] It is not possible to calculate accurately Al Shabaab's income but UN investigators estimated that at the height of the group's powers, taxes, fines and other charges brought in an annual sum of between $70 and $100 million.[19] Although Somalia has its own currency, the Somali shilling, many transactions are completed in US dollars.

Despite losing control of the major ports of Kismayo, Merca and Brava between 2012 and 2014, Al Shabaab is still said to obtain revenue from charcoal and sugar, although some reports say it has now banned the use and production of charcoal in areas under its control, hunting down charcoal traders, seizing their vehicles and imposing large fines. Some involved in the charcoal trade have even been killed. The group is said to have banned charcoal because it believed the authorities in Kismayo were making more money from the charcoal trade than it was.[20] However, UN sanctions monitors said in October 2018 that Al Shabaab was still making millions of dollars a year from charcoal, and that criminal networks were now using Iran as a transit point for illicit Somali charcoal exports.[21] A 2015 report by the Kenyan group Journalists for Justice found that the militants were still making at least $100 million a year from the charcoal industry by taxing charcoal producers and transporters as well as exports from the smaller ports still under its control. The report said that even though Al Shabaab no longer controlled Kismayo, it was still pocketing about a third of the $3 levy on each bag of charcoal that left the port. Kenyan troops based in the town and the regional administration reportedly split the remaining $2.[22]

Al Shabaab also taxes sugar as it makes its way down from Kismayo and other ports into Kenya and other parts of Africa. According to UN monitors, the group makes $12–18 million annually from taxing sugar transporters. It is said to impose a levy of $1,500 on each large sugar truck that passes through the territory it holds in Lower Juba, which is on the way from Kismayo to Kenya.[23]

The group also taxes people living in areas under its control. People report having to pay a wide variety of levies, including a house tax, a tax on any remittances they receive, a share of their harvests and a ransom for releasing forced conscripts. According to Hansen, when Al Shabaab controlled the town of Afgoye, it taxed market stalls between $20 and $40 every month and bigger business between $100 and $200.[24] Other forms of tax include a levy on trucks using Al Shabaab–controlled roads, with a $555 levy imposed each time a truck uses the road, and $1,150 for larger trucks. According to Somalia's Counter-Terror Department, other levies include $750 operating licences for heavy-duty tractors and $200 registration fees for minivans and personal cars. It costs $3,000 to register a rig for drilling a water well. Al Shabaab charges a $5 fee for bringing a camel to market, $3 for a cow and $2 for a goat.

According to Al Shabaab defectors, the group has two main tax collection departments: the 'Finance Office' and the '*Zakawaat*

Office'. A 2018 study by Somali researchers found that the group is financially self-sufficient, despite requiring substantial funds to pay for its military operations and salaries for fighters, administrators, informants and others. This includes people operating in areas outside its direct control, such as its 'shadow' or 'parallel' governors and administrative staff in Mogadishu and other government-controlled towns.

The researchers were told by a former member of Al Shabaab that foot soldiers are paid starting salaries of $30 a month. If they are married they receive an extra $30 for each wife and $20 per child. Members of the *Amniyaat* intelligence wing are the highest-paid members of Al Shabaab's armed forces, receiving at least $200 monthly.

The *Zakawaat* Office works closely with clan elders and is responsible for collecting non-monetary taxes, such as livestock and farm produce. These fees are collected once a year, traditionally during the month of Ramadan, and are imposed across southern and central Somalia, including in regions not controlled by Al Shabaab. Usually, one camel is collected for every twenty-five camels owned, and one goat for every forty owned. Livestock owners are given receipts once they have been taxed. If they fail to show the receipt the following year, they are charged twice.

Al Shabaab's Finance Office collects monetary taxes—including the religious tax, *zakat*—from businesses operating inside and outside Al Shabaab areas. Businesspeople in areas outside Islamist control say they are summoned by the group's finance officials to go to Al Shabaab areas once a year to pay their *zakat*. The 2018 study found that the militants collect at least $3.5 million annually from Mogadishu alone. In October 2018, Somalia media reported that, in a brazen operation in the outskirts of the capital, Al Shabaab distributed thousands of dollars' worth of alms to hundreds of poor people. Photos posted on pro–Al Shabaab websites showed senior Islamist officials, including Al Shabaab's main spokesman, Ali Dheere, handing out cash to men and women, especially the disabled and the elderly.[25]

Al Shabaab said the event took place inside Mogadishu, not in the outskirts.

'We can't say exactly where for security reasons, but it was deep inside the city. Of course there is danger there, but our servicemen check the area thoroughly beforehand to make sure it is safe for as high a value target as Ali Dheere to attend.'

My contact went on to say that he could go to Mogadishu whenever he liked.

'I can even go to the Peace Garden right next to Villa Somalia. But, just like you, I do not make appointments to meet people at specific times in specific locations. I never call someone up and say, "Ahmed, let's meet at Dolphin restaurant at Lido Beach." Like you, I know it is not safe to make such arrangements on the phone because you never know who is listening. I just show up unannounced.'

He then turned his attention back to the alms-giving ceremony.

'We distributed money to about seventy families. Some received $200, some $500, some $1,000, depending on how needy they were.

'We collected all this money from businesspeople in Bakara Market. As I expect you know by now, zakat is one of the five pillars of Islam. When we collect zakat in one area, we distribute it in that same area. What we take in Mogadishu, we give in Mogadishu. What we take in Lower Shabelle, we give in Lower Shabelle. What we take in Middle Shabelle, we give in Middle Shabelle.'

I asked how Al Shabaab could be sure those who received alms really needed it.

'Of course we know who is needy. We have our own administrations in every town and they know who needs what. This is because Al Shabaab staff go into the communities and conduct proper needs assessments. Mogadishu has eighteen districts so we have eighteen governors there. They make sure they know the community.

'If we see somebody who can eat at least once a day, we don't have to help them. We help those who cannot eat even once a day. Another thing we do is we give people money to start businesses. If we find someone who cannot work, we give them $1,000 or $1,500 for a start-up. This means we will not need to assist them the following year as they will be making money for themselves. This is basically a microfinance scheme and we monitor each person closely to make sure they are making the right business decisions. Some people buy auto-rickshaws with the money we give them and they generally do very well. But of course, if it is somebody like an old widow who cannot work, we give them money every year.'

I ask Al Shabaab if people ever spend the money on something like qat instead of starting businesses.

'No. This is because we assess their characters beforehand. They are not the kind of people who would chew the money away. We would never give money to those who chew the qat drug, smoke cigarettes or do not pray regularly.'

The most unpopular Al Shabaab tax is the *infaaq*, an arbitrary sum raised to fund major military campaigns or to help when the group is running low on funds. Like the *zakat*, it is collected by a special force assisted by local administrators, including clan elders.

Defectors from Al Shabaab's Finance Office have described how the militants run a tight ship when it comes to money. Al Shabaab's accountants collect the receipts issued by checkpoint personnel and tax collectors and take them to an auditor who makes sure they match the amount of money collected.[26]

Many businesspeople in Mogadishu and other areas controlled by the government complain that they now have to pay double

Fig. 1: Beach to the south of Mogadishu.

Fig. 2: Ruins in central Mogadishu.

Fig. 3: Ruins of the old Italian cathedral, Mogadishu.

Fig. 4: Boys and girls await food handouts from Al Shabaab during the 2011 famine.

Fig. 5: Children with their handouts from Al Shabaab during the 2011 famine.

Fig. 6: Private security guard at an internally displaced people's camp, Mogadishu.

Fig. 7: Crazy wires in Hargeisa, Somaliland.

Fig. 8: A newly refurbished shop in Mogadishu.

Fig. 9: Bakara market, Mogadishu.

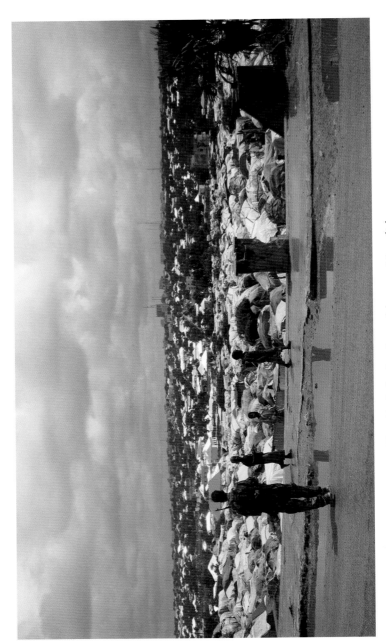

Fig. 10: A displaced people's camp, Mogadishu.

Fig. 11: A Koranic school in a displaced people's camp, Mogadishu.

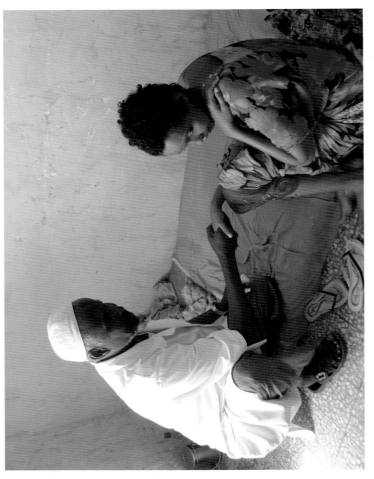

Fig. 12: Dr Habeb with one of his patients in the Habeb Mental Hospital.

Fig. 13: Patients in the Habeb Mental Hospital.

Fig. 14: Making salt, south of Mogadishu.

Fig. 15: Former Al Shabaab office, Mogadishu. Photo by Mary Harper.

Fig. 16. Old parliament building, Mogadishu. Photo by Mary Harper.

taxes: one tax to Al Shabaab, one to the government. Amina runs a large firm importing goods from the Gulf. 'When the militants were in control of Mogadishu, they used to tax us openly. Even though they withdrew from the city in 2011, they still come and ask for money. They just come at night instead of during the day. If you do not pay the money, Al Shabaab will accuse you of working for the government. You never know when they will come. They sometimes come twice a week, sometimes twice a month. If you keep refusing to pay they will kill you. A man who ran a shop next to my company's headquarters could not pay the increasingly large sums they were asking for. One evening, they shot him in the head as he was closing his store.'

It is not only the owners of large businesses in government-controlled areas who are taxed by Al Shabaab and punished severely if they fail to pay. Drivers of auto-rickshaws, or *bajaaj*, as they are known in Somalia, are also taxed. A *bajaaj* driver in Mogadishu, Farhan, said two of his driver friends had been shot dead by Al Shabaab assassins simply for failing to pay their taxes to the group.

Some Somalis working for the government have complained about being taxed by Al Shabaab. Bashir, who moved from Sweden to take up a job with the Somali government, explained how he received a phone call from Al Shabaab telling him they knew he was now living in Somalia and working for the federal administration. They said they needed to take a percentage of his salary as tax. 'I decided to quit my job and leave Mogadishu,' said Bashir. 'Al Shabaab was simply too well networked for me to stay. I have also heard that the Islamists attack restaurants, hotels and other businesses if they fail to pay extortion money. Al Shabaab is not a religious movement. It is a mafia.'

Since losing control of the larger ports, Al Shabaab has taxed people more aggressively and lost support in the process. Nomads have occasionally risen up against the group in the

Middle Shabelle, Galgudud and Mudug regions after it tried to seize some of their precious livestock as tax and forcibly recruit their children.[27] At least twelve people were killed in the region of Hiran in March 2018 after heavily armed members of Al Shabaab ordered nomads to provide a percentage of their livestock as *zakat*. They refused to give up their animals, took up their weapons and fought back against Al Shabaab.

The seizure of livestock by Al Shabaab is especially unpopular during periods of drought. In February 2017, the dozens of drought-affected Somalis arriving daily at Ethiopia's Dolo Ado refugee camp spoke of how the militants were taking their livestock and crops, leaving them with nothing to live on. Al Shabaab denied this, blaming the UN for manipulating the situation. 'No one from the areas under the control of the mujahidin has gone to Ethiopia. That is complete fabrication and a political manoeuvre by the UNHCR [the UN Refugee Agency] in order to solicit donations and to secure funds from unsuspecting donors by appealing to their emotions.'

Entertainment

Like other violent jihadi movements, Al Shabaab has a reputation for imposing harsh, austere lifestyles upon the communities it controls, erasing all fun and frivolity from their lives. Long lists have been written of all the activities it has banned, including watching movies, playing football, chewing qat and having musical ringtones on mobile phones. The media have reported that Al Shabaab has forbidden people from eating samosas because their triangular shape somehow suggests the Christian Trinity;[28] and that it banned women from wearing bras because they are a Western apostate invention.[29] Teachers have been warned against ringing bells in schools because they sound too much like Christian church bells.[30]

MODUS OPERANDI

Al Shabaab presents a somewhat different picture of what people are allowed and not allowed to do in their spare time. As one of my contacts in the group said, 'People are not allowed to gather in cafés or restaurants to watch films or foreign football matches. They must not watch the English Premier League, Italy's Serie A or Spain's La Liga. We forbid them from watching American films, sexy films and films with jokes in them. They are not allowed to watch these movies because they are against our religion and our culture. The US releases films as teaching instruments, to spread its culture and lifestyle around the world and to dominate and destroy other cultures. That is the true purpose of American films. But people living in our areas are free to watch films inside their houses. We do not interfere with that.

'The sale and chewing of qat is prohibited. We have lots of different rules about it. Selling qat is absolutely prohibited in our areas. If someone is caught buying it, well, that depends on the judge. You might get ten or twenty lashes, or you might have to pay a fine. If you are caught selling it, it is even more serious. I have seen the *Hisbah* stopping cars, trucks and motorbikes, and searching them. If they find a lot of qat they will burn the qat and the vehicle together. The qat seller will go to jail for a few days and receive ten to thirty lashes in a public place.

'When we obtain fines for crimes like chewing qat, the money cannot go towards the jihad because it is not *halal* money. The money is unclean because the person who paid the fine was doing a bad thing. That money has to be used for public services, such as maintaining roads, or it should be given to the poor or sick, or used to build a hospital or school.'

My contact scoffed at media reports that Al Shabaab had banned bras and samosas. 'We tell women to cover themselves. But we never said anything about bras. That is fake news invented by unprofessional, apostate journalists. As for the stories about samosas, these sorts of lies are spread by lazy people.

They are totally unfounded. When I saw the report about samosas, I called the journalist who wrote it to tell him he was wrong. He told me people in the town of Merca had said we banned them because they were somehow associated with Christianity. I joked with him and told him I would invite him to my house and give him lots of samosas!'

It appears that not all bans are imposed uniformly by Al Shabaab, perhaps reflecting the decentralised nature of the group, with militants in control of one area enforcing different rules from those in another. The rules around football illustrate this lack of uniformity, as in some areas it is banned completely, while in others it is allowed, albeit with certain constraints.

The Al Jazeera journalist Hamza Mohamed watched a match in the coastal town of Brava in 2014 when it was still controlled by Al Shabaab. He described a game of *halal* football, whereby: 'No shorts are allowed. Players wear tracksuits which must reach below the knee. Even though it is warm, thanks to the sun and the warm ocean breeze, players aren't allowed to play without tops or to wear vests—all jerseys must reach elbows.' Mohamed described how Al Shabaab fighters put their weapons aside and changed out of their camouflage into football jerseys. Arsenal was the preferred strip—coincidentally fitting, given that Somalis sometimes use the word 'Arsenal' as a codeword for Al Shabaab when they are speaking in public or on the phone and do not want the militants or others to know what they are talking about.

The players were subjected to severe penalties if they broke Al Shabaab's football rules:

> Balotelli-style stunts, in which a player removes his shirt, will result in a lifetime ban from playing football. It is seen as nudity and a player who removes his shirt is at the mercy of the Al Shabaab sheikhs. Roger Milla–style carousing of hip-gyrating by the corner flag will earn a player a public flogging and a life ban. Blowing kisses in triumph is a big no-no, unless you want your tongue removed ...

If an Al Shabaab player swears, he is quickly banned from the sport and taken off frontline duty. If he was in the suicide bombers' brigade he is removed from the list and put on a waiting list, which is the most shameful thing that can happen to a fighter and is seen as a delay to his 'journey to paradise'.[31]

A member of Al Shabaab told me about some of the group's football rules: 'We allow people to play football but certain conditions apply. People must not play the game during prayer time. Some parts of the body must be covered. For example, a player must cover the area from his stomach to below his knees, so he cannot wear shorts. He must wear something that reaches below his knees. The players must not insult each other. This is *halal* football and it is OK.'

A young man who lived under Al Shabaab in Merca explained how he got into trouble for wearing a famous English team's football strip. 'On one occasion I went down to the beach to play football with friends. I was wearing a Chelsea shirt. Some members of Al Shabaab saw me and told me I was a non-believer. They pointed to the logo of Chelsea's sponsor and said it was a sign of all that was evil. I told them I could take the shirt off, but they were not at all happy with my suggestion because it would have broken their rules about having to cover certain parts of the body. They then turned their attention to my shorts. I was wearing them because it was so hot. They accused me of ignorance about religious dress, saying the Koran forbade people from wearing shorts. They started asking me questions about the Koran and demanding that I recite koranic verses. I pretended to take it all very seriously and answered all their questions. Then, and I am sorry to say this because I am a Muslim, they gave me a really boring lecture about religion. They spoke for ages about how I should dedicate myself to the study of the Koran and not waste my time playing football.'

Football games, where able-bodied young men gather together without their parents, have served as ideal recruiting grounds for

Al Shabaab. I have spoken to a number of young men who have been approached by militants as they played football and ordered to come to the mosque for what turned out to be a recruitment lecture. Some told me they had then been taken away in vehicles directly to camps in the bush to begin life as jihadi trainees.

Al Shabaab also offers its own forms of entertainment, some of it macabre, some simply bizarre. When it captures spies or other 'infidels', adulterers and fornicators, it drives around with loudspeakers blaring from vehicles, ordering women from their homes, men from their fields and children from their schools. Everybody is instructed to gather in the public square to watch the shootings, amputations, stonings and floggings.

Al Shabaab says it is a religious duty to attend such events. 'In some cases, religion requires the public to be called. For example, in the case of fornication, our religion says people must be called to witness the punishment. It is our religious duty to watch the punishment being meted out.

'Also, inviting people to watch punishments is very helpful for the community. For example, if a judge rules a thief must have his right hand amputated, when people watch the amputation it will help them not to steal. It really helps a lot. I can say, without exaggeration, that as a result of this practice the areas under our control are the most peaceful in the country. Shopkeepers leave their shop doors open at all times because there is so little theft.'

Al Shabaab offers less bloody entertainment during Eid celebrations. A seventeen-minute video showed Eid al Adha celebrations in September 2017.

First there were mass prayers. On one side of a public square were the men and boys. Some toddlers faced in completely the wrong direction. Hundreds of sandals lay scattered in the sand. Women in full black niqab, or heavy black and blue robes, gathered in a different area.

Then the fun began. After prayers, the community moved to another area, which had been roped off with red string, forlorn-looking coloured balloons tied to the rope. The men and women assembled on different sides of the square.

Tiny girls dressed in black and other subdued colours, their heads veiled, sat in the sand in another area. Tiny boys, dressed up as mini Al Shabaab fighters, posed for the camera. Some wore plastic sunglasses; others had their faces almost entirely masked by black headgear emblazoned with Al Shabaab's white logo. They held large plastic guns, which they had received as gifts for Eid.

Animals were paraded around the square. It looked like a combination of a surreal dog show, a village fete and a school sports day. Grown men rode small ponies bedecked with white, blue, pink and orange pompoms. A billy goat was marched up and down. On his head was a grey trilby, on his body what looked like an ill-fitting football kit, with an orange shirt and yellow shorts. On his feet were little red socks and blue trainers. Despite his strange attire, the animal looked comfortable and confident as his proud owner paraded him around the ground.

Then came the games. First there was a sack race. Adult men climbed into sacks and hopped wildly across the sand. The winner grabbed the black Al Shabaab flag as he crossed the finishing line, waving it around in celebration. A man performed acrobatics on a yellow motorbike as another person painted white lines on the sand in preparation for another race. There were high-jump and archery competitions, a tug-of-war, and a bizarre blindfold race in which men in sarongs or ankle-length trousers walked across the sand with strips of cloth tied around their eyes. They did not look like they were enjoying themselves. The whole event had a forced and fearful air.

Al Shabaab fighters appeared wearing black masks and camouflage. They skipped around holding flaming batons. There was a fire-eater and a juggler. As the sun went down, a man on stilts marched into the square carrying the Al Shabaab flag, while other militants formed a human pyramid.

In another video, of Eid in Brava, boys in black kaftans with red-and-white *kufiya* scarves held black Al Shabaab flags as they chanted koranic songs. White plastic chairs were placed in the sand and a game of musical chairs got underway. Then there was an egg-and-spoon race, with the spoons held in people's mouths instead of their hands. People somersaulted though rings of fire on the beach, as others took part in a swimming race. The winner was the first person to reach a pole standing in the sea, an Al Shabaab flag fluttering from the top. There was a motorbike race on the beach and a competition that involved camels pulling carts along a sandy racetrack.

Al Shabaab's establishment of effective administrative systems shows that it is far more than a fighting force. It has had more than a decade to develop systems that reach deep into the lives of people inside and outside its areas of control. It is likely the group will maintain significant influence throughout southern and central Somalia unless the federal and regional governments and their allies can provide people with functioning, appealing, safe and reliable alternatives to what is provided by the Islamists.

In the Shadow

As Al Shabaab has controlled large parts of their country for years, millions of Somalis have been forced to live under its rule and influence. Some, such as the nomads who move from place to place with their livestock in search of pasture and water, have generally experienced a relatively light touch from the Islamists, although some have volunteered to fight for Al Shabaab and others have been forcibly recruited. Other people, especially those living in villages, towns and cities where Al Shabaab had or still has an established presence, have had to drastically change their way of life. Despite this, some Somalis have chosen to live in areas controlled by the group or to send their families there, deciding that, on balance, it is worth giving up personal freedoms in exchange for a degree of order, safety and predictability.

The port towns of Merca and Brava in southern Somalia were both controlled by Al Shabaab for several years. The militants have now left the town centres but maintain a presence in the outskirts and surrounding rural areas, sometimes venturing deep into the towns at night. In February 2016, Al Shabaab briefly recaptured Merca—which they had lost to AMISOM and Somali government troops in 2012—and raised their black flags over the police station and administrative headquarters.

Testimonies from residents of Merca and Brava show the extent to which their lives were changed by Al Shabaab, although the militants sometimes deny the rules they impose are as draconian as people claim.

Witnesses speak of how women were forced to put away their colourful robes of sheer, floaty material, and how men and women were forbidden from travelling in the same vehicle. One man from Merca, Mowlid, said that he had judged it to be unsafe to walk in public with his mother, sister, wife or daughter because he had feared that Al Shabaab would accuse him of immorality. He told me he lived in constant fear that the Islamists would seize the women in his family and take them off to their camps.

Mowlid said listening to the radio was not allowed unless it was tuned to Al Shabaab's station, Al Andalus. Music was banned. Girls were not permitted to play sports. Smoking was forbidden. He described how a man was caught smoking a cigarette during Ramadan. He was shot on sight and left there all day as an example to others, his body only removed during the night.

Another man, also from Merca, joked about the dilemma he faced about his facial hair now that government troops and AMISOM had taken the town from the militants. 'The question is, should you keep your beard long and risk being accused by AMISOM or the Somali army of being a member of Al Shabaab? Or should you shave it off and risk being attacked by Al Shabaab, which is still present in our city, especially at night? At least with government troops you can pretend you are too poor to go to the barber. Al Shabaab might just kill you, without asking any questions.'

Some members of minority clans said their lives improved a little when Al Shabaab first came to their towns. A young man, Hassan, described the way minority groups had been trapped in a cycle of violence, looting and prejudice before the group's arrival in Brava. 'People used to beat us, steal from us and rape our women. Then Al Shabaab came and people left us alone. Al Shabaab did not see everything through the lens of the clan. But we soon realised that Al Shabaab was little more than a change of clothes. They brought even more violence and hatred, just in a different form. Many members of minority clans went to fight for Al Shabaab, but they were mainly used as foot soldiers and were often quick to die. They were rarely given senior positions.'

Hassan described how, initially, Al Shabaab restricted itself to the mosque and did not threaten anyone. He said men were told they could no longer pray at home. They now had to go to the mosque, where they were forced to listen to long lectures about how Somalia should be united under one pure version of Islam. If people were not well enough to go to the mosque, they had to write sick notes with details of their illness and hand them in to Al Shabaab. The militants sometimes set up large screens outside, where they showed videos of their battles, their speeches and their development work. Hassan said that once Al Shabaab had gained what he described as the 'fearful obedience' of the people, they started telling them about their training camps and the glory of fighting jihad, encouraging them to join the battle to establish a caliphate.

He spoke of how a family from a minority group living close to his home was punished for playing music at a wedding.

Members of Al Shabaab went to their house and told the family that playing drums and other musical instruments was an infidel act. They picked out young women from amongst the guests and took them away, together with the bride and groom and the people who had been playing the instruments. They took them to their base, from where the screams of the women could be heard long into the night. Some of the men who had been taken returned the following day and said they had each received sixty lashes for listening to the music. The young women were never seen again.

Hassan's friend Abdi said Al Shabaab could punish people at any time, often for no obvious reason. 'One night, they stopped me and told me to open my mouth. They said they were qat monitors and wanted to check if I was chewing. Even though there was nothing in my mouth, they slapped me and forced me to lie chest down on the ground. One of the monitors said he hadn't killed anyone in the past few days and asked, "Shall I do him?" They took me to a small, hot room and left me there for days. I waited for Thursday and Friday to come, as those are the days Al Shabaab usually hands out its punishments. I was expecting a lashing, even though I had done nothing wrong. Then, one day, a local Al Shabaab leader entered the room. He told me to leave and said that if I was ever caught chewing qat, he would kill me personally.'

Abdi described how Al Shabaab would drive around Brava in cars mounted with loudspeakers that would blare out orders to gather in the public square to listen to lectures about Islam, watch executions or take part in mass prayers. During Ramadan they held koranic recitation competitions and quizzes about Islam. Prizes included laptops, hand grenades and machine guns.

He said that even though Al Shabaab officially withdrew from Brava in 2014, it maintains great influence in the town. 'By day, you see the Somali army in our town, but they withdraw to their bases at night. This is when Brava becomes Al Shabaab's city. They come out of the shadows and into our streets and houses. They lecture us about religion and tell us to give them food, threatening to kill us if we don't. In the morning, government troops come back out into the streets. If you are reported as having given food to Al Shabaab, you risk being killed by Somali soldiers. So there is no way of winning. Whatever you do in this place, you face death.'

Much has been made of Al Shabaab's disproportionate appeal to members of minority clans; of how it offers them protection and a means of seeking revenge. However, it has also been argued that, like the majority clans before it, Al Shabaab exploits these groups, especially in the Juba Valley region. According to the academics Catherine Besteman and Daniel Van Lehman, 'Al Shabaab's primary focus in Somalia is not the expansion of an extremist version of Islam but rather the continued extortion of defenceless minority groups such as the farming communities of the fertile Juba River Valley, here called Somali Bantus.'[32] They describe how Al Shabaab extorts 'a greater percentage of harvests, remittances and "religious-adherence" fines from Somali Bantus than from other Somalis.'[33] Interviewees told them how the militants confiscated about 50 per cent of Bantu harvests every year, which is more than they take from other Somalis in the area. Al Shabaab also charges the Bantu higher house taxes and *zakat*. Besteman and Van Lehman say practices such as the forced conscription of boys and the forced marriage of girls are applied more severely to Bantus than to other Somalis. Bantu Somalis employed as labourers or fighters by Al Shabaab are paid less than other Somalis, and sometimes not at all. The academics question reports that Somali Bantus support Al Shabaab because they see membership of the group as an opportunity for seeking revenge or empowerment. Members of the Bantu community have told them that they do not agree with the group's restrictive religious and governance rules, and that many have fled Al Shabaab territory to refugee camps in Kenya. Their report concludes that 'in the Juba Valley at least, Al Shabaab is a militant group misusing Islam to profit from its extortion against defenceless minority groups.'[34]

According to the Hiraal Institute, the leadership of Al Shabaab initially planned to create a relatively egalitarian organisation that would transcend the divisive and immensely complex clan politics that permeate Somali politics and society so profoundly. This represented a clear break from the norm where, on paper at least, power is carefully distributed amongst the different clans according to a strict quota system. It is in some ways ironic that, unlike almost all other countries in sub-Saharan Africa, most Somalis share the same ethnicity, language, religion and culture, yet remain bitterly divided by their clan identities.

The last person to try to dismantle the clan system was President Siad Barre, who was in power for more than two decades. For a time, he endeavoured to impose a socialist system, declaring that, 'Tribalism and nationalism cannot go hand in hand. It is unfortunate that our nation is rather too clannish: if all Somalis are to go to hell, tribalism will be their vehicle to get there.' Barre forbade people from referring to each other in terms of clan, instructing them to address each other as *jaale* instead, which means 'we are equal', 'comrade' or 'friend'. Effigies of the clan were symbolically burned or buried. But as time went on, Barre started to favour his own Darod majority clan, especially three of the group's sub-clans. His government was often referred to as the 'MOD', which stood for Barre's Marehan sub-clan, the Ogaden sub-clan of his mother and the Dhulbahante of his son-in-law.

The Hiraal Institute says that Al Shabaab 'quickly realised that clan loyalty ran deep; rather than reforming clan society, clan politics transformed the group'. The movement uses clan elders to manage and control local populations, collect taxes, raise armies and settle disputes. The Hiraal report explains how the clan system has penetrated Al Shabaab, with only a select number of clans represented in its leadership, and some sub-clans dominating entire departments. Former senior members of Al Shabaab told Hiraal researchers that the group's intelligence wing, the *Amniyaat*, is dominated by the Murursade, Habar Gidir and Duduble sub-clans of the Hawiye majority clan. They said that, although Al Shabaab has given some leadership positions to members of different clans 'in order to maintain a pan-Somali image', in June 2018 members of the Hawiye made up 50 per cent of the group's Executive Council. The dominance of the Hawiye in Al Shabaab has backfired somewhat for the group, as some of its disgruntled non-Hawiye clan members defected and went north to join Somalia's branch of the IS group, which was launched officially in 2015.

The Hiraal Institute reports that clan elders who work for Al Shabaab are given $5000 and a gun when they join and receive salaries starting at $150 a month. They are also given a camel every year and receive a share of the *infaaq*, the emergency tax raised directly from the community. While elders are used by Al Shabaab to help with recruitment and the collection of taxes, they hold some power over the group, and have been known to arrange for the release of prisoners held by Al Shabaab or to demand that the militants stop mistreating fellow clan members.

Despite its aim of being somehow 'above the clan', Al Shabaab at times has been dragged into the clan-related conflicts that have riven parts of Somalia for decades and continue to do so today. For instance, between 2008 and 2009 the Hawadle clan rose up against Al Shabaab after it killed some of its members. The Hawadle constantly ambushed Al Shabaab fighters, making it difficult for the militants to connect their southern territories with the land they controlled in central Somalia. Al Shabaab eventually signed a peace treaty with the Hawadle and paid blood money to the clan. Some years later, the Islamists wreaked their revenge by punishing Hawadle clan members when they refused to pay taxes. In 2016, they burned down an entire Hawadle village, killing about thirty clansmen and slaughtering hundreds of heads of livestock. The clan eventually started paying tax to Al Shabaab so they would stop being punished.[35]

* * *

People living inside and outside areas under the control of Al Shabaab say they face the threat of forced abduction. Ibrahim described how the militants came for him near Brava when he was walking home from his farm. They tied him up and hurled him into the back of their pick-up truck. When they arrived at their base they threw Ibrahim on the ground, dragged him to a post, tied him to it and left him there for the night. After a few days' training, Al Shabaab gave him a gun and sent him into the bush to fight.

One man, Ahmed, who lives in Mogadishu but regularly spends time in Al Shabaab areas, said the group also uses more subtle ways of winning people over to its side, sometimes targeting children as a way of trying to bring in the whole family.

'Al Shabaab is very good at intelligence gathering. If you have four children, they will identify the most active one and buy him or her sweets and maybe a mobile phone. They will give $50 to the child and tell him or her to give it to their mother. This is the way they tempt families over to their side.

'There are three parts to Al Shabaab: the head, the stomach and the legs. The head represents those who finance the movement. They are the rich Somali businesspeople who give the money to feed the stomach, which represents the implementers of Al Shabaab's policies: those who govern, who supervise intelligence gathering and so on. The legs are the foot soldiers, the minority clans and the children. They have no money and no power.'

Al Shabaab denies it abducts people or otherwise forces people to join the group. It says it welcomes those who want to live in areas it controls, including members of the diaspora and the Somali security forces. The only condition is that they abide by its rules. A member of the movement explained how, one day, two men serving in the Somali army in Brava got in touch with Al Shabaab and said they wanted to come over to the area controlled by the group. 'They didn't want to join us; they just wanted to live peacefully in our area. We told them the deal. First, they had to repent of their apostasy because they had been serving in the army of the infidels. Then, they had to sell us their equipment. They had a pick-up truck, some rocket-propelled grenades, machine guns and ammunition. We gave them $30,000 in cash. They could have got about $70,000 on the open market but we gave them less because they had been in the infidel army and because we were giving them permission to live peacefully amongst us.'

Al Shabaab affects people's lives even when they live in areas outside its control. The militants blockade towns, starving them of supplies. When they stage an attack in Mogadishu or other government-controlled towns, the whole place shuts down, disrupting trade, education and other aspects of daily life.

Al Shabaab threatens people who are in any way associated with the Somali government, the military or international organisations, no matter where they live. They can be punished, even killed, for serving food to a civil servant, washing a soldier's uniform or selling a fridge to AMISOM.

In Mogadishu, a man was shot dead in front of the headquarters of the Hormuud telecommunications company. He used to sell SIM cards and top-up vouchers for mobile phones. Sometimes he delivered SIM cards to government buildings. Al

Shabaab warned him several times to stop selling and delivering SIM cards to people in the government. He ignored the warnings and one day he was shot twice in the back.

In a camp for displaced people in Mogadishu, a man, Mustakim, explained that he had fled from Merca after being threatened by Al Shabaab. He was a member of a minority clan and used to work as a tailor. 'I made and repaired soldiers' uniforms. Al Shabaab came and told me to stop making clothes for the infidels, but I had to work in order to survive. Also, I was afraid of the soldiers, and was too scared to stop making and mending their uniforms. Both Al Shabaab and the soldiers could easily kill me if they wanted to. They were all the same to me. I could be killed for repairing uniforms and killed for refusing to repair them. So I decided the only sensible thing to do was to abandon my livelihood, leave Merca and come to Mogadishu.'

Another woman, also from Merca, had been targeted for selling tea to government soldiers. Fardowso's kiosk was near a military checkpoint and members of the Somali army were some of her most loyal customers. 'I started to receive phone calls from withheld numbers. I do not know how they got my number or how they knew who I was as I always made sure my face was covered with a full niqab when I went out. I have heard Al Shabaab forces employees of telephone companies to give out people's numbers and that it even has sympathisers in some of those firms, like it does in the army. I knew my job was risky because the way Al Shabaab operates is to do what is easy for them. They kill people who do menial jobs that are somehow associated with the government, however loosely. Selling tea to Somali soldiers is enough of a connection. They said I should stop making tea for the infidels, otherwise they would kill me. I carried on because that was the only way I could feed my family.

'I knew there was no point in going to the police or the army as some of them sympathise with Al Shabaab, while others are indifferent. They do nothing to protect us, and sometimes accuse us of having sympathy with Al Shabaab when we report that members of the group are harassing us. Then, one evening, two men came to my home. Their faces were wrapped in scarves. They wrote down my name. One of them took my photo with his phone. It was like a death sentence. That was when I decided to flee to Mogadishu with my whole family, as I was afraid that if I left them there they would be targeted instead of me. Al Shabaab often goes after the family members of individuals it wants to punish. I am afraid they will track me down here in this camp. They have my name and my photo, and nobody can hide in Somalia. Everyone knows everyone else's business and it is easy to track people down using their clan identity, no matter how lowly or insignificant they are in society. There is no sanctuary in my country.'

Dozens of people have recounted how they receive threatening phone calls from Al Shabaab via withheld numbers. They include people in Kenya, Somaliland and further afield. A woman working in Somaliland's capital, Hargeisa, showed me a text message she had received from Al Shabaab warning her to stop working for a telecommunications company because it meant she had to share an office with men. A Somali journalist in London was sent an email by Al Shabaab: 'Hey, we know where you are. We know where members of your family live, including those here in Somalia. One day you will get the punishment you deserve, which is that we will kill you. This is because you lied about Islam and spread propaganda spearheaded by non-Muslims and non-believers. This is our last warning to you, you follower of unbelievers.'

A man in Mogadishu who used to repair computers in government buildings explained how the phone calls became more threatening over time. 'The first time they called me they said that if I gave up what I was doing, if I stopped fixing things for the government, I would be spared. The second time they said if

I didn't stop what I was doing, I should consider myself a dead man. The third time they sent me money on my mobile phone for my burial clothes. That was it. I gave up the work and they stopped threatening me. Now I am unemployed.'

People describe how members of the *Amniyaat* have terrified them by telling them what colour and type of clothes they are wearing on a particular day, or what kind of transport they use to get to work and at what time.

As one young man in Mogadishu said, it is more frightening now that Al Shabaab is no longer in control of the city because you never know who is who. 'Before it was easier because Al Shabaab was controlling particular areas of this city. Now they have agents everywhere without the obvious beards or distinctive dress. The most normal person you know can be a member of Al Shabaab. They play football with you; they are your neighbours; they own coffee shops. Al Shabaab is everywhere. The group has recruited many, many people from every walk of life. It is impossible to know who is an informant. These Al Shabaab people, they are like *jinns*—they work magic; they appear and disappear. They don't have a particular uniform. You don't even know if the person working alongside you is one of them. They know everything you are doing. They even know in advance the route you are going to take.'

It is very rare for Somalis speak to me about how living with violence and the threat of violence affects them emotionally. If they do, it is usually because I push them. I try to do this as gently as I can, but, in almost all instances, the initiative comes from me.

The most memorable exception happened in London, late in the evening of 12 November 2018. Earlier that day, I had posted on Twitter and Facebook that today was my deadline for submitting the final draft of this book to the publishers, and that I was worried as I still had so much more to do.

After I sent the document to Hurst, I received a phone call from a Somali friend whom I first got to know when he worked as a journalist in Mogadishu. He was an extraordinarily brave reporter. Some would describe him as reckless, as he always seemed to go the extra mile, travelling to places deemed too dangerous, even by Somali standards. He obtained all the gory detail about attacks, and would often phone me with vivid accounts of the horrors he had seen. His information was rough and raw. Al Shabaab did not like his style. One day my friend forwarded me an email sent from a well-known Al Shabaab account, warning him that if he continued to report in this way he would be killed. 'Don't think you can escape us. We know where you are at any time of day, and we know where you live. We know you are newly married and that you have a baby on the way.'

The journalist fled to the UK and applied for asylum there. His application was successful and some time later he brought over his wife and children. The couple had more children, with a new baby arriving almost every year. He found a job in hospitality and thrived. Whenever I saw him, he was cheerful and confident.

That evening, he encouraged me to deliver my book on time and told me he had some good news that he wanted to tell me before sharing it with others. His whole family had just been granted permission to remain in the UK indefinitely, and would soon be eligible for British passports.

'I want to talk to you about something else too. I have been living in London for the past five years and recently all the violence I witnessed in Mogadishu has been flashing through my mind. It is as if I relive each death I experienced, including the first, which happened when I was about eleven years old. This was when I saw my next-door neighbour being gunned down during the civil war of the 1990s. It is as if the whole incident, and the many, many others I witnessed, are being replayed again and again in front of my eyes.

'I spent what should have been the best years of my life, from the age of eleven to the age of thirty-three, living with killings all around me. It meant very little to me when people died. Now, all of a sudden I am feeling the pain. I think it is because I feel so safe here in London that all these memories are flooding back. I cannot watch any violence on television. I cannot look at all the photos and videos posted on social media of attacks in Somalia. I have to turn my head away. It is the same when I hear ambulances or see blood. My wife bled severely during the birth of our latest child and I could not bear to see red blood on the hospital floor. I have spoken to my doctor about this and he says it is normal to feel this way after what I have seen.

'I feel guilty, heartless and ashamed because I felt nothing about all those deaths I saw in Somalia. In the UK, life is precious and respected by all. In Somalia, life is worthless. It is cheap. Here, I have the same rights as the prime minister, Theresa May, when it comes to things like the law, public transport and the National Health Service. We will both be treated the same. It is not like that in Somalia. In my country, there is only one punishment, which is killing. There is no other form of sanction. If you have a row with a business rival, a squabble over land or any kind of dispute with anyone, you risk being shot.'

Islamic State

Although Al Shabaab remains the dominant violent Islamist group in Somalia, it has existed alongside, and at times faced competition from, similar movements, including a local extremist group Hizb-ul-Islam and the Somali branch of Islamic State (IS).

As the fortunes of Al Qaeda started to decline and IS gained in strength and prominence in Iraq, Syria and elsewhere, speculation grew that either IS would start to take hold as the dominant Islamist force in Africa or that Al Shabaab would switch allegiances and spearhead the formation of an East African branch of IS. One study found that in 2014, IS:

> began to make both formal and informal approaches to al Shabaab, seeking to wean it away from allegiance to al Qaeda and instead swear loyalty to the new 'Caliph', al Baghdadi ... From early 2015, the Islamic State began also to appeal directly to the al Shabaab rank and file, in particular by having Somali members portray a life that seemed far superior, in jihadi terms, to that offered by al Shabaab.[36]

However, Al Shabaab remained loyal to Al Qaeda, purging IS sympathisers from its ranks, killing some of them.

In 2015, the leader of a group of a few hundred Al Shabaab fighters in the Golis mountain range in Puntland, northern Somalia, Sheikh Abdulqadir Mumin, declared allegiance to the IS leader Abu Bakr al-Baghdadi, although security experts say this was not coordinated with the IS leadership. Mumin is a British citizen, who lived in Sweden and the UK before returning to Somalia to join Al Shabaab, and later IS. The formation of this small 'IS Somalia' (ISS) branch led to concern that it would serve as a rallying point for Somali extremists and foreign IS fighters fleeing Syria and Iraq. However, this did not come to pass and by mid-2018 the Somali National Intelligence and Security Agency estimated that ISS had no more than about 200 fighters across the country. In November 2018, AMISOM said there were roughly 100 to 200 men in ISS, which it said operated mainly in Puntland and was 'for hire' in Mogadishu.[37]

The Somali branch of IS has stayed small for several reasons. Its base is hard to reach, for both Somalis further south and for international jihadis. It has periodically been engaged in intense conflict with Al Shabaab, losing fighters and becoming distracted from its principal purpose of defeating the 'apostate' government and forming a caliphate. Also, unlike Al Shabaab, but like many other armed groups in the country, it is mainly composed of just one clan. Like Mumin, most of its members are from the Ali

Salebaan sub-sub-clan of the Majeerteen sub-clan of the Darod majority clan, which dominates north-eastern Somalia as well as areas in the far south of the country. In some ways, ISS is more like a clan militia than an ideological movement:

> A senior police commander in Puntland, interviewed in May 2018, estimated that around 90 per cent of the Ali Salebaan supported ISS, largely in order to use ISS as a way to gain more economic power and political influence in the state as part of a common phenomenon evident in many parts of Somalia whereby clans ally with other groups in temporary arrangements driven by short- or mid-term commercial or political interest rather than any deeper or long-lasting affinity. Similarly, some Ali Salebaan members support it [ISS] merely because their clansmen are in charge, regardless of the nature of the group, its actions or objectives.[38]

Despite its weaknesses, ISS has conducted several attacks, mainly in Puntland. These have included assaults on government buildings, hotels and police posts, as well as targeted assassinations of government officials, members of the security services and others associated with the 'apostate' authorities. ISS is also active further afield, including Mogadishu, where it claimed its first attack in April 2016 when it used an IED to target an AMISOM convoy. It has carried out several assassinations in the capital, and is said to have established strongholds in the city's Bakara Market area and in Elasha Biyaha, an area on the outskirts of Mogadishu. Between 27 February and 27 July 2018, ISS carried out at least eleven deadly attacks in or near Mogadishu, killing at least fifteen people, including policemen, soldiers, government officials, tax collectors and a traffic policeman. In one of these incidents, it claimed to have killed or wounded fourteen soldiers in an IED attack on 24 July 2018.[39]

Although Al Shabaab is responsible for dozens, if not hundreds, of targeted assassinations every year, ISS is beginning to catch up. In the third quarter of 2018, security analysts said the group carried out a fifth of all such assassinations in Somalia. ISS has also become more active in terms of tax collection, extracting payments from businesses in Mogadishu as well as in Puntland's port city of Bossasso. Indeed, several of the assassinations carried out by ISS in the capital's Bakara Market were prompted by the refusal of some businesspeople to pay taxes.[40]

Al Shabaab is strongly opposed to ISS. One Al Shabaab official said of ISS: 'We see them as bad people because they say they are part of IS but they are not. Yesterday, they were part of Al Shabaab and we are the true Islamic people. We believe in unity under one emir. As it says in the Koran, "Allah loves people who fight alongside one another". Anyone who tries to break this unity must be killed because if we are divided we will be weak. Dividing the mujahidin is a red line for us. We won't talk to them about this; we will not lecture them. We will just execute them on the spot.

'ISS is trying to take over our voice, our men, our weapons and our people. We do not care if Somalis go to fight jihad with IS over there in Libya and Syria. We will even give them money to do so. But bringing IS here to Somalia is bad because it sows division.'

As Al Shabaab is relatively self-sufficient, able to raise its own taxes and other income, as well as to recruit or forcibly abduct fighters and other members, the fortunes of Al Qaeda elsewhere in the world are almost irrelevant to the group. As long as it is able to survive as a fighting force, raise and extract funds, and provide essential services, it is difficult to imagine how the group will be eliminated, unless it decides to disband, perhaps by signing peace with the government. ISS is a far more fragile venture, vulnerable not only to attack by Somali forces, AMISOM and US drones, but also its senior 'cousin', Al Shabaab.

4

RESISTANCE

A few weeks after Donald Trump was elected president on 8 November 2016, government officials asked a series of questions about Africa. One asked, 'We have been fighting Al Shabaab for a decade. Why haven't we won?'[1]

The team had good reason to ask. Despite being outgunned and outnumbered by Somali federal government troops, Somali regional forces, Somali militias, African Union soldiers, Ethiopian troops, US drone operators, Western special forces and foreign military advisers, Al Shabaab still held swathes of territory and continued to attack government-controlled areas in Somalia and Kenya.

The Somali authorities like to claim that Al Shabaab is on the way out. Shortly after they came to power, I interviewed both the former Somali president Hassan Sheikh Mohamud, who served from September 2012 till February 2017, and Mohamed Abdullahi Farmajo, who succeeded him. I asked them how things were progressing in the fight against Al Shabaab. Both told me the group would be defeated within two years. Both were wrong.

EVERYTHING YOU HAVE TOLD ME IS TRUE

In a paper written in 2018, a Mogadishu-based think tank painted a stark picture of the group's enduring strength, which contrasted sharply with claims by the Somali federal government that Al Shabaab was on the verge of defeat:

> The war against Al Shabaab has been at a stalemate for the past three years, with a slight territorial gain for the group. The group currently controls territory in 11 of 18 Somali regions and parts of Kenya's Coast and North Eastern provinces—total territory that is almost half the landmass of Somalia. Almost all major cities in southern Somalia are besieged by the group, with widespread starvation and inflation causing inhabitants to seek shelter in Al Shabaab territory.[2]

An internal African Union Mission in Somalia (AMISOM) document, released at the end of 2018, came to a similar conclusion, although it said Al Shabaab controlled a smaller amount of territory:

> Commanding between 4000 [and] 7000 active combatants, including foreigners, the group still maintains control of about a fifth of Somalia, mainly in ungoverned rural areas and small towns in southern and central Somalia, with strongholds in the Juba Valley, Lower Shabelle, Middle Shabelle, and Upper Gedo. Al-Shabaab continues to recruit children and women and attract foreign fighters especially providing in Somalia a potential safe haven for ISIS elements leaving Syria and Iraq to regroup.[3]

In March 2017, President Trump eased US combat rules in Somalia, giving the American military more freedom to carry out offensive air strikes and raids by ground troops. Deaths of civilians were permitted if deemed necessary and proportionate. The number of US air strikes went up significantly, more than doubling from fifteen known strikes in 2016 to thirty-one the following year. There were forty-seven known strikes in 2018.[4]

On 19 January 2019, the US military said it killed fifty-two members of Al Shabaab in an air strike, in response to a militant attack on a Somali army base near Kismayo in which eight soldiers died. Shortly afterwards a Somali intelligence expert sent me a series of images on WhatsApp. With no warning whatsoever, ten photographs and one video appeared, showing Somali soldiers picking their way through the charred remains of men's bodies. The dead were wearing camouflage and khaki, some still clutching their guns as they lay scattered around the truck they had been travelling in, by now a blackened wreck. Some of them were still on fire, flames and smoke rising from their lifeless bodies. One soldier stood on the remains of the vehicle, passing the dead men's weapons to another soldier, who carried them off with his bare hands. The intelligence expert said the images had been taken by the regional Jubaland forces, and that the American claim of fifty-two dead Islamist militants had not been independently verified.

Although Al Shabaab has remained active, carrying out at least thirty-three car bombings in Mogadishu between January and November 2017,[5] it has been argued that by 2018 'the increasingly lethal air campaign by Somalia's allies' had forced Al Shabaab to change its tactics. The group appears less able to conduct complex attacks in which its fighters bomb, raid and besiege military bases and other targets. It has been focusing instead on bombing government offices and businesses that do not pay taxes and other fees demanded by the militants, and on the assassination of politicians, municipal officials, police officers and others linked to the government in some way. Most of these bombings and targeted shootings occur in Mogadishu, although they also take place in other parts of Somalia and across the border in Kenya.[6]

Every so often the BBC, in detailed consultation with journalists on the ground in Somalia, produces a map of who controls what in the country. The map drawn up in February 2018 showed Al Shabaab had moved back into stretches of territory along the southern coast, land it did not hold in November 2016 when the previous BBC map was produced. It had also regained control of a number of key routes between strategic towns and cities. This meant that the militants could blockade government-held urban areas, move in more easily to conduct suicide bombings and other attacks, and retake towns more quickly when they were abandoned by Somali troops and AMISOM forces.

The outsourcing of security to foreign powers has in many ways kept Somalia in an infantilised, dependent state, unable to meet one of the basic prerequisites of a functioning nation: guaranteeing the safety of its own people. After difficult early years, the 22,000 AMISOM troops posted to the country began to make significant gains against Al Shabaab, returning a number of Somalia's towns and cities to their people. However, AMISOM's hold on these places is fragile.

AMISOM's first six-month mandate to deploy to Somalia was approved by the United Nations Security Council in February 2007. It was to become the African Union's 'longest running, largest, most costly, and most deadly operation'.[7] The following month, the first batch of Ugandan soldiers arrived, with Burundian forces deploying later the same year. Sierra Leone sent troops in 2013. Although the initial plan was not to include any troops from Somalia's neighbours, this was rescinded by a UN Security Council resolution in 2007,[8] and Djiboutian soldiers joined the force in 2011. Another neighbour, Ethiopia, which has for years had a military presence in Somalia, agreed for more than 4,000 of its soldiers already stationed in the country to be absorbed into AMISOM in 2014. Kenyan troops poured across their eastern border into Somalia in October 2011. Operation *Linda Nchi*, which means 'Protect the Country' in Kiswahili, marked the first time Kenya went to war in another country since independence in 1963. AMISOM assumed formal command of the nearly 5,000 Kenyan troops in Somalia in 2012.

Ghana, Kenya, Nigeria, Sierra Leone, Uganda and Zambia have all contributed to AMISOM's police force.[9]

AMISOM's achievements have been made at considerable personal cost, with hundreds of African Union soldiers losing their lives, especially during militant assaults on their forward-operating bases. In the deadliest attack, on 15 January 2016, Al Shabaab stormed a Kenyan military base at El Adde in southwestern Somalia. Despite promising a full account of the battle, the Kenyan government is yet to release full details of the dead and wounded. It has also failed to disclose whether Al Shabaab took prisoners of war, as claimed by the group. Media reports suggest at least 173 Kenyan troops were killed, with another thirteen taken hostage. The academic and AMISOM expert Paul Williams believes the reports are probably accurate: 'My research suggests these figures for the Kenyan troops killed and captured at El Adde is plausible ... I suspect that the battle at El Adde was the deadliest encounter in the history of modern peace operations.'[10] It is probably no coincidence that Al Shabaab chose the third anniversary of the El Adde attack to lay siege to Nairobi's luxury hotel complex at 14 Riverside Drive.

Somalis were initially hostile towards AMISOM troops, but they became more accepting after seeing the progress they were making against Al Shabaab. However, there have been reports of misconduct, with human rights groups accusing the force of mistreating civilians, including raping women.[11] African Union troops have also been caught and arrested for selling military equipment to civilians.[12] These weapons, ammunition and other instruments of violence are then used for personal protection, for criminal purposes, or by private security companies and militias, or they are sold on to other armed groups, including Al Shabaab. UN investigators have reported that arms imported by the federal government for use by the Somali military have found their way into the hands of weapons dealers in the markets of Mogadishu.

The merchants said some of the guns were bought by Al Shabaab agents.[13] This violates the terms of a UN arms embargo on Somalia, which was partially lifted in 2013 to allow the government to import weapons in order to equip its military in their fight against the Islamists.

Some AMISOM soldiers say they do not like Somalia or its people, whom they describe as arrogant, rude and racist. They complain of the unrelenting heat and say the only things they look forward to are their wage packets and trips back home. They say that they are always scared because 'Somalis are not afraid of death' and Al Shabaab lurks around every corner. Some speak of dead and captured comrades, others of the early days in Somalia when their living conditions were so bad that 250 AMISOM troops became malnourished, many of them showing signs of beriberi. Fifty were airlifted to hospitals in Kenya and Uganda; four of them died.[14] Some Ugandan and Burundian soldiers say they do not see the point in fighting a war that has little bearing on events back home, apart from making their leaders look good and earning their countries funds for their contribution to the operation in Somalia.

Al Shabaab says most people serving with AMISOM are there for the money. 'African Union troops receive a salary of $1,200 every month. They get $900 of this amount. The rest goes into the personal pockets of their presidents and government ministers. But even $900 is a lot of money in a country like Uganda. And you know Africans. They are very simple people but they are greedy. One of their favourite expressions is "Let's get rich or die trying". The troop-contributing countries do not care when their men die in Somalia. They even throw their widows on the trash heap.'

Somalia, the 'southern front' in the War on Terror, has become a testing ground for global powers to deal with violent Islamist extremism, 'failed' or 'fragile' states and the African continent. It is also a place where foreign policy has become increasingly confused. While in the 1990s foreign intervention in Somalia was essentially led by the US, today a growing number of African and non-African powers have taken an interest in the country. This has led to a lack of coordination on the ground. In December 2017, the African Union's Special Representative to Somalia, Francisco Madeira, warned that Somali forces were not ready to take over from AMISOM, which had already started a gradual pull-out from the country with the withdrawal of 1,000 troops. He said that in addition to being severely under-equipped and short of troops, the Somali security forces were being trained by a bewildering number of countries, including Turkey, the United Arab Emirates (UAE), Britain and the US. There was no joined-up plan, he said, resulting in a dangerous level of confusion. Madeira added that many of the soldiers trained by foreign countries were serving in regional armies, which were often at odds with federal troops. Others ended up working for the multitude of private security companies that operate in Somalia.

This confusion of foreign powers is visible as you fly in low over the Indian Ocean to the seaside airport in Mogadishu. Stretched along the beach, there is a gleaming new Turkish base, Turkey's largest overseas military training facility. Other foreign military bases and training grounds are clustered around the airport, where every day the disconcerting sound of weapons firing at a shooting range mingles with the noise of aircraft landing and taking off. Far up the coast in Somaliland's port town of Berbera, the UAE is building a military facility. This has provoked rage from the Somali federal government, which has accused the UAE of violating the country's sovereignty and territorial integrity. In the south-western town of Baidoa, British troops train the regional police force. In Mogadishu, US special forces have trained an elite group of Somali commandos, known as *Gaashaan* or 'the Shield', who wear black balaclavas to hide their identities and protect their families from reprisal attacks.

Despite all the millions of dollars spent on training and all the talk about Somalis taking responsibility for their own security, the local military and police are in no way capable of doing so. Between September and December 2017, at least sixty Somali soldiers were killed and large quantities of arms and ammunition seized when Al Shabaab overran four military bases. A government investigation into the attacks found that a third of the soldiers in these bases did not even have weapons. It also found that of the 26,000 Somali troops on the payroll, only about 10,000 were fit for active service. The rest had already retired, or were too old or disabled to fight. It is difficult to imagine how such a shambolic, poorly equipped, divided and undisciplined force will be able to take over security responsibilities from AMISOM in December 2021, which is the date set for such a handover to take place.[15]

In a forthright article for *The New York Times* following the devastating truck bombing in Mogadishu in 2017, Somalia's then head of the National Intelligence and Security Agency, Abdillahi Mohamed Sanbalooshe, pleaded for a new international approach to the security situation whereby Somalis would be given more autonomy and control. He said it was time for 'a new paradigm of cooperation between Somali security services and our international partners' and argued that Somalia 'cannot any longer outsource our investigations and intelligence analysis to private contractors driven by the profit motive'. Somali security services needed their own equipment and to develop their own expertise: 'In early 2017, we had just four overworked police teams with no post-blast investigation kits, no forensic laboratory and just one borrowed device for the exploitation of captured cell phones.' Somalia's government was struggling to pay regular salaries for police and soldiers, let alone training and equipping specialised bomb units.

We have been operating almost completely blind. International partners offered to provide 'technical assistance,' but their good intentions served to blind us even more: the evidence gathered from bombing scenes is handled and removed by foreign 'mentors' who treat intelligence as a commodity rather than as a shared asset in our battle against a common enemy. Once taken away, it is rarely, if ever[,] returned. Only fragments of power-blast investigations are shared with us; often, we get no information at all.[16]

In 2018, Somali analysts criticised their government for giving Al Shabaab 'financial and operational freedom':

All things remaining constant, the war against Al Shabaab will continue in its fluid nature, with a slight advantage for Al Shabaab. While the group is still reeling from a leadership and membership crisis, it is facing disparate and poorly coordinated Somali security forces, making it easier for them to at least keep the status quo, or even gain more territory in the next two years.[17]

As well as trying to defeat Al Shabaab militarily, the authorities are also trying to woo defectors, using different approaches for high-, medium- and low-ranking members of the group. Somalis complain that some high-level defectors, such as Al Shabaab's former deputy leader and spokesman, Mukhtar Robow, lived in hotels in Mogadishu instead of facing justice.

Al Shabaab says it now considers Robow to be an apostate. 'He is doing something that is not Islamic. He is a hypocrite. He has joined those he used to kill and describe as apostates. As our spokesman, he used to inspire our fighters to go and slaughter the infidels. Now he has gone over to the enemy side. But people won't trust him. They know that tomorrow he could change sides again.'

Somalis ask why some of those who defect from Al Shabaab are given money while soldiers in the Somali army are sometimes not paid at all. Social media was ablaze with criticism in January 2018 when a regional minister in Baidoa gave $15,000 to Mohamed Hassan Aden Sandhere for defecting from Al Shabaab, taking with him a combat vehicle and heavy machine gun.

Another problem with the dominant international security strategy towards Somalia is that it tends to focus too closely on Al Shabaab and the terror factor. It largely disregards the other conflicts in the country, which are generally related to clan, property and business disputes. There are also deep tensions between the regional states and the central government, and between some of the regions themselves, which have on occasion erupted into violent confrontation. The tortuous process of establishing a federal system only began in earnest after multiple interim administrations were replaced by an internationally recognised central government in 2012. The situation in Somalia was so dangerous that some of the transitional governments that formed after the fall of President Siad Barre in 1991 were based outside the country. Others were based in Somali towns other than the capital, Mogadishu, such as Jowhar and Baidoa. Even the moderate Islamist and former chairman of the Islamic Courts Union (ICU) Sheikh Sharif Sheikh Ahmed was elected and sworn in as head of state outside Somalia in 2009. The Somali parliament, which was responsible for electing the president, held the voting session in Djibouti as it was judged too dangerous to hold such a meeting in Somalia. The swearing-in ceremony also took place there. Shortly after the election, the then UN special envoy to Somalia, Ahmedou Ould-Abdallah, implored Somalis to stop fighting and give the new president a chance to govern. 'It is up to you, the fathers, mothers, brothers and sisters to prevail on your children, your young brothers and friends to stop the violence. For the last twenty years, it has not helped any group to win lasting victory.'[18]

In time, international and local policy-makers may come to regret their grand project for a federal Somalia, whereby the country has been divided up into five regional states—six if the self-declared republic of Somaliland is included—each with its own president and legislature. On a number of occasions some or all of the regional states have severed ties with the federal government. Some fear the federal model could lead to the greater balkanisation of an already fractured country. It is likely that Al Shabaab and other armed groups will take advantage of these tensions and distractions, if they are not already doing so.

* * *

One country that has taken an enthusiastic interest in Somalia in recent years is Turkey. Centuries ago there was an Ottoman presence in Somalia, and there are still remains of Ottoman-era buildings in parts of the country today. The relationship was renewed during the famine of 2011 when the then Turkish prime minister, now president, Recep Tayyip Erdogan, flew to Somalia. This was the first visit by a non-African head of state in more than twenty years. At the time, most other foreign powers were maintaining a safe distance from the country, preferring to conduct most of their Somali-related business from air-conditioned offices, hotels and villas in neighbouring Kenya. Erdogan and his wife walked through the streets of Mogadishu, visiting camps full of people affected by the devastating drought. He did not wear body armour. He wore a suit.

Somalis still talk of how Erdogan kissed dirty, hungry children and how his wife cradled starving babies. This was the beginning of a love affair between the two countries. Somalis started to name their boys 'Erdogan', their daughters 'Istanbul'. Millions of dollars were raised in Turkey to help those in need. Ankara named an ambassador to Somalia, Dr Kani Torun, who set up shop in a converted villa in the heart of Mogadishu, unlike most other foreign missions which were based in Kenya or behind the wire at Mogadishu's airport. On one of my visits to Somalia during Ramadan in 2012, Dr Torun insisted on inviting my Somali driver, guide and bodyguards into the grounds of his embassy to sit together with him and his staff for *iftar*, the breaking of the fast. We all sat at a long table in the open air, eating food mainly purchased in the local market. Somalis are usually kept well away from foreign missions and UN compounds unless they go through a lengthy vetting and screening process. Much of the food and drink in these places is imported.

After he visited Mogadishu, Erdogan wrote an emotive article for *Foreign Policy* magazine entitled 'The Tears of Somalia'. He argued that the world's first twenty-first-century famine tested 'the notion of civilization and our modern values'. He wrote that: 'The tears that are now running from Somalia's golden sands into the Indian Ocean must stop. They should be replaced by hopeful voices of a country where people do not lose their lives because of starvation and where they express their eagerness to develop and restore peace and stability.'[19]

During this honeymoon period, it was hard to find a Somali who would criticise Turkey, even amongst my contacts in Al Shabaab. Somalis said the Turkish people treated them as equal Muslim brothers and sisters. Unlike other foreigners, they lived and worked in the heart of Mogadishu, rebuilding the shattered infrastructure, treating the sick and educating the children. Such affection for a foreign country is highly unusual in Somalia, where people are generally fairly hostile towards outsiders and have all sorts of abusive nicknames for them. But as time went on, criticism of Turkey increased. Turkey was too focused on Mogadishu, was striking self-interested business deals, handed out money to government officials without questioning how it was spent, and did not coordinate with other donors.[20]

Turkey, like many other countries, is keen to lay its hands on Africa's natural resources and to exploit new markets as the continent develops. But by focusing on Somalia, classed by many as one of the most dangerous countries in the world, it has chosen a highly eccentric gateway into the continent.

I visited the port in Mogadishu, a key source of revenue for the Somali government. It was now being run by the Turkish company Al Bayrak. Where once rival militias battled for control of the lucrative docks, giant container ships now lined up neatly to discharge their cargoes of cement, paint, vehicles, shoes, pasta, ketchup and rice. Huge cranes swooped up and down, some operated by Turks, others by Somalis.

As a container swung uncomfortably close above my head, the sprightly Turkish port manager explained that since Al Bayrak took over in September 2013 it had been bringing in a monthly revenue of $4 million and rising. He said 55 per cent of the money went straight to the Somali government.

The Turks seem to be everywhere in Mogadishu. They run schools and provide hundreds of scholarships a year for Somali students to study in Turkey. They convert houses into hospitals and run the airport, where they have built a glossy new terminal and are constructing an airport hotel. Turkish Airlines flies to Mogadishu several times a week, the first major commercial airline to do so in more than twenty years. Its first flight was in March 2012, less than a year after Erdogan's dramatic visit to the Somali capital. The flights are generally full and, due to the lack of competition, tickets are expensive, with a return flight often costing more than $1,500. Prices are likely to fall now that Ethiopian Airlines and a few others are venturing into South Central Somalia.

Turkish engineers are hard at work on the streets of Mogadishu, building dozens of kilometres of new roads. Even the garbage trucks trying to get rid of the decades' worth of rubbish and rubble come from Turkey. On one visit, I counted more Turkish flags in the city than Somali ones. In many ways, the Turks are engaged in their own form of resistance to Al Shabaab and other armed groups simply by living and working in the city, driving their own vehicles and mixing with the local population.

At a gleaming new hospital, built by Turkey, Turkish doctors wore simple white polo shirts. On one sleeve was an image of the

Turkish flag; the Somali flag was on the other. Near to the hospital, Turkish builders in cowboy hats worked alongside Somalis as they put the final touches to a huge Ottoman-style mosque in the hospital grounds with room for 2,000 worshippers.

On the seafront, a huge new Turkish embassy has been built. Most of the builders were Somalis. They said the Turks had taught them new skills, which they would put to use in the reconstruction of their country. Some of the Turks who lived and worked in the compound whilst the embassy was being built said they were not very fond of Somalia, mainly because of the insecurity. They were counting the days till they could go home. The supervisor explained that they had had to increase the height of the compound's perimeter walls after a mortar was fired into the embassy grounds.

Many Turks in Mogadishu seem to have a different attitude from most other foreigners in Somalia towards danger, continuing to work and otherwise go about their business during times of heightened insecurity. On the day of a suicide bombing in the city, I was refused access to the airport, where I was due to meet the British ambassador. Nearby was a Turkish school, guarded by two lightly armed Somalis. Turkish children scampered about, playing hide-and-seek amongst the papaya trees. They shared classes with Somali students, who the Turkish teachers said were especially good at computing and languages. The Turks have paid a price for this more relaxed attitude to security. Some have been killed and injured in attacks by Al Shabaab, while others have been shot dead in business and other disputes.

The day after the suicide attack, I managed with some difficulty to get into the airport compound, this time to meet officials at the UN, which is based in a sterile, grey complex of containers. Somewhat to my embarrassment, I did not have a pen. A member of the UN staff kindly lent me a pencil. I forgot to give it back, and later on I gave it to a Somali friend.

Wielding the UN pencil, he rushed off to his friends shouting: 'Look! This is all the UN has to offer us, after more than twenty years and billions of dollars. In just a few short years, the Turks have helped transform our man-made earthquake of Mogadishu into a semi-functioning city. They have brought their own engineers to stand in the hot sun and build roads. This has helped to reawaken business in Mogadishu as auto-rickshaws and wheelbarrows can now function on the smooth roads, delivering people, fresh fruit and bread to different parts of the city. Previously only 4x4 land cruisers and other tough vehicles could use our shelled-out, pot-holed roads.'

Of course, it is not as simple as that. The UN and others are contributing massively to Somalia, often in less obvious ways than the Turks, who have opted for highly visible projects.

Al Shabaab has become progressively more hostile towards Turkey. In November 2014 a member of the group said: 'The Turks in Somalia have two faces. During the famine of 2011, they said they were coming to help the Somali people. They came to areas controlled by Al Shabaab and we welcomed them. They gave money, food and water. That was good and we welcomed it.

'But now they have switched sides. They are helping the Somali government, giving them money every month and helping with security. They are working with the apostates. As long as they are helping the infidels, we will consider them a legitimate target.'

The Al Shabaab official went on to criticise Turkey for what he said was too close a focus on its own pockets and on the Somali elites. 'The Turks are now building roads, but only roads which lead to the presidential palace. They are rebuilding the Maka al Mukarama road where the apostates gather to eat, drink and shop. Why are they doing that? If they really wanted to help the Somali people, they would build other roads, not the one from the airport to Villa Somalia.

'Turkey is now fighting a cold war against the Somali people, both economically and politically. A Turkish company has signed a contract with the president to run the port. As soon as the ink was dry, the Turks fired 5,300 Somali port workers. They brought people from Turkey instead, forcing economically desperate Somalis to cross the desert to Libya and die in the Mediterranean Sea. They did the same thing at the airport, creating jobs for Turks and firing Somalis. They are as bad as the UN, which comes to Somalia with dozens of expatriate staff. Turkish businessmen are bringing food to Somalia and destroying the local market. This is an economic cold war. That is why we now attack the Turks. Not all the attacks on Turks are by Al Shabaab. Some are organised by angry, jealous Somali entrepreneurs who accuse them of taking their business. Others are by criminal gangs, maybe even politicians. But it is good that they kill them.'

* * *

The areas controlled by Al Shabaab shift constantly, as do those where it has a presence or an ability to stage regular attacks. Any attempt to produce a map showing which parts of Somalia are controlled by which group draws criticism, sometimes simultaneously, from AMISOM, the Somali government, Al Shabaab and international security advisers. I once received a string of angry phone calls from Al Shabaab's communications department because a BBC online map of Somalia said the group had only a 'presence' in certain shaded areas, rather than 'control'. AMISOM has also asked why the BBC maps look so different from its own, which tend to show African Union forces controlling ever larger parts of the country, squeezing Al Shabaab into smaller and smaller areas.

Equally problematic are the maps that confine the areas of Al Shabaab's presence or control within Somalia's borders. A more accurate depiction would have shaded areas, or perhaps coloured dots, well inside Kenya's borders. They would be concentrated in the coastal regions, parts of the capital Nairobi and North Eastern province, which abuts Somalia. There would be arrows stretching across the sea to Yemen, where for some years Al Shabaab and Al Qaeda in the Arabian Peninsula have periodically shared arms, intelligence and fighting men. There might be vague coloured splashes in Somaliland, which suffered a major Al Shabaab attack in 2008 and where the militants are said to retain a quiet presence. The movement's influential and charismatic former leader Godane came from Somaliland.

But it would be much more difficult to insert any shaded areas in Somalia's other neighbour, Ethiopia, even though, like Kenya, it has a large indigenous Somali population, hundreds of thousands of refugees from Somalia, and a long border with the country. Ethiopia is Al Shabaab's prime target. It has been a declared enemy since the group's inception, whereas Kenya only became a major focus after invading Somalia in 2011. Local and international security specialists say Al Shabaab is trying very hard to attack Ethiopia, but has failed so far, largely because of the effectiveness of the country's security and intelligence services.

When I ask people in Ethiopia how their country has managed to avoid attacks by Al Shabaab, they look at me as if I am stupid. They then point to their eyes, and often refer to this part of their anatomy in their answers. 'We have eyes in the back of our heads.' 'Our community never sleeps. Its eyes are always open.' 'We have eyes everywhere, always on the lookout for potential enemies.'

No matter whom I ask, be it a government minister, member of the intelligence services, foreign diplomat or woman selling mangoes on the roadside, the answer usually includes the words 'security' and 'intelligence'. People often talk about Ethiopia's *kebele* system—referring to the country's smallest administrative unit—whereby people are organised into wards or neighbour-hoods and all know each other's business. The community essentially spies on itself. The police are informed of new arrivals, landlords report new tenants, calls and conversations are monitored, and everybody is being watched all of the time. As Ethiopia's former information minister Negeri Lencho told me: 'Here in Ethiopia, security is within the people. You cannot underestimate our security and intelligence services. They penetrate society. They even know the colour of your bed sheets.'

Mention the words 'Al Shabaab' in Ethiopia and people shut down. Once, while sitting in a restaurant with expatriate friends, I overheard them whispering, 'Mary is researching a book about Al Shabaab. We better not talk about it here. It could compromise our positions in this country.'

Al Shabaab's failure to attack Ethiopia is not for lack of trying. The group is said to have a special brigade which focuses on the country and has had at least two near misses. One was a plot to blow up at least one shopping mall in Addis Ababa in 2015, the other a planned double suicide attack on a World Cup football qualifier in the capital in 2013. While they were preparing for the stadium attack, the bombers blew themselves up by mistake. A security official said the first person to be arrested in connection with the botched attempt was the landlord who had rented the accommodation to the would-be bombers. He was accused of failing to alert the authorities about his new tenants.

It is possible that Al Shabaab will try to take advantage of the tremendous changes that have occurred in Ethiopia since the appointment in 2018 of the trailblazer prime minister Abiy Ahmed. His lightning-fast reforms have catalysed ethnic convulsions in parts of the country, including the eastern Somali Regional State, which was previously known as Zone Five or the Ogaden. More than 95 per cent of its population is Somali. With an area of about 250,000 square kilometres, the state is the second largest in Ethiopia.[21] It has a long border with Somaliland and Somalia.

In Addis Ababa, the area of Bole Mikael is often referred to as 'Little Mogadishu', as are the Eastleigh district in Nairobi and the Somali-dominated part of Minneapolis in the USA. In Bole Mikael the distinctive script of the Amharic language slips away from storefronts and signs, replaced by the double letters—xx, cc, oo and aa—so often seen in the Somali language, which was first written down in 1972. Restaurants offer Somali dishes of rice, pasta, meat and bananas, to be washed down with fresh fruit juice or camel milk. Somali music blares from the roadside kiosks and stalls. Many of the residents are either Ethiopian Somalis or Somali Somalis, all blended in together. Some Ethiopians see Somalis as a good thing, at least for the economy. As one ethnic Oromo resident of Bole Mikael said: 'This area is not Ethiopia. It is Somalia. I worry that if the Somalis leave here, we Ethiopians will become much poorer. Ethiopians rent buildings in Bole Mikael to Somali businesses and families. It would be an economic disaster if they went back to Somalia. Also, Somalis are good at gathering information on other Somalis. They understand the language and culture and mix in well with the community.'

A senior Ethiopian intelligence official described the Somalis as a crucial resource in the fight against Al Shabaab: 'Of course there are Islamist extremists and Al Shabaab sympathisers here in Ethiopia. But in some ways we see the Somalis in Ethiopia, at least the decent ones, as the best protection we have against militant Islamism. We just have to be clever about the way we deal with them. Unlike Kenya, which treats Somalis, especially those who come from Somalia itself, as a negative force, as undesirable aliens, we try to integrate them. It is best to win them over to the Ethiopian way of doing things. We believe that empowering them, at least to a degree, will de-radicalise them. But we always keep a close eye on their madrassas and all their other activities.'

In Bole Mikael I met a Somali, Abdinur, who had initially fled from Somalia to Kenya in the mid-2000s. He said he was treated in such an intolerable way there that he left for a new life in Addis Ababa. 'Ethiopia is better than Kenya. In Kenya, there is massive prejudice against us. We suffer collective punishment just for being Somali. The Ethiopians will punish viciously a Somali who does wrong, but will leave the law-abiders alone. I hear the Ethiopians don't even bother to put Al Shabaab suspects on trial. They just kill them. They disappear into thin air. But the rest of us are pretty much left to get on with our lives as best we can. Some Ethiopians say that they owe us Somalis a favour because of the support we gave to the rebel forces that drove out the Ethiopian dictator Mengistu Haile Mariam in 1991. Some of those former rebels are now in government and other powerful positions.'

The Ethiopian security forces have a long history of operating in Somalia and know the territory and its people well. Ethiopian soldiers have maintained a presence along the long shared border for decades, regularly basing themselves inside Somali territory, even though they often refuse to admit to this in public. Unlike the Ugandan, Burundian and Kenyan forces, who have suffered heavy casualties in Somalia, the Ethiopians seem to have suffered less, although it is always difficult to be sure as they are so secretive. For instance, in June 2016, Al Shabaab said it killed sixty Ethiopian troops in an attack on their military base in Halgan in central Somalia. AMISOM said 110 Al Shabaab fighters were killed in the incident, while Ethiopia denied it had lost any soldiers at all.

A member of Ethiopia's intelligence service said his country's security services are less corruptible than their Kenyan counterparts. 'The problem with Kenya is that the military and police are corrupt. And once the security forces start to accept bribes, they have lost the war.' The same intelligence official, who spends a great deal of time embedded deep in Somali territory, expressed immense frustration with the Kenyans. 'Time and again we have told the Kenyan security forces the names of the hotels in Kenyan border towns like Mandera where Al Shabaab members are staying. We have even given them the numbers of the hotel rooms where they sleep. They do nothing with the information we give them. Maybe Al Shabaab pays them off, or maybe they are just lazy and incompetent.'

During my conversation with the intelligence official, he frequently used the word 'bulldozer' when describing Ethiopia's approach to Al Shabaab. 'Al Shabaab doesn't attack Ethiopia because of the "bulldozer" deterrent. They know not to provoke us with an attack on home soil because the cost would be too high for them. The Ethiopian response would be devastating. We would bulldoze them out of existence. Look at what happened at Halgan. Al Shabaab lost hundreds of fighters. They know Ethiopia would chase them to the bitter end. Al Shabaab does not want to meet the same fate of the Somali Islamist group Al Itihad Al Islamiya, which was destroyed by Ethiopia in the 1990s.' I noticed the intelligence official failed to mention the 2006 Ethiopian invasion of Somalia. Aimed at eliminating the Islamic Courts Union, the invasion had helped give rise to a stronger and more determined Al Shabaab and ended with a humiliating Ethiopian withdrawal in 2009, in some ways echoing the departures from Somalia of the US military and UN peacekeepers in the mid-1990s.

For its part, Al Shabaab says it is just a matter of time before it attacks Ethiopia. 'We have a clear strategy. We cannot operate on multiple fronts at the same time. For now, our principal targets are the apostates in Somalia and Kenya. When the right time comes, we will focus our attention on the Ethiopian crusaders. One day we will absolutely, no doubt, target Ethiopia. The Ethiopians say they are very good at security and intelligence but they are not. One day, sooner or later—we are not going to say when, how or where—we will punish them. One day they will see us, *inshallah.*'

In recent years, the Ethiopian government has distributed significant resources to the Somali Regional State. Its strategy differs significantly from Kenya's, which has traditionally starved Somali-dominated areas of resources. For instance, before the Somali Kenyan MP Yusuf Hassan intervened to bring about improvements, Nairobi's Eastleigh district was much neglected. Despite its relatively central location, its roads were full of potholes, its drains stinking and open, while its huge piles of rubbish lay uncollected.

Ethiopia's former prime minister Meles Zenawi used to describe the country's Somali Region as a 'bucket with holes', as money sent to the area would quickly disappear into the hands of the clans, never to be seen again. The region was affected by an insurgency led by the Ogaden National Liberation Front, which demanded more autonomy for the Somalis of Ethiopia. But the situation changed under the regional strongman Abdi Mohamoud Omar, nicknamed Abdi Iley, who was president of the Ethiopian Somali Region from 2010 to 2018. Under his rule, the Somali Region went from being the most troublesome part of the federation to one that offered help to more unstable states, especially the Oromo and Amhara regions, where there were widespread anti-government protests from 2015 to 2018. As president, Omar offered to send his region's security forces to help quell the disturbances. He also sent assistance to drought-affected people in Tigray region.

The increase in resources to the Somali Region has made a big difference to its capital Jijiga. When I flew to the town in 2013, the dilapidated airport was closed. Immigration control consisted of a single man in a tin shack who glanced at my passport and waved me through. Now there is a properly functioning terminal. One of the first things you notice as you drive into town is a huge walled compound, which houses the rather grand palace. People would point at the building, saying it housed the terrifying President Omar, who was arrested in August 2018, accused of instigating violence and other human rights abuses.

Although Jijiga has a small-town feel about it, the roads are newly paved with freshly planted flowers in the roundabouts and central reservations. New buildings are being constructed, including a large stadium. Blue auto-rickshaws buzz about, as donkeys in harnesses decorated with garish bouquets of red plastic flowers pull wooden carts loaded with large plastic drums of water. Women push wheelbarrows filled with yellow jerry cans, while nomads lead their camel caravans through town, each lumbering beast attached to the other with a stretch of rope.

A statue of the Somali warrior poet Seyyid Mohammed Abdulle Hassan on horseback stands in the centre of town. He was called the 'Mad Mullah' by the British after he declared jihad on the colonial powers in the early years of the twentieth century. It took twenty years for the Europeans to defeat him. His poems remain popular to this day, including one he wrote after his forces killed the British commander Richard Corfiel in 1913:

How the valiant Dervishes have slain you;
How they have abandoned your rotting corpse,
with its gaping dagger-wounds to the carrion-eaters.
Tell them how the hyena
Has dragged your carcass to its grisly den;
Tell how it tore the muscle and fat from your skeleton;
Tell how crows plucked your sinews
And tendons from the bare bone...[22]

When I posted a photo of the Jijiga statue of Seyyid Mohammed Abdulle Hassan on my Facebook page it drew an angry response from Somali friends. They said Ethiopians had no right to claim the Seyyid as their own, as he was a Somali and had fought against Ethiopia's colonial ambitions in their country. 'He would be sorry if he knew his statue was under the Ethiopian flag as that is what he fought against.' 'What a joke, Ethiopia is trying to own Somali history.' 'Ha ha, Mad Mullah. He killed Richard Corfield. The mad one was Richard, not the Seyyid.' 'Correction. Jijiga is part of Somalia, not Ethiopia.' 'This is NOT the place he should be. The statue should be in Mogadishu or Talexh, which is where he actually came from.' 'Mary Harper, you know that legend is not an Ethiopian, he is a Somali.'

Security in Jijiga is tight, with several police forces deployed. The federal police wear blue camouflage, the state police are in green camouflage and the city police wear bright blue shirts with baseball caps. As dusk fell one evening, I saw people in fluorescent bibs patting down everybody on the streets, turning out their pockets and giving them a thorough search. It is the same at hotels, where all guests are screened, their bags carefully searched, unlike the often perfunctory glances of the Kenyan security guards posted at the entrances to malls, hotels and other buildings in Nairobi. I was in the Kenyan capital four days after the Riverside Drive attack. Guests at my hotel had to ask for their bags to be screened as there was nobody manning the X-ray machine when they arrived.

The Ethiopian police can be brutal. Outside the airport, I saw them beating and punching a man simply because he had failed to park his vehicle correctly. A number of people in Jijiga said they wanted to move to nearby Somaliland because it had more freedom, although it was not as developed as Ethiopia.

I witnessed the full impact of Ethiopian security on the road from Jijiga to the border town of Togwajaale in Somaliland. I somewhat regretted that I had accepted a lift when I saw the amount of qat the driver had in the car. It was a bone-shattering ride as the black pick-up sped through the parched landscape, dust devils rising like smoke against the blue horizon. Ethiopian music was on at full blast, as the driver rapidly shook his shoulders up and down in time with the rhythm. His eyes were either on his phone or the giant pile of qat on the seat beside him, as he picked out the most tender leaves to chew. The car swerved dangerously as it dodged skinny cows, goats, sheep and camels on the road. Nomads suffering drought in eastern Somaliland had brought their livestock here to Ethiopia in search of pasture, although there was hardly any vegetation to speak of.

We passed some thorn trees. Two grown men had climbed to the uppermost branches of one of them, and were peering out over the horizon. 'They are looking for their camels,' the driver said. 'They must have fallen asleep or got so high and wild on qat that they lost their flock.' Now I know why so many Somali goats and sheep have phone numbers hennaed onto their sides: their owners can be reached if they became separated from their herds.

Up ahead, not far from the border with Somaliland, I spotted what looked like some kind of multi-vehicle accident or a frantic roadside market. The driver drew to a sudden, screeching halt. About forty white minibuses were lined up along the road. Women and children were standing in one queue, men in another. Every individual was being thoroughly searched. One woman started shouting, pointing at the baby on her hip. 'They even checked inside my child's nappy,' she said. 'They had a good look at my phone, including my messages. Have you heard of Al Shabaab? It is because of them that we are being treated like this. The Ethiopian police are looking for bombs, weapons and other suspicious material.'

Everything the minibuses were carrying had been thrown out onto the road. Each bag and suitcase had been opened, the contents emptied out. There were great piles of colourful clothes. Shoes were scattered around. There were empty boxes of cheap

Chinese goods, the brand new items tipped out unceremoniously into the dust. People were busy unstrapping mattresses and chairs from the roofs of the buses. I found it difficult to believe that so much could fit into—and on top of—these vehicles.

I looked out across the landscape and saw a group of nomads in the distance. 'Surely Al Shabaab could come in that way?' I asked a forlorn looking man. 'Nobody is guarding the border there and there is no fence.'

'They could, but even Al Shabaab is afraid of the Ethiopians,' he said. 'If they come and they are caught they will simply disappear; they will be killed almost immediately.'

* * *

The situation is somewhat different in Kenya where, in addition to the headline-grabbing attacks, especially those at Westgate Mall and Garissa University and Riverside Drive, Al Shabaab has carried out numerous other assaults. For a time, these attacks were so regular they barely made the local news. Al Shabaab has slaughtered people in churches, and has dragged teachers out of minibuses and killed them one by one. It has ambushed the police and the army. Its fighters have attacked villages and towns, sometimes filming the killings as they go. They invade towns at night, force people into the mosque and lecture them for hours.

Al Shabaab says the two main reasons for its attacks on Kenya are to pressurise the government to withdraw its troops from Somalia and to treat Kenyan Muslims better. Shortly after Garissa, Al Shabaab sent a statement to the Kenyan authorities warning them of more attacks: 'Do not dream of security in your lands until security becomes a reality in the Muslim lands, including the North Eastern province and the coast, and until your forces withdraw from all Muslim lands. We will, by the permission of Allah, stop at nothing to avenge the deaths of our Muslim brothers, until your government ceases its oppression and until all Muslim lands are liberated from Kenyan occupation. And until then, Kenyan cities will run red with blood. And as we said, this will be a long, gruesome war in which you, the Kenyan public, will be the first casualties.'

Al Shabaab has invested significant resources in appealing directly to possible recruits in Kenya, producing videos and online magazines in the Kiswahili language. In one video, produced by Al Shabaab's Al Kataib media department, militants chant the names of locations in Kenya, including the coastal towns of Mpeketoni, Mombasa and Lamu. 'You, my brothers in front of me, if you put your trust in Allah only, then regardless of your few numbers, you have the ability to conquer the whole world.'

After its devastating raid on Kenyan troops at El Adde base in Somalia, Al Shabaab sent out a press release. The paper was headed with the logo of an open Koran with two crossed guns beneath it. It read:

07 Rabi' Ath-Thani 1437 (17/01/2016)—Following Friday's raid on a Kenyan base in the town of El-Adde, Gedo region, the death toll of the Kenyan crusaders massacred in the base has now risen to 100, as confirmed by the Mujahidin's Military Intelligence department. Mujahidin fighters from the *'Commander Saleh An-Nabhani Battalion'* stormed the Kenyan base in the early hours of Friday morning, killing more than 100 Kenyan invaders, seizing their weapons and military vehicles and even capturing Kenyan soldiers alive ...

This audacious attack—the largest single attack against the Kenyan military inside Somalia—comes as a response to the aggressive Kenyan invasion of Muslim lands and the Kenyan military's continued persecution of innocent Muslims, particularly in the North East and Coastal regions ...

Harakat Al-Shabaab Al-Mujahideen vows to strike the African crusaders, by the permission of Allah, until all the crusaders are expelled from the Muslim lands that they've occupied, Islam's Shari'ah is fully implemented and the religion becomes all for Allah alone. *'And fight them until there is no more Fitnah (disbelief and polytheism) and the religion will be for Allah Alone'.* [Koran, Al Anfaal, 39.]

Decades before Al Shabaab started to attack Kenya, the authorities there had treated both Kenyan Somalis and refugees from Somalia as second-class citizens. The presence of Al Shabaab sharpened Kenya's resolve. In April 2014, following a string of attacks in Mombasa and Nairobi blamed on Al Shabaab, Kenya launched Operation *Usalama Watch*. Somalis were rounded up, with dozens incarcerated in a stadium in Nairobi. Some, including people with refugee status in Kenya, were deported to Somalia. This indiscriminate crackdown angered many Kenyan Somalis and other Muslim communities in the country. According to the International Crisis Group, Al Shabaab took advantage of this, 'stepping up recruitment and staging more attacks'.[23]

In 2016, Kenya announced plans to close down the giant refugee camps at Dadaab in the east of the country, home to hundreds of thousands of Somalis. It argued the camps, with their tens of thousands of young, idle Somali men, were a fertile source of recruits for Al Shabaab. Others have argued that the camps are no such thing, and are in some sense a defence against militancy.[24]

In 2012, I visited the Dadaab refugee settlement, one of the biggest complexes for housing refugees in the world. At the time it had a population of more than half a million people. Divided into four huge camps, it has been there for more than twenty years. Recent attacks on the camps and the kidnapping of foreign aid workers meant humanitarian agencies had dramatically scaled down their work.

The first thing I noticed was the smell. It hung over the camps, stale and miserable, trapped in the air. A mixture of smoke and old clothes. Of bodies in need of a good wash, in a place where water, soap and privacy are scarce.

Most people lived in tents on the sand, unable to go home and forbidden from leaving the camps to try to build a life elsewhere. As one man said, 'We live in an open prison.'

The second thing that struck me was the way people moved and the expressions on their faces. Their bodies appeared beaten down, shoulders hunched as they walked listlessly through the camps, dragging their feet through the red dust. There was a death of spirit. A boy in pink flip-flops, far too small for him, scuffed his way onwards, as a white land cruiser raced past, churning up a cloud of sand that beat against our faces.

We stopped to talk to a young man who emerged from what was now his home, a flimsy construction of sticks and ragged cloth. Like everyone else, he had built a low fence of thorns around it, to separate himself from the families crammed around him. He said his name was Abdullahi and that he was twenty-five years old.

'I walked here with my mother, from far inside Somalia. I hate this place, especially the hot, dirty wind, from which I cannot escape. Worse still, there is nothing to do and nowhere to go.'

No wonder some young men leave this place, returning to Somalia to fight Al Shabaab or venturing to Nairobi in search of work, where they are at constant risk of being detained for having no documents and needing to bribe the police to let them go.

Although some have lived in the camps for more than two decades, they said they were still not allowed to use stones, concrete or other robust materials to build their homes. Dadaab, the authorities say, is a refugee camp, not a permanent settlement. The strongest-looking buildings were the mosques made out of metal sheets and the tin toilets standing like sentry boxes at regular intervals between the mass of cloth tents, stained red with dust.

Things cheered up a little in what my companions described as Ifo High Street, the main shopping area for one of the camps. Kiosks made entirely from empty, flattened tins of food donated by the USA sold batteries, small bottles of perfume, and mobile phones. There was a barber's shop, an internet café and a money transfer business.

We drove past some freshly dug graves as we left the camps, heading up towards the Somali border. We reached a place where, in material terms, people had far less than those in the camps, even though they were native Kenyans, not refugees. They had no shops, no mobile phone coverage, no clinics, and no free food and water rations. Until recently they had had to walk their livestock for three days and three nights from their grazing grounds to reach water.

One of the people I was with, a Somali businessman from outside Kenya, who understood how difficult things were for the nomads, had donated money for a borehole, which had just started working. We watched as cows, sheep and goats quenched their thirst. They no longer had to go on that long walk to water.

We visited another settlement, where another of my companions, who originally came from the area and had done well for himself, had got together some wealthy friends and in a single day raised $100,000 to pay for a school. Lively boys with closely shorn heads scampered about and showed us where their school used to be. It was just a tree in the sand, where they and their teacher used to sit in its shade. Now they had three strong new buildings freshly painted in cheerful colours.

The money had also been used to buy a vehicle, which was rented out for $2,000 a month to an international aid agency in Dadaab. This was used to pay the teachers' salaries, to keep the school going.

It was time to say good-bye and to head back to Dadaab. It was early evening, and the refugees were venturing out to the periphery of the camps to look for firewood. A man paced past, a small axe swinging lethargically by his side. A group of children played a half-hearted game of football.

I was struck by the contrast in energy levels between the refugees and the people we had just visited outside the camps. One was a place where, with a bit of appropriate help from its own people, the community was doing things for itself, with a sense of pride. The borehole and the school, which had so obviously transformed their lives, had been built exactly where they needed them, with no need for international development assistance, feasibility studies, expensive consultants or project managers. The other place, the refugee camp and its atmosphere of resigned hopelessness, remained hostage to the lumbering machinery of foreign aid.

A report by the peacebuilding group Saferworld found that there are places where Kenya has adopted a different approach to its 'Somali problem'.[25] The study focused on the town of Garissa, which hit the headlines during the Al Shabaab attack of April 2015. Garissa had already suffered many smaller Islamist attacks, mainly in response to Kenya's invasion of Somalia in 2011. Whenever a police post, a hotel, restaurant or other target was attacked, the Kenyan security forces came down hard on the local population. In November 2012, according to Saferworld researchers: 'Following the killing of three of its men, the army reacted by burning the market in Garissa town and shooting local residents. There was a moment when indifference became untenable. We were told how "anyone who looked like a Somali or a Muslim" was taken into custody.'[26]

After the university attack, a new regional co-ordinator, Mohamud Saleh, was appointed for the North East region. He worked hard to improve communications between the community and the authorities, giving his phone number to the public and asking people to call him personally if they saw anything suspicious. He also involved the community more closely in security. It seems to have paid off. According to Saferworld:

Kenya has a community policing system called 'Nyumba Kumi'—meaning 'ten households'—under which clusters of households are supposed to report suspicious behaviour. In many parts of Kenya, the public has good reason not to trust the Nyumba Kumi model. However in Garissa, trust in Saleh enabled people to trust in Nyumba Kumi.[27]

The authorities also made efforts to change their approach towards Muslims on the coast by involving local communities more closely in security provision. This, together with a new constitution in 2010, which devolved power and resources to regional governments, led to some improvements for Kenya's Somali and other Muslim populations. Intelligence gathering also improved, all of which led to a reduction in the number of Al Shabaab attacks in the country.[28]

Just as joint AMISOM and Somali army offensives against Al Shabaab's major strongholds in southern and central Somalia forced some insurgents to move further north into Puntland, the increased successes of the Kenyan military against the group have pushed it south into Tanzania and possibly Mozambique. Since around 2015, the number of Islamist attacks in Tanzania has increased. It is not clear how many of the assaults are perpetrated directly by Al Shabaab and how many by pre-existing domestic militant organisations.[29] Unlike in Kenya, it is hard to work out how serious the threat of militant Islam is to Tanzania because the authorities are so tight-lipped about jihadi attacks. Since the election of President John Magufuli in 2015, the Tanzanian authorities have made it more difficult for journalists to operate freely in the country.

As well as increasing its presence in Tanzanian territory, Al Shabaab also recruits Tanzanians to train in Somalia, in order to fight in the country or to take their newly acquired skills back home to carry out attacks there. A senior Tanzanian security official told the International Crisis Group that Tanzanians made up the second largest cohort of foreign recruits after Kenyans between 2009 and 2012.[30]

* * *

One part of the Horn of Africa that is especially vulnerable to attacks by Al Shabaab is the self-declared republic of Somaliland. The territory declared independence from the rest of Somalia in May 1991 following a civil war which flattened its capital, Hargeisa, and left tens of thousands dead and hundreds of thousands displaced. Despite tireless efforts by campaigners, Somaliland has not been recognised internationally. Its government and security services are weak, there is a long and highly porous border with Somalia and some of Al Shabaab's most senior leaders have come from Somaliland.

There are those who say Al Shabaab is present in parts of Somaliland, especially around the western city of Bur'ao, but that it prefers to keep a low profile, using the territory as a place to rest and recuperate, to plot and plan in peace. Others say some in Somaliland's government sympathise with the Islamists and have made deals with them. Whatever the truth is, Al Shabaab has not attacked Somaliland since 2008, when several people were killed in triple suicide bombings targeting the presidential palace, a UN compound and the Ethiopian consulate.

A senior Ethiopian intelligence official in Addis Ababa predicted Somaliland would soon be a disaster area. He said Al Shabaab was being pushed steadily north by AMISOM offensives and US airstrikes. He was worried about the growing number of religiously conservative schools in Somaliland funded by Gulf states, which he said were breeding the next generation of violent jihadis. 'Every year, thousands of young Somalilanders graduate from high school and university, some of which are funded by Wahhabis in the Gulf. Unemployment is even higher in Somaliland than it is in Somalia, so these young people do not have a future. I imagine some of them would fall eagerly into the hands of Al Shabaab, as they are already familiar with its rhetoric and are desperate to earn some money.'

Many in Somaliland disagree with this pessimistic assessment. Like Ethiopians, they often point to their eyes when asked about

Al Shabaab, to show that everyone is watching everyone else. They say that their strongly oral culture ensures that everybody knows each other's business and that there are no strangers within their community.

A soldier explained that in Somaliland members of the community report suspicious behaviour to the security forces, unlike in Somalia where they are often more frightened of the police and military than they are of anyone else. He knit his fingers together to show how tightly he believed the community in the territory is intertwined with the security forces there.

There are glaring weaknesses in Somaliland's security forces, and it is difficult to imagine how they would cope if Al Shabaab moved in as a fighting force. Some might be tempted to join for financial reasons as security personnel are poorly paid. As in Somalia, some in Somaliland's military moonlight for private security companies in order to make ends meet. An army captain, Karim, said he received a $150 monthly salary from the government, which was not enough to feed and educate his nine children. He supplemented his army income by working as a guard for an international charity during his spare time, where he received $350 a month. He said he would be tempted to join any other armed group if it offered better pay.

Although unemployment is high in Somaliland, there are jobs that cannot be filled locally because of a lack of skills or a refusal to engage in certain types of work. Locals are employed to do basic construction jobs, but foreigners are flown in to perform the finishing flourishes. The situation is the same in Somalia. In Mogadishu, a Somali businessman who built a luxury apartment complex shipped in 100 Kenyans to do much of the work. Pakistani engineers were brought from Karachi to install the lifts. Syrians and Yemenis fleeing war at home are finding well-paid employment in Somaliland, as dentists, doctors, cooks, construction workers and engineers.[31] A Somali friend who is building a huge hotel in Hargeisa, which he describes as a 'resort', told me he had flown in Pakistanis and Indians from Dubai to do the sophisticated construction work, as the Syrians and Yemenis already living in Somaliland were too expensive. Foreigners also work in the hospitality industry. The espressos and cappuccinos in an Italian-style café in Hargeisa are made and served by Kenyans, many of the staff at one of the city's main hotels are Oromos from Ethiopia, and some of the best food in town is found in Yemeni restaurants. Some of the beauticians in the high-end beauty salons come from Kenya.

Books for Peace

Another less obvious way of resisting Al Shabaab is by presenting people with alternative ways of thinking, and giving them space to express themselves freely. One place where this approach is very apparent is the annual Hargeisa International Book Fair, which was launched in 2008 with about 200 participants. It has been going ever since and attracts thousands of visitors. Authors, poets, film-makers, publishers, musicians, dancers and other artists are invited from all over the world to participate in an event held in a territory that does not officially exist as an independent country. Every year a different African country is invited as a guest, with speakers often overwhelmed by the size and enthusiasm of the audiences. A gentle poet from Kenya told me that usually a handful of people turn up for her readings; in Hargeisa there were hundreds in the audience. Several had already bought her books, which were on sale at the festival, and had read her poems. They quoted lines from her work, comparing her writing with the rich, oral poetry tradition of the Somalis.

The event is the brainchild of the mathematician, publisher, computer analyst and inventor Jama Musse Jama. Although pioneered in Hargeisa, book fairs are now held in other parts of Somalia, including Garowe, Kismayo and Mogadishu.

EVERYTHING YOU HAVE TOLD ME IS TRUE

When I wrote an article about the Hargeisa book fair, a journalist from a respected international publication asked if I was joking and accused me of making the whole thing up. For many outsiders, the idea of a book fair on Somali territory is impossible to imagine because for them the word 'Somali' is associated with piracy, terrorism, war and famine. Somaliland suffers from a similar image problem; most people don't know it exists, and have no idea that it is relatively peaceful, with a functioning economy, society and political system.

Somali politicians, elders and members of the religious community hold a near monopoly on debate, and almost all of them are older men. Book fairs create spaces for young people, women and creative individuals, allowing them not only to express themselves, explore new ideas and push boundaries, but also to challenge one another and question the dominant narratives about their societies. At times, imams and other senior members of Somaliland's religious community have criticised, and even threatened, the Hargeisa book fair, accusing it of encouraging immoral behaviour with its music, film and theatre shows. Religious leaders tried to have the festival shut down in 2015 after it invited as one of its main speakers a British feminist who supported gay rights and equal marriage.

Enthusiastic young members of book clubs from all over Somaliland are given the stage, as are young singers, dancers and actors. The Hargeisa International Book Fair is about far more than books. There is poetry, music, song, dance, theatre, art, photography and more.

There is such enthusiasm for the fair that, from day one of the week-long event every summer, there are always far too many people to fit inside the large hall where the presentations are held. The organisers show a typically Somali innovative spirit, technological know-how and ability to think on their feet by immediately setting up large screens outside the building so people can gather around them to see and hear what is going on inside.

The fact that so many young people come to the book fair not only reveals a thirst for knowledge, but also highlights the lack of activity and entertainment for the youth of Somaliland. Being young and having nothing to do can be a dangerous combination. Just a few hundred kilometres to the south of Hargeisa, many young Somalis are finding distraction by taking up arms and joining the various militia groups tearing apart Somalia, including Al Shabaab and the small offshoot of IS.

I found myself thinking of this as I watched boys dressed in animal print costumes sailing through the air, forming giant human pyramids and throwing fire. They were members of the Somaliland Circus, which traditionally performs on the last day of the fair. They were the same age as those being forcibly recruited into Al Shabaab and other armed groups across the border in Somalia.

As well as trying to revive Somali cultural life, much of which was destroyed by the long years of conflict, Jama says he started the book fair for the youth: 'At the end of the day, I did it for young Somalis. Literature and culture give young people a wonderful way of growing up, and allow them to make up their minds for themselves. The book fair offers the Somali youth an alternative to guns; it gives them a platform to come together and express themselves. It helps fill the vacuum left behind after the war. It frees their minds and promotes alternative ways of living to that offered by Al Shabaab.'

Like so much in Somaliland, the book fair only works because of volunteers, from those who give of their time to plan and organise the events, to the contributors who fly in from abroad. Young Somalis, with book fair baseball caps perched on their heads, run the stalls with great professionalism, writing out a neat receipt for every purchase. Each time I attend the fair, I end up with a large pile of these meticulously written receipts, as I cannot resist the books on sale. Among my purchases are a trilingual physics book, in Somali, English and Arabic; Somali translations of Anton Chekhov's short stories and George Orwell's *Animal Farm*; and a book called *Somalis Do Not Lie in Proverbs*, which was launched at one of the fairs by the Russian Somali expert Georgi Kapchits.

The Somali diaspora plays a prominent role in the festival. Many of the organisers are based in Europe, and several of the speakers come from abroad, including the novelist Nuruddin Farah, the poet Said Salah, who is based in Minneapolis, and the London-based author Nadifa Mohamed, who explained what the event means to her: 'The book festival is a chance for Somalis in the diaspora to witness and partake in the cultural renaissance of the region. Everything seems exploratory, exciting and hard-won. I particularly like it when students or elderly women pluck out their self-published books from their bags and give me a quick sales pitch.'

Much has been written about how the diaspora helps Somaliland economically, mainly through remittances, and how, by contrast, some members of the diaspora return to Somalia to blow themselves up as suicide bombers for Al Shabaab. The involvement of the diaspora in the book fair adds another dimension, showing how the global Somali community can enhance cultural life in Somaliland.

The diaspora can also play a negative role by meddling destructively in politics from abroad or running irresponsible media operations. 'Those who stayed behind' sometimes feel resentful towards members of the Somaliland diaspora who jet in from overseas to take up political posts or flash their money around during the summer holidays. But such feelings are not much in evidence at the book fair, where both 'sides' seem to bring out the best in each other. The passionate engagement of the expatriate community in the fair and other activities and the amount of time its members spend in Somaliland suggest that the word 'diaspora' is in some ways misleading in the Somali context, as so many people have at least one foot almost permanently in both worlds.

The Hargeisa book fair attracts a growing number of foreign writers, publishers, film-makers, artists and musicians, as well as curious people looking for something a little different. One year, a Scandinavian supermodel spent several days at the festival, a black headscarf draped somewhat awkwardly over her blonde hair. For the jazz clarinettist from New Orleans, Evan Christopher, who played with the 'King of the Somali lute', Hudeidi, his trip to Somaliland was the first he had ever made to Africa.

'In America,' he said, 'most people don't know what Somaliland is, let alone where it is. The country is much greener than I expected. I thought it would be a desert! I didn't expect to find so many similarities between the culture of Somaliland and the culture of New Orleans. It's strange but both locales are dealing with a large exodus after, in our case, the devastating flooding of our city, and, in the case of Somaliland, of war. But, remarkably, in terms of the role of culture in the rebuilding process, I have found a lot of similarities.'

The book fair shows how much people can achieve with a little money and a lot of passion, imagination and commitment. In this way, it resembles Somaliland itself, which in a short space of time and with a confident, can-do attitude has built itself up from the rubble of war into a functioning polity. It also shows what a crucial role art, literature and culture can play in society, not just as forms of entertainment, but, in the case of Somaliland, by offering an alternative vision to violence and instability.

The relative safety of Somaliland gives young people, even those with few resources, the freedom and opportunity to be creative. On a day off from the book fair, I met a group of young men from the Amazing Technology Company a few kilometres outside Hargeisa as they filmed their latest adventure movie.

It was the middle of nowhere and cars were pursuing each other in tighter and tighter circles, sending thick clouds of dust into the hot air. It was a truly spectacular chase. Mohamed Saleh was at the wheel of the wildest car. With a cool demeanour and an Afro hairstyle, he was the movie's main stuntman. Like everyone else on the film set, he was completely untrained.

'One time the car nearly flipped over,' he said. 'It was vertical, balancing on two tyres. But far more frightening was the fact that the cars did not belong to us! The company we hired them from had no idea we were using them in an action movie. They thought we were just going for a leisurely drive.'

In the Amazing Technology Group's tiny one-roomed office in the capital Hargeisa, a giant Hollywood-style movie poster covered a whole wall. The group's chairman, director, producer and cameraman, Ibrahim Mohamed, sat behind the desk.

He reached under the table and presented me with a large, crumpled bundle of green cloth. This was the green screen, used as a neutral backdrop when filming to be filled in with different backgrounds later on. He pointed to a battered camera perched in the corner. 'It is the only one we have,' he said, 'but it is an improvement from before, when we had to rent or borrow one.'

'We have to make do with whatever we have,' said the vice chairman and main actor, Hersi Abdirizak. 'We don't have the money for costumes, so we borrow clothes from our friends. For pistols, we buy plastic guns in toyshops and paint them black. Our friends in the police lend us the knives, axes and machetes.'

On set for their latest film, the gun they used was a real AK-47. It too came from a friend in the police. 'I hope it's not loaded,' said Adam Konvict, a local rap artist who, together with an off-duty policeman, was helping out as an extra. The company relies heavily on the generosity of others. In its newest action movie, a Somali take on cops and robbers, some of the actors were on loan from the Somaliland circus troupe, performing incredible acrobatics as they raced through the city streets.

What the Amazing Technology Group lacked in resources was more than made up for in imagination, confidence and get-up-and-go attitude. This group of seven young men aimed high, right from the start. While still in their teens at university, they made their first movie. It was not a short, student-style video but a full-length action film. With romance, violence, an evil gangster and thrilling car chases, *The Lost Diamond* proved a huge hit when it was shown on local television.

'We learned everything we know by watching Hollywood and Bollywood films,' said Hersi. 'I love playing the villain. I get to do all the fun stuff. My role model is the Joker in *The Dark Knight*.' So convincing was Hersi as a gangster that he said people were frightened of him when they saw him in the street.

'We want to dig out the treasure that is here. Through our movies, we want to show the whole world our Somali treasure,' he said. 'Our goal is to launch a booming Somali film industry. We could call it "Sollywood".'

Some of the group's films contain serious messages. One focuses on relations between members of the diaspora, who pour into Somaliland in the summer, and those who stayed behind during the territory's long and difficult years of conflict. The film, which went viral in Hargeisa, was a hot topic of conversation in the city's coffee shops and restaurants.

It was over a wickedly sweet milkshake and vanilla cake, thick with colourful icing, that I first heard about the film. Somali friends collapsed with laughter while telling me about scenes in which slim locals mock a bulky diaspora man, instantly identifiable by his rolling swagger and flashy clothes. But they also discussed the serious points raised about growing tensions between the two groups.

The dynamic and daring spirit of these young men is typical of Somalilanders. One man was blasting a road through the mountains to the sea. A woman had converted her house into a luxury restaurant, where diners sit under the stars on the rooftop. A businessman talked of bringing in a funfair and building a municipal swimming pool, where men and women would be able to swim on different days.

But that stunt man with the cool hairdo was quite the heartthrob of Hargeisa. I discovered this after the Amazing Technology Group posted photos of our meeting on its Facebook page. Lots of young Somali girls came to me in great excitement when they realised I might be able to introduce them to their idols. Most of them asked for 'the one with the Afro'. When he agreed to pose with them for selfies, they positively swooned.

Many in Somaliland's population do not like the fact that their daughters develop crushes on local film stars and disapprove of events like the book fair, where young people of both sexes gather together to debate, watch plays and sometimes even dance. But some probably understand that such forms of distraction are safer than the alternatives available further south across the border in Somalia. They would prefer their children to be attracted by literature, theatre and music over what some young people perceive as the adventure, and sense of purpose and belonging, offered by Al Shabaab and IS.

From Within

I have met some Somalis who believe the only way to deal with Al Shabaab is to go into the areas they control and talk to them. One such person is Ahmed, who works for a local NGO in Mogadishu.

'It started during the famine of 2011 when Al Shabaab was not allowing food aid into the areas it controlled. I travelled to their area and spoke to them. I told them we would give them 20 per cent of any food we delivered to the hungry people. Some time later, a man came to me and took me to Al Shabaab's office in Bakara market. Even though the group had officially left Mogadishu by that time, they still had an office right in the heart of the city. They told me they did not want any United Nations or United States logos on the bags, so we transferred the food out of the sacks with UN and US logos and put them into bags with Arabic logos. Then I grew a beard, put on Islamic dress and went into Al Shabaab–controlled villages.'

For a while, this system worked. Ahmed was able to deliver food to starving people in Al Shabaab areas, always giving 20 per cent of the supplies directly to the Islamists. But his luck ran out in 2013, when he says he was abducted by Al Shabaab and accused of working with the Somali government and international NGOs.

'I was walking on the streets here in Mogadishu when two men approached me and put a pistol against my arm. They were not wearing masks or anything. I was terrified but tried not to show it. Al Shabaab kept me in a small room for eighteen days. They did not tie me up. Every morning they came and asked me lots of questions, accusing me of working for the government and of talking to people from the World Food Programme. I insisted that I had done no such thing, that I was just an ordinary Somali civilian. They asked me for $10,000, which I did not have. Eventually I gave them $3,500 and they let me go.'

Ahmed said that, after some time, he returned to Al Shabaab areas, and that he has not been bothered by the group again. He continues to deliver food and other essential supplies, including medicine, and still gives 20 per cent of every delivery directly to the militants.

Several influential Somalis, including at least three recent heads of state, agree in private that the only realistic way to end the conflict with Al Shabaab is dialogue. Many of those who have worked inside government or the security and intelligence services know that the situation is not clear-cut or black and white, but is rather grey and formless. Somalis who have worked closely with Al Shabaab defector programmes have told me the group is not ready for talks. However, they say that with a great deal of work, patience and compromise, Al Shabaab can be brought around to talk, even though the group says publicly it will never negotiate. The former national security and counter-terrorism adviser to the Somali government, Hussein Sheikh-Ali, who created and coordinated Somalia's high-level Al Shabaab defectors' programme, argues openly that the only way forward is dialogue and that bringing the insurgents to the table is possible. He has great insight into the minds of Al Shabaab's leaders, having spent hours speaking to senior members of the group. On the first anniversary of the October 2017 truck bombing of Mogadishu he wrote an opinion piece for *The Guardian* newspaper, saying:

> I believe we have to compel and convince al-Shabaab to come to the political negotiating table. ... To outsiders, al-Shabaab might seem like an unreasonable party to negotiate with, but from warlords to Islamists, successive Somali governments have always found room to accommodate opposition groups, violent and nonviolent alike. ... Ahead of negotiations, it will be key to assess the personalities of al-Shabaab's current leaders, and identify what motivates them, as well as establish who is open to reconciliation and who is not. ... President Mohamed 'Farmajo' Mohamed has promised to deliver a new constitutional order before the next elections—and this could potentially accommodate some of al-Shabaab's demands.[32]

Other Somalis have used their oral traditions of poetry and song to try to get their messages through to Al Shabaab, often at great personal risk to themselves and their families. One man who has done this is Abdi Shire, who left his home in the UK after becoming an MP in Somalia.

RESISTANCE

'It was 3 December 2009. I came back from work in London and my wife was watching a Somali satellite TV channel. There was blood, gore and screaming. I thought she was watching a Hollywood movie, but it was the news. A suicide bomber had blown himself up at the Shamo hotel in Mogadishu where the first set of medical students in years were graduating as doctors. Al Shabaab had created a human abattoir.

'That was the trigger. I come from a family of poets and song-writers. I went to a room and just started writing a poem on the computer. It was in the Somali style, with alliteration. Every sentence started with the letter Q. Then I went straight to my brother's house and we put the words to music. We recorded and released the song immediately which we called Qaylodhaan, meaning "alarm" or "siren." It is a word used by nomads when they are being attacked by an enemy to alert people that they are in mortal danger. Somalis watched it and cried. Shortly afterwards I received a voicemail on my phone. It was a death threat from Al Shabaab. I took my phone to Tottenham police station and played them the message. They asked if I was afraid and I said "no". The Shamo hotel attack and that song marked the end of public support for Al Shabaab.'

5

THE PROPAGANDA WAR

The Echo of Jihad

'I am a white Western woman. I am not a Muslim. Surely there is nothing you hate more?'

It was a glorious summer's day in London and I was on the phone to a member of Al Shabaab. I had arrived too early for a meeting in the Houses of Parliament and was sitting in the shade of its grand buildings in a park by the River Thames. My phone rang, the words 'Al Shabaab' flashing across the screen. It felt strange to be speaking to a member of a designated terrorist organisation as I sat just metres away from parliament, the very institution that had outlawed the group in 2010.

'Indeed you are all those things. But your reporting on Somalia, which we monitor closely, is quite fair. You give different sides of the story, unlike many of your apostate colleagues who are little more than mouthpieces for the crusaders.'

By this stage in the conversation, the tone of the man's voice had changed completely. It was relaxed, even warm. Just minutes before, it had been clipped and cold as he told me about Al

Shabaab's latest attack on the Kenyan coast, how many men and women had been killed, and how glorious this massacre had been. When he had finished, I had asked him how Al Shabaab could justify the killing of civilians in a coastal village. He launched into the usual spiel about how every Kenyan was a legitimate target because it was the Kenyan people who had elected the government that had declared war on Al Shabaab.

The man from Al Shabaab did not like it when I challenged him and told him I did not understand his argument. He repeated the same phrases in a mechanical way, as if he had learned them by rote. He became angry when I interrupted him. He knew he was right; he believed in the twisted logic. There was no room for discussion.

Towards the end of our conversation, he sounded genuinely concerned. His voice became gentle, almost caring. 'Have you ever thought about the afterlife? You know, Mary, you will not be around in twenty, thirty or forty years' time. I seriously recommend you consider converting to Islam. You seem to be a good person and this will definitely be the best thing for you to do. It will be the right and proper thing.'

This was not the only time Al Shabaab had expressed concern about my welfare. Once, members of the group found it difficult to reach me as I was away on a foreign trip and not using my usual mobile number. When an Al Shabaab official finally got through on my return to the UK, I explained I had been in Nigeria. 'Please don't go there again,' he said. 'Nigeria is a very dangerous country, and anything could happen to you there.'

When I put it to him that Somalia was also a dangerous place, in large part due to the existence of his group Al Shabaab, he said, 'We would not target you deliberately, Mary. If you happened to visit a place populated by the apostates, such as a government building or a hotel, that would be your own fault. Or you could just be in the wrong place at the wrong time.'

Another time, in June 2018, on the day after I returned to London from Somalia, I received a call from a member of Al Shabaab.

'Mary, you have been in Mogadishu. How was it?'

I was shocked that he knew. During the visit, I had stayed in secure accommodation near the airport and had only made trips to and from the airport compound. Unlike during my usual visits, I had not gone into town. I had not walked about in the streets, markets or anywhere else. I had hardly met anybody, and about half of those I had met were foreign diplomats, foreign bodyguards, foreign advisers and foreign administrative staff.

'How on earth do you know that?' I asked. 'My movements were very limited. I did not meet many people, and many of those I met were foreigners.'

The man from Al Shabaab chuckled.

'You are well-known in Somalia. We have eyes and ears absolutely everywhere. It is my job to monitor journalists and their work, so when you show up here, our people tell me you're in town.'

I told my contact that this made me very scared. His voice took on an almost tender tone. 'You don't need to be afraid of us. Our organisation does not have a special problem with you. Of course our friends will tell us, "That BBC lady, Mary Harper, is in Mogadishu, is in Baidoa," or wherever you happen to be, but you don't have to worry about it. Nobody will waste their time trying to kill Mary Harper. We have hundreds of enemies in Mogadishu but Mary is not one of them. Cool down.'

I said not everybody in Al Shabaab knew who I was and what I looked like, so they could kill me just for being a white person. 'Oh, we don't want to kill every white person in Somalia. Some of them are Muslims and have nothing to do with the Somali government and its allies. We do not target them.'

Communicating with Al Shabaab is the most uncomfortable part of my job. As a BBC journalist with a special interest in

Somalia, I am useful to the group when it wants to get its message out into the world. It is my duty to tell every side of every story, so if Al Shabaab contacts me to confirm it carried out an attack, I include this information in my report along with any details I receive from the Somali authorities, the African Union Mission in Somalia (AMISOM), eyewitnesses and others.

Since the early days of its existence, Al Shabaab has operated a highly effective PR machine, cultivating relationships with key individuals in international media organisations. It has developed such contacts in Al Jazeera, Channel 4, Reuters, the Voice of America, the BBC and elsewhere, and delivers its information swiftly, in neatly packaged form. The group has similar contacts in Somali media houses and there are sympathetic websites that publish its statements and gory battlefield photographs in full.[1] Al Shabaab also has sympathisers on social media. It often gets its side of the story into the public domain way ahead of the Somali military, AMISOM, the Kenyan authorities and its other battlefield rivals.

Al Shabaab is persistent. Members of its press department call me non-stop until I answer. On my phone, there are records of missed calls from Al Shabaab: seventeen in a single hour of a single day, fourteen on another day, ten, fifteen and so on. There are demanding text messages too: 'When should I call you back? In thirty minutes, one hour or when...?'

When I do answer the phone, the caller usually asks, 'Are you at work today, Mary? Do you have a pen?' With efficient clarity, he then launches into details of Al Shabaab's latest attack, how many people the group claims to have killed and wounded, how many foreign soldiers it has taken hostage, and the quantity of weapons, ammunition and military vehicles seized. Apart from inflations of the number of people killed and quantity of equipment taken, the information released by the militants usually proves to be accurate.

THE PROPAGANDA WAR

If this information is not broadcast on the BBC, Al Shabaab will call back to ask why. If there is an error in the information broadcast, someone from the group will call to correct it. Sometimes, when the BBC broadcasts a report attributing an attack to Al Shabaab, a contact will call to say the group had no role whatsoever in that particular incident. Or I will receive a text message to clarify confusion: 'Hi Mary. There's no Twitter handle currently belonging to HSM [Harakat Al Shabaab Al Mujahideen, the full name of Al Shabaab]. All who claim to speak in our name are no doubt FAKE.'

If the person I am speaking to does not know the answers to my questions, he says he will call me back as soon as he has them. He usually does so within the hour. At other times he will ask me to email the questions. I usually receive a written response within a few hours, written in perfect, grammatical English.

Whenever Al Shabaab releases a new video, I receive a phone call asking me if I am near a computer. The official gives me a list of links and codes which take me through several websites. This will eventually lead me to the latest film, which I am advised to download quickly before it is removed from the site. Some of the videos are blood-ridden accounts of raids on Somali and Kenyan towns, military bases and other targets filmed by Al Shabaab's cameramen, who are embedded with the frontline fighters. I was told by a British communications expert specialising in counter-terror messaging that one film of an Al Shabaab raid was shot by six cameramen, some of whom were killed in the battle. Some of the films have animated sections in the style of violent video games.

Propaganda has played a central role in the insurgency since its inception. Although Somalia is often portrayed as a failed, broken state, its people are enthusiastic, super-modern communicators. Al Shabaab is no exception. The country's vibrant traditional oral culture has been married with the latest information technology to ensure Somalis stay in touch with each other no matter where they are in the world.

Communications have played a central, indeed exaggerated, role in Al Shabaab's strategy. Al Shabaab was pioneering among jihadi groups in its use of social media, especially Twitter. It has stated that the media war is one of the most important elements of its campaign: 'The media battle waged by the mujahidin is one of the hardest and most important in our war against the Zionist-Crusader unbelievers, which make us, as the caretakers of the media jihad in our beloved battlefront of Somalia, strive harder to report the truth to the people from the battlefields.'

The group's communications department has several objectives, including increasing Al Shabaab's visibility locally, regionally and internationally; spreading its ideas and vision; masking setbacks; and attracting sympathisers, funders, and active recruits. The movement recognises and exploits the media-savvy nature of Somalis, for whom rapid information flows have always been crucial to their existence and can be a matter of life and death, especially in times of war or drought.

The group has developed a sophisticated, multilingual media operation, designed to appeal to its multiple audiences. It communicates mainly in Somali, Kiswahili, Arabic and English, but has also used Norwegian, Swedish and Urdu. It uses a broad range of media platforms, including radio, online magazines and films, as well as social media. It has developed recognisable brands; for example, its films open with a yellow logo against a black background, complete with dramatic, rousing sound effects. Like the group as a whole, Al Shabaab's media department has proved nimble and resilient, quickly adapting to changing circumstances and circumventing efforts to prevent it from communicating with its target audiences.

Just as they fight each other on the ground, Al Shabaab and its adversaries engage in a virtual media war, battling for control of the narrative. The multiple actors, including Al Shabaab, Islamic State (IS), the federal government, regional administrations, AMISOM, the US military and the Somali diaspora, all jostle for space in the dynamic and highly internationalised media environment.

I remember the day Al Shabaab took its war into the Twittersphere. It was 8 December 2011. At exactly 5.35 in the afternoon, an email dropped into my inbox from Al Shabaab's press office, inviting me to follow the group on Twitter. I did so straight away, and there, with its distinctive white logo on a black background, was an image of the Al Shabaab flag.

The first tweet was in Arabic, 'b-ismi-llāhi r-raḥmāni r-raḥīmi', which translates as 'In the name of God, the most gracious, the most merciful'. After that, Al Shabaab switched to English and got down to the serious business of military propaganda.

The first messages gave a hint of what was, within a few hours, to become the most intense bout of fighting in Mogadishu in several months between the Islamists and government troops backed by African Union forces.

The tweets spoke of an attack by Al Shabaab on an AMISOM base in the north of the city. A few months earlier, in August 2011, Al Shabaab had announced a 'tactical withdrawal' from Mogadishu, although it has never completely left the city. What Al Shabaab described as a mere 'withdrawal' was labelled as a massive victory by AMISOM and the transitional federal government.

The tweets then changed subject, focusing on what Al Shabaab described as the utter failure of Kenya's military intervention in Somalia in October of that year. One quoted a BBC story about a plan for Kenyan troops to join AMISOM. It said this was proof that Kenya had run out of money to pay for its military operation, so needed to beg for foreign funding instead. Al Shabaab's advice to the Kenyan soldiers was condensed into one word, in capital letters. It said simply 'FLEE'.

Al Shabaab then engaged in a Twitter battle with Kenya's military spokesman, Major Emmanuel Chirchir, himself an enthusiastic proponent of social media. He sent regular tweets to his thousands of followers giving details of what he claimed were Kenya's spectacular military successes in Somalia. On one occasion, he took to social media to warn Kenyans not to sell donkeys to members of Al Shabaab, who he said were using the animals to transport weapons. In one tweet, he warned that 'any large concentration and movement of loaded donkeys will be considered as Al Shabaab activity', suggesting the animals should be targeted by Kenyan firepower. The militants hit back immediately: 'Like bombing donkeys, you mean! Your eccentric battle strategy has got animal rights groups quite concerned, Major.' Another anti-Kenyan tweet was crassly poetic: 'Funny how bitter Kenyans witter on Twitter as KDF [Kenya Defence Forces] boys in the forest wildly flutter with hopes of glitter now down in the gutter—what a pity!' Al Shabaab also posted an ironically mocking tweet referring to the need for Somali government soldiers to sober up, accusing them of being intoxicated by the narcotic leaf qat, and therefore of being incapable of fighting properly.

In 2015, the Somali authorities called on the local media to stop referring to the Islamists as 'Al Shabaab', but to call them 'UGUS' instead, a Somali acronym that stands for the 'Organisation for the Slaughter of the Somali *Umma* [community of Muslims]'. Al Shabaab hit back almost instantly with its own acronym for the Somali federal government, which it also called 'UGUS', in this case meaning the 'Organisation for the Humiliation of the Somali *Umma*'.

Just as Al Shabaab has used Twitter and other forms of social media to mock and taunt its enemies, opponents of the group have used the internet to stand up to the Islamists. As Menkhaus explains, social media has been a double-edged sword for the movement:

New communication technologies have hurt Al Shabaab as much as they have helped it. The organisation has exploited the internet and social media to recruit, fundraise, issue threats, monitor enemies, amplify its messaging, and reinforce its narrative. It has used remittance and telecommunications sectors to move money and raise revenues. At the same time, this technology has exposed the militant group to lethal armed counterinsurgency strikes, broadcast its internal feuds, and rendered it impossible for Al Shabaab's leadership to control its image and message.[2]

Social media has also been used to counter content from false accounts published by Al Shabaab's adversaries. In 2014, Kenya's military spokesman, Major Chirchir, posted a tweet saying, 'Al Shabaab spokesman Ali Dhere (alias Ali Mohamed Raghe) finally succumbs to last courtesy call injuries! Focus on Al Shabaab leadership targeting continues.' The news was picked up by the media, but shortly afterwards a tweet appeared dismissing the reports. 'The guy you're saying is dead just called me! He didn't sound dead to me.' It then quoted Ali Dheere as saying 'He (Maj Chirchir) is doing what he always did, lying to his people. I'm well. Very well.'

* * *

I have been speaking to members of Al Shabaab for years and always feel uneasy when I see their numbers light up my phone because I know what is coming. A callous announcement of another attack, news of more deaths, and claims of responsibility for massacres, sieges and suicide bombings. One time, the caller said: 'Our fighters are having such great fun in the hotel, Mary. They are killing really well. They have been there for hours, and they will not stop until they die; something they are very much looking forward to it as they will become blessed martyrs.'

The different ways Al Shabaab has communicated with me over time mirror the organisation's changing fortunes.

At first, statements arrived unsolicited in my BBC email inbox, laid out in the form of conventional press releases and written in impeccable English. I would email back my questions and receive prompt, considered replies. I do not know whether someone gave Al Shabaab my email address or whether they simply guessed it. These early communiqués, mainly outlining military operations, were also posted in Arabic on jihadi websites.

Then came the phone call.

I was in Covent Garden, a popular shopping area of London, when I received a call from a Somali number. As I made my way through the crowd, the caller explained in English that he was from Al Shabaab and that he had some information for me. I took down his details and immediately phoned a trusted journalist in Mogadishu, who told me he recognised the number and confirmed that, yes, the caller was a genuine member of the group's media department. He had met this man in person and been struck by his intelligence and polite, professional manner. My journalist friend said he found it hard to understand how such a man could represent Al Shabaab.

I called the man back and he proceeded to give a detailed account of a major attack by the group, which I was later able to confirm was accurate.

In 2009 and 2010, during the height of its success, Al Shabaab upgraded its propaganda operation, rebranding it as Al Kataib Media Foundation. It ran radio stations known as Al Andalus and the Al Kataib Media Channel, as well as a news agency, online sites and Twitter accounts. It started to make polished videos which, unlike its earlier amateurish attempts, were in HD format and slickly produced, often involving a gripping narrative. In March 2009, it released a new recruitment film, *Ambush at Bardale*, which introduced the American jihadi Omar Hammami, also known as Abu Mansoor Al Amriki. He sang jihadi rap songs and became something of a celebrity for the group and its sympathisers, especially those in Western countries. Before Omar Hammami was killed in a purge in 2013 he let the outside world know he was in trouble by posting on social media the details of the claimed threats against him and photographs of injuries he said he had suffered at the hands of rival members of Al Shabaab.

During the Somali famine of 2011, Al Shabaab lost substantial public support after it blocked the delivery of humanitarian aid to starving people in the areas it controlled. It went on an international media offensive, bombarding journalists with photos of militants in full battle-dress handing out food parcels to the hungry. It filmed neat rows of children lined up in tents. Boys sat on one side, girls on the other, as they waited to receive their handouts. The group accused aid agencies of attempting to spread Christianity in Somalia. It said they were undercutting local farmers and nomads by distributing free food and flooding the market with cheap imported goods. Al Shabaab stressed that it knew more about the real needs of the Somalis and said that it had its own development projects that were far more successful than those run by the government and international donors.

I temporarily lost contact with Al Shabaab around the time it lost control of Mogadishu in August 2011. There were no phone calls and no emails. I began to imagine my English-speaking contacts in the group had been killed.

Some months later, the phone calls began again. My contacts were alive and well, had survived what they described as 'a bit of difficulty' and were now based in a different part of Somalia. Access to the internet was patchy, so we communicated mainly by phone and continue to do so. Communications with Al Shabaab also became less frequent after the US intensified air attacks under the Trump administration. I found myself having to initiate the call more often, and was regularly greeted with a recorded message saying the person's phone was off.

There are lots of text messages from Al Shabaab stored on my phone.

Some are very brief. Monday, 21 April 2014: 'An apostate Somali MP just killed in Mogadishu.' Tuesday, 25 October 2016: 'Mandera attack: We did it.'

Others are longer. Wednesday, 25 March 2015: 'The attack which lasted almost 20 hours resulted in the perishing of dozens of apostates and their allies. Some of the Mujahidin attained martyrdom during the operation.' Thursday, 8 June 2017: 'The Mujahidin have this morning stormed an apostate military base in the town of Af-Urur in the Northern Bari region. By the permission of Allah alone, the Mujahidin have completely over-run the base and secured the town. A preliminary count puts the number of dead apostate Puntland troops at 61 ... All praise is due to Allah alone.'

At times I receive a short phone call to let me know that I will be receiving what the caller describes as a 'text message press release'. One morning, when I was on holiday in Wales, Al Shabaab called to say it had carried out its first ever attack in Djibouti, killing at least three people at La Chaumière restaurant, which is popular with foreigners. I was told I would receive the press release in five parts, and sure enough, within minutes, five texts came through:

'SMS PRESS Release: "Djibouti Explosions" (27/05/2014)

1. In the name of Allah the Most Merciful, the Most Beneficent. As part of the ongoing Jihad against the Western-led Crusade against Islam, Harakat Al-Shabaab Al-Mujahidin forces have on Saturday night carried out a successful operation against the coalition of Western Crusaders based in Djibouti. Two explosions targeted a restaurant frequented predominantly by French Crusaders...'

Each part was carefully numbered, the first four had the word 'Cont'd...' at the end, and the final part of the release was clearly marked:

'The archers are ready, the arrows are poised and the target clearly defined; it's time to strike back. ### End of SMS PRESS Release "HSM Press Office".'

I then received another phone call to check I had received all five messages.

From the many messages on my phone, it is possible to chart the history of Al Shabaab attacks.

'SMS PRESS RELEASE: "The Mpeketoni Raid" (16/06/2014).

In the name of Allah the Most Merciful, the Most Beneficent, HSM Commandos have last night carried out a successful raid on the town of Mpeketoni in the Lamu District. In a daring raid that commenced shortly after 20.00 hours Sunday night, the Mujahidin descended upon the town in the cover of darkness and, following a short battle, fully secured the town and its perimeter...'

At times, the group responds to world events. For example, on 6 December 2017, minutes after Donald Trump's landmark recognition of Jerusalem as the capital of Israel, I received three missed calls from Al Shabaab. A two-part text message followed, calling upon 'all Muslims to take up arms and defend Al Aqsa from the US-sponsored Zionist occupation'.

In some respects, the group's communications department operates like a modern, international media body. The advent of the smart-phone, which serves simultaneously as a stills camera, video camera, voice recorder, editing facility, transmitter and distributor, has enabled even poorly resourced people operating in hostile, difficult places to produce and distribute relatively high-quality media on multiple platforms. It means Al Shabaab can project an exaggerated, glossy image of itself and its activities, leading some people to believe it is more powerful than it really is.

The group's media operations are highly agile. Its websites, films and radio station pop up in other locations, physical and virtual, almost as soon as they are shut down, as do those of its affiliates and sympathisers. In some ways this is part of the group's appeal. Some members of its audience probably find excitement in playing cat-and-mouse games for the forbidden fruit of a graphic Al Shabaab video, complete with rousing music, animation, blood, gore and martyrs' testimonies.

Al Shabaab uses videos to undermine confidence in the ability of the government and its international partners to protect people, even in Mogadishu. On 31 May 2018, its media wing, Al Kataib, released a new thirteen-minute video detailing the bloody activities of its hit squad in the capital, known as the Muhammad bin Maslamah brigade. The unit mainly carries out assassinations of people working for the government and the security services. The film starts by showing the battalion's training camp, named after two dead Al Shabaab leaders, Muhammad Ismail Yusuf and Hassan Abdullahi Hersi, also known as Hassan 'Turki'. It shows trainees practising drive-by shootings and other methods of killing individual targets in urban environments. The video shows in graphic detail what it claims are assassinations carried out by the brigade in Mogadishu of figures such as members of local government, security and intelligence personnel, and off-duty policemen. It provides a list of those it claims to have killed in the city, including some of the clan elders who selected MPs for the federal parliament, army officers, local government officials, policemen, an intelligence officer accused of being a CIA spy and members of regional assemblies. The film features a speech by Al Shabaab's deputy leader, Abdirahman Mahad Warsame, also known as Mahad 'Karate', who urges government officials and members of the security forces to repent, saying: 'Let not the support of the crusaders that are with you deceive you; by God, they will be of no benefit to you. If you reject and choose disbelief, then get the good news that our swords will be unsheathed on the necks of all apostates. Our gallant assassins will pursue you everywhere. The Muhammad bin Maslamah brigade will

continue to pursue you until your filth is cleansed from the land.'
The video concludes with the voice of the former Al Shabaab
leader Ahmed Godane.

As one young man in Baidoa told me, the availability of cheap,
reliable internet services in Somalia means Al Shabaab videos can
'go viral in our city and elsewhere'. Paradoxically, this is because
Al Shabaab material also offers entertainment for those who hold
no sympathy for its ideology or methods. A university student
said: 'The frequent explosions and lack of social activities here in
Mogadishu mean I don't go out very often. I just sit in my room
and watch YouTube videos. Some of them are produced by Al
Shabaab. I watch them because they are in my language, they
show my people and they are in some ways entertaining, even
though I don't agree with their messages and would never want
to have anything to do with the group.' This reminded me of
Ali, the young man I met in a London suburb who had been
served with a deportation order after committing multiple
crimes. He too found some kind of solace or distraction in Al
Shabaab videos.

The Somali government has also attempted to take its war
against Al Shabaab onto the airwaves. It has produced films showing elite government troops fighting the militants, all set to a
dramatic soundtrack. As the academic Peter Chonka, who has
written extensively on communications in the Somali context,
writes, 'The FGS [federal government of Somalia] has frequently
broadcast footage of its battlefield or intelligence successes, including interviews with captured operatives and judicial processes (up
to and including executions) of either alleged Al Shabaab members
or government forces accused of killing civilians.'[3]

* * *

Al Shabaab delivers its specially tailored propaganda to multiple
sources, ranging from journalists in the headquarters of interna-

tional media organisations in London, Washington and Doha to people in the smallest village or nomad camp in rural Somalia. I heard stories of how it uses information to recruit, intimidate and manipulate the poorest and most marginalised of Somalis when I went to the cathedral in Mogadishu.

On the way, we drove past skeletons of the city's other fine buildings. The remains of the old parliament rose up from battered, bullet-scarred blocks of concrete and low, green thorn bushes. Flights of stairs ran up the inside of its smashed-out tower, open to the breeze and the blue sky. It was like nothing on earth, more akin to a dystopian movie set than anything one could imagine existing in reality.

A few shots rang out. A family of goats darted behind large pieces of rubble, ducking down until calm returned. 'Goats are Mogadishu's great survivors,' said one of my bodyguards. 'They eat paper, cloth and sticks during times of famine. They even chew the qat leaves and stalks discarded by chewers and get high like we do, running around and bleating all night. Even the baby goats do this, driving their parents crazy. They know how to take cover, dodging bullets during gun battles. They skip over the remains of collapsed buildings and find shade in unexpected places. Goats are the masters of our city and will survive all other living creatures here.'

He pointed to a thin brown cow nosing its way through an ocean of rubbish. 'That animal just stood there when the shots were fired. It is slow and stupid, and it will die young.'

Our vehicle stopped and we got out near a large yellow metal bin. I heard a rustling sound and peered inside. In the bin was a tiny child, scavenging amongst the scraps. She looked similar to other children I had seen in Mogadishu, some of whom wandered around in bands like packs of feral dogs. They had ashen, lifeless skin and expressionless eyes, and many seemed physically and mentally stunted. These were Somalia's street children.

THE PROPAGANDA WAR

The Catholic cathedral, built by Italian colonialists in the 1920s, was one of the grandest in Africa. Its last bishop, Salvatore Colombo, was murdered by Islamist extremists in 1989 as he was giving mass.

By the time of my visit, the gigantic building was in ruins. The roof had been completely blown off.

The guards drifted away from me as we entered what remained of the cathedral. Most of its walls were gone so we were exposed to danger, but somehow felt safe. Enough remained of the elegant stone arches and religious symbols to remind us we were in a sacred place. One guard crouched down, lost in thought. Another stood still, gazing upwards to the sky.

High above us, sculpted in stone, was Jesus on the cross. Bullet holes scarred the carving, the colours faded. The guards, who were Muslim and Somali, were especially upset by the statue of St Francis of Assisi, the Christian patron saint of animals. His head had been blown off and the sheep around him reduced to vague shapes of shattered stone. As livestock is the mainstay of the economy and very dear to the hearts of Somalis, the guards were unhappy that representations of animals and their saint had been so horribly damaged.

In one corner was what looked like a pile of discarded cardboard and cloth. Slowly, I made out the figure of a man so deeply asleep he appeared not to be breathing.

Suddenly, there was noise and movement, the sound of giggling. Two boys, completely naked, rushed in and poured water from plastic jerry cans onto their bodies. They scrubbed themselves as best as they could, without any soap. Then they darted into a dark corner, emerging soon afterwards dressed in tattered shorts and singlets.

An old man noiselessly appeared from behind a battle-scarred pillar. 'I fled here with my relatives some years ago. I came from the port of Merca, which was taken by the Islamists. I would not

201

have survived under their rule. I have no food. I have no water. The only thing I have is time.'

He gestured through one of the open arches. Outside, in the grounds of the cathedral, were the familiar small dome-shaped dwellings made from sticks, tattered plastic and scraps of cloth. There are similar settlements of people forced from their homes on almost every spare patch of ground in Mogadishu, although the government has been trying to shift them to the northern out-skirts of the city. Many Somalis, especially those from minority groups and weaker clans, have lived like this for nearly thirty years.

Inside the camp I met a woman, Fartun, who was breastfeed-ing her baby. She called me over and explained how she had come to Mogadishu quite recently from an Al Shabaab village in southern Somalia. She was a member of a despised minority clan and had a distant cousin living here in the camp. Apart from her baby, she had lost everyone in her family.

'My two boys, one nine, the other twelve, came home from school very excited. They said, "Some men came and told us that if we came to the city of Kismayo with them they would teach us how to drive brand new white land-cruisers. They would give us laptops and mobile phones."'

The woman warned her boys that these men were members of Al Shabaab, and that they were dangerous people, full of false promises. But a few days later, the boys were gone. In the night, they had taken the few clothes they had and disappeared.

'I went to Al Shabaab's local headquarters and asked to speak to the head of the administration. I waited for hours, and refused to leave when they told me to. I kept coming back day after day. Eventually some of the militants took me to a room and locked me inside. They returned with hot knives, glowing orange, and pressed them onto my skin.'

Fartun showed me the shiny scars on her arms and legs where she had been burned, the deep dent in her forehead caused by the smash of a rifle butt. From time to time, she picked ragged scraps of Somali pancake from a plastic bag and put them in her mouth. 'I feel ashamed. I am eating and have nothing to offer you, but if I do not eat, I will have no milk for the baby.'

She explained how Al Shabaab later came to her house and took her husband away. She said she had heard he was dead, but had never heard anything about her sons.

A young man came and crouched down beside us. He said he too wanted to tell me his story, but only if I promised not to use his name. He was also a member of a minority clan and had a large, livid scar on his leg. He spoke quietly, and kept looking around to make sure nobody was listening.

'Al Shabaab took me from my village when I was a teenager. They put me in a group of other boys, and the first thing they did was talk to us. They spoke to us for hours every morning about how Somalia is controlled by non-believers, and about how hard our struggle would be to defeat these infidels, but said that we would win in the end. They clearly believed in what they were preaching. Different people would speak to us each morning but they always had the same message. They were on the right path and everyone else, especially those in government and those who supported it, was on the wrong one.'

Tiny beads of sweat covered the young man's forehead. His knee jiggled frantically.

'They told us the reason they were making us run and train so hard was so that we would become men and fight for the cause. They said the Kenyans and Ethiopians wanted to take Somalia by force so we should fight them. That if we fought and died for the cause we would end up in paradise. They seemed to think we were buying into what they were saying. If you did not nod along to their words, you knew you were going to be killed. So the other boys and I kept nodding our heads and saying positive words to try and show that we agreed with them.'

The young man explained how he and the other boys followed the same routine every day, of getting up early, running and training, then listening again and again to the lectures. Afterwards they were sent to wash clothes and dishes, and clear up the base.

'I do not think any of the older men really thought Al Shabaab had anything to offer. That is why they are only successful with young people because they sometimes fall for what the Islamists tell them, or get attracted by its promises. Al Shabaab says it will give people money, but for most young men it is the lure of marriage that attracts them. But as the situation became more desperate for Al Shabaab, as they started losing territory and fighters, they no longer bothered preaching to people and persuading them to join with their words. Now they just come and abduct young men and women by force.'

Counter-narratives

Despite, and perhaps because of, its military setbacks Al Shabaab continues to run a relatively slick, efficient and adaptable information department. Its communications are often more compelling and relevant to its multiple audiences than those of its opponents. Al Shabaab's adversaries have invested significant money, time and human resources to combat the group's information war. This is a less demanding and certainly less life-threatening part of the effort to defeat Al Shabaab. But many Somalis I have spoken to doubt its efficacy.

A government minister admitted how far behind the administration is in terms of its communications strategy. 'Al Shabaab has won the propaganda war,' he said. 'It has been ahead of us right from the start.'

Although so many resources have been invested in trying to counter Al Shabaab's messages, some of those involved in these campaigns are sceptical about their impact. The head of a Somali NGO told me how he was benefiting from international funds directed at combating Al Shabaab propaganda: 'I have received tens of thousands of dollars from international donors for counter-messaging projects which I know are almost entirely ineffective.' A Western diplomat, who has spent years in the region, said, 'These information campaigns are almost completely pointless because hardly anybody pays any attention to them.'

AMISOM, one of Al Shabaab's main battlefield rivals, struggled to come up with an effective communications strategy when it first arrived in Somalia in 2007. According to the AMISOM expert Paul Williams: 'For its first two years, AMISOM had virtually no media presence or proactive communication strategy and operated with a "bunker mentality" whereby media briefings were sporadic and poorly organised, the messaging confused and the tone defensive.' The African Union force has made some cringeworthy mistakes, such as in March 2014 when Somali media quoted a Burundian AMISOM officer as saying, 'I don't want to defeat Al Shabaab. I would rather scatter them to prolong my mission.'

AMISOM's initially ineffective communications system not only allowed Al Shabaab to dominate the information space, but also adversely affected its already delicate relationship with the Somalis. Initially, Somalis saw the force's presence in their country as almost entirely negative. In an effort to improve AMISOM's image, a consortium of three private firms was hired, at great expense, to develop a strategy which would serve its multiple audiences more effectively. It produced 'positive' films, videos and other material such as *Gate of Hope*, 'Somalia Back from the Brink' and 'AMISOM Hospital'. In 2014 the Ugandan military released a twenty-three-minute film entitled *Heroes in the Horn*. A flood of anti-Al Shabaab propaganda was produced, including a radio drama called *The Misleaders*, which focused on how Al Shabaab tells lies when it is trying to recruit people. Another radio series was called *Happy People Can't Be Controlled*.

This new communications strategy had some success. In a poll conducted in Somalia in January 2010, almost a third of the respondents said AMISOM was in the country to cause harm. By December 2011, this figure had dropped to 9 per cent. This shift in public perceptions of AMISOM may have been connected not only to an improved communications strategy, but also to the fact that Al Shabaab withdrew from Mogadishu in August 2011, partly due to the active involvement of AMISOM. Williams found that AMISOM's reputation dipped during periods when the communications consortium was not working effectively: 'This coincided with polling evidence that showed AMISOM's reputation with local Somali civilians reduced significantly during 2015 and 2016.'[4]

Some members of the intended audiences of these messages appear fully aware of who is behind these operations and who is profiting from them. In their present form, many of these messages do not seem to be making much of an impact, and may even backfire at times. According to a senior Western military official, some anti-Al Shabaab information drives are entirely counterproductive, indeed dangerous, as they can draw people's attention to the existence and philosophy of violent Islamist extremism. He said these campaigns could also unwittingly highlight the failure of Al Shabaab's competitors to provide adequate security, health facilities, employment, education and legal services, which can incentivise people to join the movement.

Some Somalis are adept at recognising which anti-Al Shabaab information campaigns are devised by foreigners. They react to these messages with a mixture of hostility, sarcasm, amusement and scathing cynicism. Some feel they are part of a neo-colonial project, while others say the campaigns are pointless and simply serve as a moneymaking industry for those involved. While many Somalis have a healthy dose of scepticism in their attitudes towards the media and other forms of communication, others, including some women and members of rural populations, are more impressionable.[5]

Some Somali and non-Somali individuals involved in these activities appear to believe in what they are doing, and to work hard and thoughtfully. Others are more sceptical. As one member of a Somali NGO said: 'We distribute US-funded comic books and put up billboards promoting tolerance. Their impact is minimal. Nobody changes their minds about Al Shabaab because of our billboards in Kismayo.' Some non-Somalis, especially those based in Somalia, say they enjoy the extra 'danger money' and frisson of working in a conflict zone. Some are purely cynical and say they are in it for personal profit.

A number of Somalis involved in internationally funded information campaigns have boasted about how effective they have become at extracting money from donors. According to the head of a Somali NGO who has been involved in multiple information campaigns: 'I know which button to press. I have pressed the buttons of FGM [female genital mutilation], HIV, gender awareness and whatever else was in fashion at the time. Now the most lucrative button is migration, where foreign funders, especially the EU, have more money than they know what to do with.'

Al Shabaab's energetic media department contrasts with the more hands-off approach of the Somali government, AMISOM, the UN and others involved with Somalia, who tend to send generic press releases that are often deleted unread from journalists' overcrowded inboxes. Some communications specialists offer sophisticated training and advice to Al Shabaab's many opponents, but in most cases this does not appear to have been heeded effectively. Several Somalis participating in foreign-funded workshops on how to use information to counter violent Islamist extremism have told me the main reason they attend is the per diems and free lunches.

EVERYTHING YOU HAVE TOLD ME IS TRUE

Al Shabaab and the Somali Media

Al Shabaab threatens Somali journalists working in Somalia, East Africa and the Horn, and further afield. This can be face-to-face or by email, text message or a phone call from a withheld number. As one Somali journalist said: 'A man approached me in a tea shop near the radio station where I worked. He asked me why I had not broadcast as breaking news the full recording Al Shabaab had released the previous night of its leader Ahmed Godane. His speech was forty minutes long but I only broadcast it for five or six minutes, and not as breaking news. The man threatened me and said next time I must play the entire recording. Otherwise I would pay the ultimate price.' Another journalist explained that, after he broadcast a report on a failed Al Shabaab attack, the militants abducted him and cut his chest open with a knife.

Somali journalists are not only under threat from Al Shabaab. Friends in the Somali media have told me that sometimes the authorities say a journalist has been killed by Al Shabaab when, in all likelihood, the murder has been ordered by a government official, powerful businessperson or other individual who does not like what the journalist has been reporting. It is relatively easy to organise such a killing as guns for hire come cheap in many parts of Somalia. According to the media rights group, the Committee to Protect Journalists, for five years in a row—from 2014 to 2018—Somalia came top of the list of countries with the worst records for prosecuting the killers of journalists.[6]

On at least one occasion, Al Shabaab has infiltrated Somali media. A well-known journalist, Hassan Hanafi, was executed by firing squad in 2016 after he was found guilty of colluding with the militants in the murder of five fellow journalists. While working in the media, he is said to have run a secret bureau, identifying, threatening and colluding in the killing of journalists who portrayed Al Shabaab in a negative light.

Al Shabaab also appears to have sympathisers working in foreign media houses. I have met a handful of Somali journalists working in the international media who say they believe the group is the best option available when it comes to governing their country. They seem to revel in sending me links to reports extolling Al Shabaab's latest activities and pointing me in the direction of the most blood-soaked images of places and people they have attacked. Sometimes they tell me to be on the alert for a major militant attack, claiming to have prior information about it.

With their enduring oral culture, profound and active relationship with broadcasters, including the BBC, whose Somali service is more than sixty years old, and the 'life-and-death' necessity of knowing what is happening around them, Somalis are arguably one of the most media-literate populations in Africa. They have embraced enthusiastically digital media, with the number of Somali news websites exploding from twenty in 1998, to 527 in 2006, and 748 in 2014.[7] Many of these sites emanate from the diaspora.

However, some Somali 'journalists', including those working for Al Shabaab and its affiliates, are highly experienced creators of 'fake news', of parallel universes that bear little relation to each other or to events on the ground. Al Shabaab presents distorted stories for all of its audiences, be they local, regional or international. These include films of its claimed military achievements shot in the style of war movies or violent video games. These are largely aimed at international viewers and would-be recruits, funders and sympathisers. For local consumption, it distributes glowing reports of its humanitarian work during times of drought, and more rustic films of rural idylls, Eid games and happy farmers.

Equally unrealistic are the sanitised, airbrushed images created for the Somali government, internationally funded projects and AMISOM. These include the #SomaliaRising and

#MogadishuRising initiatives whereby films and airbrushed photos of beautiful beaches, happy schoolchildren, female MPs and bustling markets were tweeted around the world. As one Somali businesswoman said: 'These images are even more evil and unfair than Al Shabaab's propaganda. They make Somalia look like a place where everybody spends their time on the beach, playing football and eating ice cream and lobster.' One man was so influenced by these messages that he decided to move to Somalia from Denmark: 'I came back to Somalia because of these messages, after living abroad for nearly twenty years. The reality is completely different. I have had three near-misses from explosions, and part of my home was blown up in an Al Shabaab attack.'

Much of Somali broadcast, print and digital media is unreliable and untrustworthy. Diaspora and local outlets often serve the interests of a particular region, clan, or religious or political group. Many Somali media houses are corrupt, serving as little more than money-making opportunities for the editors and journalists involved.[8] There are multiple instances of Somali journalists demanding money for positive reports to be published or broadcast and for negative ones to be removed from websites. Somalis and non-Somalis have paid for positive and biased media coverage. Somali media workers based overseas operate in relative safety and with near complete impunity, unlike those at home, many of whom have been killed by Al Shabaab and others. The international media is also problematic as it tends to lack nuance, slipping into simplistic stereotypes about Somali pirates, warlords, terrorists and famine victims, and sometimes giving undue prominence to Al Shabaab's activities.

People say how worried they are about the current state of education in the Somali territories. They say Gulf states have too much influence and are funding schools and universities. 'These institutions are breeding the next generation of Taliban,' a rights activist said. 'They are doing the jihadis' job for them, whether they are Al Shabaab, Islamic State or Al Qaeda. This is the new

Cold War. It is a battle of ideas and one side, the West, is not even aware it is happening. The best way they could help fight Islamist extremism in Somalia would be to fund schools that encourage independent and critical thinking.'

A student in Hargeisa, who attends a Kuwaiti-funded school, told me how much happier she was now that she had moved permanently to Somaliland from London, where she was born and raised for the first sixteen years of her life. 'I came here less than a year ago and it is so beautiful,' she said. 'This is due to the religion. I no longer read Western books as they are against Islam. Now I wear the full niqab and follow my religion as closely as I can. I have come to realise that the way people live in the West is immoral and decadent.' She then proceeded to tell me off for bringing a bag of carefully chosen novels from the UK as a gift for one of her friends. She told me I was a bad influence and that the books I had brought would pollute the mind of her friend.

There are some home-grown spaces, such as book fairs, cafés and music venues, which offer an opportunity for more marginalised Somalis, including minority groups, women and youth, to be heard. They also provide a space for a broader range of ideas to be explored and for dominant, rigid norms to be challenged. However, these are under increased threat from religious conservatives, including in Somaliland.

Although Al Shabaab has suffered military setbacks, losing crucial territory and access to resources, its propaganda machine continues to thrive. Despite the significant resources poured into countering its propaganda, Al Shabaab remains ahead of the game in the communications war. It is possible that the weaker it gets, the more committed it will become to investing time and other resources in its media operations. In this way it is able to project an image of power and success. As a result, even though this is only in the virtual world, many inside and outside Somalia are likely to perceive Al Shabaab as bigger and stronger than it really is, and therefore to respond to it as such.

6

THE INDUSTRY

Whenever a car bomb explodes in Mogadishu, a scruffy-looking man will rush to the scene along with the ambulance drivers, security forces and journalists. He will go immediately to the burned-out remains of the vehicle, eyes scanning the wreckage, hands darting here and there as he salvages spare parts that he will later sell.

Later on, when the body parts and twisted metal have been removed—samples carefully collected and taken away in plastic bags by foreign security operatives dressed in khaki and dark glasses—a Somali woman in colourful clothes will appear wearing a white face mask. She will sweep away the broken glass and other damage, then hose down the area to remove the blood and other stains.

Then the repairmen will come in and do their best to make it look like nothing ever happened.

These jobs—the vehicle scavenger, the road cleaner and the rapid repairman—are just some of the opportunities created by the long years of violence in Somalia. They are the unintended consequences of the Al Shabaab insurgency. Suicide bombs create surprising forms of employment.

There are people sitting at desks in London, Washington and Nairobi who have also benefited directly from Al Shabaab, writing reports on how to counter the extremist threat in Somalia and raising funds for projects in a country they may never set foot in. A whole industry has built up around Al Shabaab, and many people are earning a good living from it.

Making money out of war is nothing new in Somalia. In his book *The Real Politics of the Horn of Africa: Money, War and the Business of Power*, Alex de Waal devotes a chapter to Somalia entitled 'A Post-Apocalypse Workshop'. He describes elegantly how successive governments have profited from conflict and insecurity, and how reconciliation conferences have become vehicles 'for the Somali elite to conduct every conceivable business and charge the costs of hotels, per diems, transport and security to the hosts and donors.'

The long years of insecurity have resulted in a lack of accountability and oversight. It is simply too dangerous for donors to monitor accurately the billions of dollars poured into Somalia for peacebuilding, development and other projects. De Waal describes how political elites use foreign aid as 'personal cash dispensers'. He reveals a shocking level of diversion of domestic revenue and foreign funds: 'Between 2000 and 2011, successive governments raised $53 million from domestic sources (principally port and customs dues) and received $304 million in bilateral aid from Arab countries, of which only $124 million could be accounted for.'[1] In other words, over a period of eleven years, more than a third of aid and tax revenue went straight into politicians' pockets.

Menkhaus has a similar assessment, describing the transitional national government established in 2000 as 'in essence a piece of paper on a fish hook, thrown into international waters to lure foreign aid which could then be diverted into appropriate pockets.'

One sector that is positively booming in Somalia is that of private security. The streets of Mogadishu are full of bullet-proof land cruisers, escorted by pick-up trucks crammed with armed private security guards sitting with their legs dangling over the backs and sides of the vehicles, guns pointed down towards the road as they dash through the city, bumping wildly on the uneven, pot-holed roads. The colour of their uniforms depends on which company they work for. The backs of the pick-ups are fitted with special wooden seats for them to sit on, a steady line of work for the city's carpenters and joiners. According to Menkhaus, 'it is widely believed that private security is one of the fastest-growing sources of employment in Mogadishu and a generally lucrative business. "Private security services are the oxygen of the capital," noted one local observer.'

Menkhaus argues that 'Somali non-state armed groups are stronger than nascent state security forces, and they intersect freely with the national army and police, blurring the line between state and non-state actors. ... Their current relationship with the formal security sector is thus not so much integration as it is penetration.' He says Somalia is a classic example of a 'mediated state', whereby, in order to function, the weak central government must forge deals with the multitude of militias and other non-state armed groups that operate within its borders.[2]

Some powerful Somalis believe that travelling with heavy security makes them conspicuous and therefore more vulnerable to attack, so they choose to take the lower-profile but potentially more dangerous option of driving around in ordinary vehicles. This is not an option for most foreigners, who have to pay hundreds, if not thousands, of dollars a day for vehicles, guides, bodyguards and fortified accommodation.

Security companies charge up to $2,000 a day for protection in Mogadishu. One outfit, which offers an expatriate 'close protection officer' or 'CPO', an armoured vehicle and two armed escort vehicles, charges $1,607 for a full day outside the safety of Mogadishu International Airport, and $1,017 for half a day. For movement inside the airport compound, which involves an expatriate CPO and an armoured vehicle, it charges $944 a day and $632 for half a day. I do not understand the need for armoured protection within the airport, which is a kind of 'green zone', crammed with foreign forces and surrounded by fortified perimeter walls, apart from on the side that opens directly onto the beach and the Indian Ocean. I have been driven around this area in unprotected minibuses and cars. At other times, I have simply walked.

I have driven around Mogadishu with expatriate bodyguards, including Croatians, South Africans and Estonians, and have felt significantly more vulnerable than when I am with Somalis. I feel far more visible with a big white man in a bullet-proof vest sitting in the front of the car than with a Somali. Although I am no security expert, I find it disturbing that they cannot understand the radio conversations that take place in Somali between the driver of the bullet-proof car and the local armed guards outside in the escort vehicle. It is disconcerting to travel in convoys where the expatriate CPOs have no way of communicating with the Somali guards accompanying us because the local guards only speak Somali and the CPOs do not. Although my Somali is poor, I can understand enough to work out that sometimes the Somali guards are saying it is not safe to travel down a particular road or to go to a particular destination, but the foreign security guard insists that we do, and, as he is in charge, they have to obey him.

Some private security companies are run by Somali businesspeople, others by foreign firms. Some are highly professional, while others are more casual. Many of the guards are active members of the Somali security forces, seeking to top up their meagre or non-existent government wages. The peacebuilding group

Saferworld estimates that 50 per cent of Somalia's security forces double up in some capacity in the private security sector.[3]

I have spent long evenings in the communal areas of 'secure' hotels in Mogadishu talking, or trying to talk, to foreign private security guards. They often sit alone or silently in small groups as they work their way through plates piled high with large servings of protein and carbohydrates. The only time I elicited any warmth from a taciturn Croatian was when I asked about his breakfast, which consisted of a huge bowl of porridge topped with about a third of a jar of imported peanut butter. He said the peanut butter gave him 'power', much needed in this 'hot, hostile environment'. When he was not out escorting foreign visitors around Mogadishu he was in the hotel gym, smacking his fists into a punch bag or lifting weights. The more communicative security operatives, all of whom have served in the military, share gruesome war stories from Afghanistan and Iraq. Some have families back home in Croatia, South Africa, Scotland or elsewhere. Many live strange, single lives, and seem locked eternally into a military mindset, seeing everything through the prism of conflict and insecurity.

These foreign-run security outfits and hotels—or 'camps', 'secure accommodation' or 'secure residential facilities', as they are sometimes called—also have foreign support staff. In one such facility, Filipinos ran the accounts and administration. They sat together in the evenings, giggling quietly as they poured sauces from home onto the bland meals prepared by the Indian cook. Most were women, and they told me how much they missed their children back home in the Philippines. 'I have worked in Afghanistan, Iraq and now here in Mogadishu,' said a finance officer, whose husband is looking after their three children in Manila. 'I earn five times more than I would back home and I want my children to have a better life than me. I want them to work for the United Nations. The money I earn here pays for them to attend a good private school. Of course I miss them desperately. I get to go home every few months, but every day I wake up thinking about them, whether they have the right clothes, stationery and other items they need for school, and whether their father has prepared their packed lunches.'

One time, in a different facility, I could not sleep and went into the restaurant to see if I could find a banana or other snack. It was about three o'clock in the morning. There, sitting alone at a table in front of the television, was the Kenyan cook. He was watching football. At first he did not see me. I could not help staring at his face because he looked deeply, deeply sad. He turned and smiled when he noticed me in the room. I sat with him for a while and he told me how much he hated Somalia:

'I am not allowed to go out of this compound at any time, day or night. The only time I am allowed to leave is when I travel to the airport to fly to Kenya for my holiday. I am the only African member of staff and I have no friends here. I asked my boss to let me work seven days a week because there is no point in having a day off here in Mogadishu, as there is nothing for me to do and nobody for me to talk to.

'I feel the white people who work here look down on me and, as everybody knows, the Somalis hate most other Africans. Behind our backs, they call us "Bantu" or "slave". They crack cruel jokes about our wide noses and tight, curly hair. One time, I saw a Somali girl make a face with her lips, somehow turning them inside out so they became very large and took up almost half her face. She also pushed her nose up with her finger, so the nostrils were showing. She did this to mock the way I look.

'Once, a Somali guest called me over to where he was sitting with his friends, who were also Somalis. He told two jokes. One was about how a Somali made the terrible mistake of opening a bottle of expensive perfume and allowing a "black African", as he put it, to have a smell. "All the perfume in the bottle disappeared," the man said. "The African's nostrils were so big that all the perfume went up his nose as soon as he took his first sniff from the bottle." The man then pointed at my nose, and fell about laughing.

'The next joke was just as bad. The man asked his friends why "black African" babies cried so much that even their mothers could not quieten them down by offering them the breast. "It's because their hair is so wiry and tightly curled that when it grows in for the first time it is agonisingly slow and painful, like having a corkscrew twisted through their scalps." Once again, the man pointed at me, this time making spiralling motions with his finger as he thrust it near my head. If Somalis make these kinds of jokes about me, imagine what they say about AMISOM.'

* * *

Many Somali businesspeople and politicians, especially those in South Central Somalia, currently stand to profit more from war than peace. In order to keep their business and political models intact, these individuals need to block the state security forces from developing in any meaningful way. Some powerful politicians have stakes in private security companies. Menkhaus argues that some of those who have invested in the security sector have gone so far as to provoke violence themselves: 'There is no question that at least some Somali non-state security providers have staged insecurity in order to provide protection, and have worked to undermine the revival of an effective central government and security sector.'4

Private security has been good business in Somalia since the government of President Siad Barre collapsed in the early 1990s. International humanitarian agencies working in the country at the time started to hire armed guards to protect their personnel and equipment. In order to avoid embarrassment, some agencies, which officially had a 'no arms' policy, listed these expenses under the neutral area of 'technical support'. This gave rise to the word 'technical', the name Somalis give to the pick-up trucks mounted with big weapons that have become such a hallmark of the conflicts in the country. Some are fitted with anti-aircraft guns. During the civil war of the 1990s, I saw civilians with horrific injuries, their bodies blasted apart by clan militias who used anti-aircraft guns for street fighting, firing them horizontally at people rather than pointing them up into the air to shoot at planes.

As laws and regulations are weak or non-existent, some private security companies have significantly overstepped the mark. One example is that of Saracen International, a firm reportedly linked to Lieutenant General Salim Saleh—the half-brother of the Ugandan president, Yoweri Museveni—and Erik Prince, the founder of the controversial security giant, Blackwater Worldwide, although he denies any links with the company.[5]

Saracen and its offshoot, Sterling Corporate Services, allegedly sent dozens of South African mercenaries to train an anti-piracy force in the semi-autonomous region of Puntland. This was during the heyday of Somali piracy when small groups of armed men in tiny skiffs threw ladders up the sides of vast tankers, boarded them and seized the crew. The sailors and their vessels were only released once hefty ransoms were paid, often amounting to millions of dollars. UN investigators accused the company of violating the arms embargo on Somalia and documented the abuse and killing of Somali trainees. They alleged that in October 2010 a trainee was beaten, his arms and feet bound behind his back. The UN monitors said he later died from his injuries, although the firm denied this.[6] Puntland suspended its contract with the company in 2011, leaving more than 1,000 half-trained and well-armed members of the 'Puntland Maritime Police Force' to fend for themselves in a desert camp. It is unclear what happened to them, although locals speculate some joined pirate gangs, clan militias and Al Shabaab.

THE INDUSTRY

It is not just private security firms that are doing well out of conflict and instability in Somalia. Many foreign countries have troops based in the country. At its height, the African Union Mission in Somalia (AMISOM) provided paid roles for 22,000 African troops, much of this funded by the European Union (EU). Soldiers and police officers from Uganda, Burundi, Kenya, Ethiopia, Djibouti, Sierra Leone, Nigeria and Zambia have received better pay than they would at home, although in some cases their governments siphoned off a portion of their wages for 'running costs'. Former police officers from Britain make a good living training the security forces in Somaliland. The US, the EU, Turkey, the United Arab Emirates and other foreign powers have sent troops to the country to train and advise the Somali security forces, while other Somalis are sent abroad for military training. It is not unusual to see Western security 'advisers' directing Somali government troops as they battle with Al Shabaab.

British spin-doctors, paid for by UK taxpayers, have lived in Villa Somalia with the Somali president and other senior government officials, writing speeches and press briefings. Other communications experts live in shipping containers at the airport designing messages to counter Al Shabaab's enthusiastic propaganda machine. At least three British PR companies have made sizeable profits providing services for the governments of Somalia and Somaliland, and for Somali businesspeople.

Some years after Al Shabaab established itself as a dominant and enduring force, 'CVE' became the buzzword for Somalia. At first I had no idea what it meant, but quickly learned that the acronym, which flew so frequently from the tongues of foreign diplomats, analysts and aid workers, stood for 'Countering Violent Extremism'. CVE became an essential component of funding applications for projects in Somalia and other countries affected by violent Islamist extremism. The world was suddenly awash with CVE 'experts'. Critics say the money poured into CVE projects diverted funding from more meaningful, long-term development work. A former British army officer who has worked for years in the Horn of Africa said that, in some cases, the obsession with CVE was hitting the availability of funding for useful projects, such as training young people in marketable skills so that they would have some hope of finding a job instead of drifting into crime or militancy. The latest fashion was CVE and that was what donors were interested in, often engaging in nebulous information campaigns that appeared to have little or no impact on the target population.

Some in Somalia have become very adept at 'milking the development cow'. A wall surrounding an NGO compound in Hargeisa tells this story very well. One can track the current donor buzzword by reading the list of names painted on the wall, of which all but the most recent have been crossed out with a simple X. 'Combating female genital mutilation', 'Mine clearance', 'AIDS awareness charity', 'Sustainability and development NGO', 'Counter-radicalisation programme', and the latest one, 'Tackling illegal migration'. It appeared that whoever was behind these messages was obtaining foreign funding for whatever was the most fashionable development theme at any time. Unscrupulous local NGOs can profit from instability in Somalia, since, for many donors, the country is deemed too risky for them to send in experts to perform proper evaluations and audits.

Of course, there are highly qualified, committed individuals, Somali and non-Somali, who are doing exceptional work in this difficult, dangerous, complex and contradictory environment. I have met UN staff, communications consultants, psychiatrists, security personnel, water engineers and others who are using their impressive skills to make things better for Somalia and its people. Between 2015 and 2018, for instance, the UN and other agencies helped to prevent a devasting drought from becoming a famine.

* * *

THE INDUSTRY

Many of the internationals working in the 'Somalia industry' are based at Mogadishu International Airport, or 'MIA' as it is known locally. There are now two Mogadishus: the one confined inside the airport, the other sprawling outside.

On one visit in 2018, I did not set foot outside the MIA. It felt like another country. It is a vast complex that houses not just one but two airports, as the UN has its own facility, which is out of bounds for most Somalis. Kenyans deal with the tickets, security checks are performed by Ugandan AMISOM troops, and logistics are facilitated by Nepalese. Even the tea is made and sold not by Somalis but by Indians.

At the other airport, all travellers are instructed to deposit their suitcases, bags and purses in long lines on the floor. A Somali appears in a royal blue boiler suit, his face wrapped almost entirely in black cloth, his eyes hidden behind wrap-around dark glasses. He is leading a dog. He releases it and points to the line of bags and cases. The dog sniffs each one, darting back and forth. Later, a Turkish dog handler carries out the same procedure on the same bags, which this time are lined up on the tarmac directly outside the plane. All with good reason, as became clear in February 2016, when a laptop bomb exploded aboard Daallo Airlines Flight 159 to Djibouti, blowing a large, jagged hole in the side of the plane and hurling the bomber to his death below. As the aircraft had not yet reached cruising altitude and the cabin was not fully pressurised, the remaining seventy-three passengers and seven crew members survived, and the plane was able to make an emergency landing in Mogadishu. Shortly afterwards, residents of the town of Balad, 30 kilometres north of the capital, told police they had found the body of a man who had fallen from the sky. Daallo's chief executive, Mohamed Ibrahim Yassin Olad, said the laptop bomber and most of the other passengers on the flight were scheduled to take a Turkish Airlines plane that morning but it had been cancelled due to bad weather.[7] Al Shabaab later said it carried out the attack.

The zone around the airport is filled with clusters of container-built embassies, UN compounds and accommodation blocks, like some sort of giant children's toy. At the British embassy, there is a black door with a number 10 screwed to it, just like the front door of the prime minister's residence in Downing Street. The East Africans guarding the embassy work for the private security company Bancroft, which has a significant presence in Somalia. In 'The Village' restaurant, where internationals, many of whom rarely set foot outside the airport, meet their Somali visitors, the waiters and waitresses come from Kenya. Burly Nigerian AMISOM police stroll around the UN compounds, sweating profusely.

UN and other diplomatic staff, as well as their foreign advisers, spend their evenings at the *tukul*, a collection of round thatched-roof buildings with tables set out in the open air around them. A good bottle of wine costs $8 and alcohol flows aplenty. Newcomers are eyed up, with burly men in tight T-shirts telling young women about 'the ratio' in MIA, whereby males significantly outnumber females.

One of the more bizarre spots at the airport is 'Chelsea Village'. This is a complex of sand-coloured shipping containers surrounded by a thick, sand-coloured wall. The facility, which can accommodate more than 180 people, advertises itself as 'your home in the heart of the Mogadishu International Airport zone' and prides itself on 'the comfort and safety of our rooms, the quality of our catering and the peace of mind provided by our security'. It charges $175 a night.

Chelsea Village has a gym, also within a shipping container, a bunker in the event of attack and a rooftop area, complete with sun loungers laid out on artificial grass. There is a wooden 'pirate ship' for parties and a large outdoor TV screen showing football matches, ice-skating at the Winter Olympics or whatever else might take your fancy.

Each guest has his or her own individual shipping container for a hotel room. These have been 'carefully crafted by respected Croatian shipbuilders. ... We know that you'll sleep well at Chelsea Village'. Inside each container is a double bed, a very small window, a desk, a chair, a wardrobe, a satellite TV and a compact bathroom. Guests are instructed not to try to adjust the air-conditioning and the rooms are uncomfortably cold compared with the hot air outside.

The containers are arranged in a grid system, separated by avenues, each one with a metal plaque bearing the name of a London street. 'While we're not sure which "road" you'll be staying on at Chelsea Village—Oxford Street possibly or Covent Garden—one thing is for certain: your room will be of an exceptional standard.' Other 'roads' include Harley Street, Regent Street and Savile Row.

In the restaurant, cooks from Asia berate Somali cleaners for failing to take their jobs seriously. Most of the food is imported, despite the abundance of fresh meat, fruit and vegetables available in the markets just beyond the outer walls of the MIA. According to the Village's website, 'Our food is imported from one of Europe's top suppliers who supply 65% of the world's cruise line industry'.

Chelsea Village says its catering staff are used to working in difficult places. 'Our chefs are hand-picked not just for their proven ability and passion for cooking but also for their experience in extreme environments. All have served in Iraq, Afghanistan and/or across the African continent. They are used to emerging from a bunker and still getting a three-course meal with at least three options out on the service line in time for lunch or dinner!'[8]

At about ten o'clock one night in Chelsea Village, I was going to my container to sleep when I came across a Somali woman struggling to manoeuvre two large suitcases down a series of concrete steps. I stopped to help her and asked what she was up to. 'I cannot stay in this place a moment longer,' she said. 'I am a Somali woman and I need fresh air to sleep. That small window in the metal container does not open, and the air-conditioning is freezing. I cannot use that tiny bathroom because I am a good Muslim woman and it is not sharia-compliant.' I asked her where she was planning to go at this late hour. 'I will go into the city and find a hotel.' I suggested she wait until morning, as it would be unwise to move around Mogadishu at this time. 'I am a Somali and I will manage,' she said, before disappearing into the black night.

Al Shabaab knows about Chelsea Village and other similar facilities in MIA. 'That place and others like it, they are there to make money for foreigners, pure and simple. The whole of the airport zone has become a foreign business. It is proof of the true purpose of the UN and other apostate organisations. They are not in Somalia to help Somalis. They are here to help themselves with their fat "danger money" wage packets and their sinful, obsessive consumption of alcohol in our Muslim land. The whole complex based in the MIA is about making money for foreigners while, outside the barricades, in the real Somalia, people are dying of hunger.'

Controversy has surrounded some of the companies which, like Chelsea Village, provide accommodation at MIA. One is Bancroft Global Development (BGD), which provides many services in Somalia, including overseeing mobile clinics and mentoring AMISOM personnel. Its airport accommodation site is called 'Mogadishu International Campus'. The company says it has also made 'entrepreneurial investments' in Somalia, making it 'one of the country's largest real estate investors and developers'.[9]

In 2013, the UN conducted a risk review of BGD as it planned to increase the number of its staff staying in Bancroft accommodation from a handful to more than fifty. The review concluded that there was a 'high level' of reputational risk to the UN if it entered into an accommodation facility contract with Bancroft.[10] It gave three main reasons for its findings. The first related to concerns about the ownership of the land Bancroft was building on. While not referring to BGD directly, the review noted that 'in many cases land has been developed without the consent of its owners'. More disturbingly, the UN said it had received anecdotal information that BGD 'has been using its medical facilities, "clinics", throughout Mogadishu for the purpose of gathering intelligence. When individuals seek medical assistance they are asked to provide information on the whereabouts of Al Shabaab and of militant activities.'[11] Thirdly, the UN expressed 'concern over the military activities that were being staged from the Bancroft facility'. Bancroft has stated that its personnel act as mentors, that they are officially assigned to troop-contributing countries and that they do not take a direct part in hostilities. The company says that, in most cases, Bancroft personnel do not carry weapons.

An earlier UN risk report, of July 2010, stated that there were indications that BGD was 'also supporting general operational activities with AMISOM against Al-Shabaab/insurgent entities'. It concluded that BGD posed a 'potential reputational risk to the United Nations in Somalia' and that it was 'certainly possible that BGD is undertaking operational activities against Al-Shabaab/insurgent activities while working in partnership with United Nations entities'. The report stated that the overall level of risk was perceived as 'HIGH'.[12]

It is not just well-placed Somali politicians and businesspeople, international relief organisations, conflict experts and foreign security companies who do well out of the situation. Exploiting the existence of Al Shabaab for personal gain also occurs on a very local level, deep inside Somali territory.

Mohamed is twenty years old, comes from a minority clan, and lives in a village in central Somalia.

'I know people who were threatened by members of the government security forces who said, "Either you let me marry your daughter or I will tell the authorities that you are members of Al Shabaab". Also, I noticed in my area that all the koranic teachers were disappearing. Government soldiers make money out of them because they have long beards. They say they will present the bearded teachers to the Americans as terrorists and get a reward. I heard about one koranic teacher whose clan paid the soldiers hundreds of dollars to let him go. But I have heard of others who were handed over to the government or even to neighbouring countries. If you are a minority-clan member and you have a big beard you are good business for government troops.'

A senior Ethiopian security official, who spends most of his time working in Somalia, told me that the Somali intelligence agency, NISA, 'has become a supermarket for intelligence' whereby intelligence operatives will sell information to people, including Al Shabaab, if they pay the right money. If this is the case, it is not surprising that Al Shabaab has such accurate information about who is in a hotel or other building and when they are there, and is therefore able to conduct such ruthlessly accurate strikes on its high-value targets. The Ethiopian official, who is ethnically Somali, said that some businesspeople and politicians have paid Al Shabaab to kill their rivals in hotels, restaurants and other locations. These incidents bear all the hallmarks of an Al Shabaab attack but the motivation for killing has nothing to do with the Islamists' ideology. Once again, there are blurred lines, this time between Al Shabaab, members of the business community and Somali politicians.

Some people have used the situation to trick foreign powers into killing their enemies by pretending they are members of Al Shabaab. In September 2016, for example, officials in Galmudug region accused the authorities in neighbouring Puntland of duping the US military into believing members of its regional security forces belonged to Al Shabaab. The US conducted a drone strike in which Galmudug said seventeen members of its forces were killed. Initial reports that they were members of Al Shabaab were denied by the Islamists who said they had no fighters in the area. Although the US initially refused to give further details,[13] it later issued a draft statement, seen by the Reuters news agency, saying, 'the armed fighters were initially believed to be al-Shabaab but with further review it was determined they were local militia forces'.[14] The US said ten members of Galmudug's regional force were killed in the drone strike and three others wounded.

Neighbouring countries have also benefited from the war in Somalia, although, of course, they have also suffered from the overflow of insecurity, Al Shabaab attacks and huge influxes of refugees. Perhaps the most brazen example is the story involving Kenya, charcoal, sugar and Al Shabaab.

Despite Al Shabaab killing hundreds of people on Kenyan soil, damaging the essential tourist trade and recruiting many locals to fight on its behalf, Kenyan troops have been accused of collaborating with the Islamists for personal gain. Troops based in Somalia, who are supposed to be fighting Al Shabaab and creating a buffer zone to prevent them from entering Kenya, have ended up colluding with the group, all in the search for money.

The Kenyan campaign group Journalists for Justice conducted a study, *Black and White: Kenya's Criminal Racket in Somalia*, which exposed the extent of profiteering by Kenyan forces in Somalia. It found that Kenyan troops in and around the port city of Kismayo had not only taken over the lucrative charcoal-exporting business from Al Shabaab, but were also actively working together with their supposed enemy in the sugar-smuggling business.

According to the report, since September 2012, when the Kenyan Defence Forces (KDF) pushed Al Shabaab out of

Kismayo, 'control of the port is the central activity in which KDF troops are engaged and illegal export of charcoal has continued in significant volumes in flagrant violation of the UN Security Council's ban on the trade which contributes directly to the financing of al-Shabaab.' Somali charcoal is highly prized in the Gulf, where it is used to burn incense and in shisha pipes, a national pastime in some countries. As well as providing tens of millions of dollars a year to Al Shabaab, the charcoal trade has led to environmental devastation in Somalia, where trees are recklessly cut down and burned to produce the lucrative export.

When the Kenyan troops took over Kismayo, they inherited a stockpile of about 1 million sacks of charcoal. Requests from the UN and the federal government of Somalia not to export the charcoal were ignored. According to the Journalists for Justice report, both the Kenyan forces and the regional authorities in southern Somalia earned significant profits from the illegal trade.

The report accused the Kenyan military of imposing a $2 levy on every bag of charcoal exported from Kismayo and every sack of sugar imported through the port. 'A conflict economy has emerged around the cross-border trade where, conversely, insecurity is good for business.' The study found that as much as $250,000 a week is made from sugar imports to Kismayo, amounting to some $13 million a year, with the total value of the sugar trade between $200 and $400 million. Port workers told researchers that about 230 trucks, each carrying 14 tonnes of sugar, leave Kismayo every week, a total of more than 3,000 tonnes. Al Shabaab taxes each truck $1,025 for safely crossing its territory into Kenya, giving the driver a stamped receipt that allows him to pass safely through areas under Islamist control. The report said Al Shabaab makes more than $12 million a year for allowing sugar to pass through its territory. As the report concludes: 'No wonder the KDF [Kenya Defence Forces] and Jubaland authorities do not want to cut off al-Shabaab's revenue streams—if they did, they would be cutting off their own.'[15]

THE INDUSTRY

With so many groups and individuals profiting so handsomely from Al Shabaab, it will be difficult to reach a stage where even the possibility of ending the conflict emerges. Too many people have too much to gain from the status quo. It is unfortunate, and unfair, that those losing the most are Somalia's farmers, nomads, office workers and small businesspeople. The Somali elites, many of whom have foreign passports and can leave the country at the slightest whiff of danger, often profit from the insurgency, as do many of the foreigners based in the country or living abroad and working as experts on Somalia, security and/or violent extremism.

CONCLUSION

Over nearly thirty years reporting on and from Somalia, I have seen the very best and worst of humanity. I have seen what happens to people in the near total absence of a functioning central authority and where the possibility of violence lurks around every corner.

I have seen what happens to people who have been born and brought up in conflict; who have no idea what peace looks, smells or sounds like. For decades, Somalis have had to live with the stark and ever-present risk of a premature, violent death.

Maybe the reason why Somalis are such brilliant entrepreneurs is that their environment forces them to spot and seize opportunities, think on their feet, act fast and take risks. Through creative ingenuity and a refusal to take no for an answer, they have ensured that water is delivered and electricity keeps running in shell-shattered parts of town; and that money from abroad reaches the poorest people in the most far-off villages and nomad camps—even in areas severely affected by long years of conflict and violence.

Al Shabaab has taken hold in Somalia and endured because it has helped fill giant gaps in security, governance, justice, education and employment. In some areas of life if has offered the best choice available. That is why Somalis who hate everything the group stands for still travel outside their home areas to use its courts. It is why Somalis, even some who live in Kenya, have sent their families to live in areas controlled by Al Shabaab. And it is why some people who seek revenge decide to join its ranks of fighters.

The movement provides services for Somalis. Some, like the use of its courts, are voluntary. Others, such as income redistribution through *zakat*, are obligatory, even in cities, towns and other areas ostensibly controlled by the government and the African Union (AMISOM). However violent, cruel and ideologically inflexible it may be, Al Shabaab has a degree of legitimacy whereas most state institutions do not, because they are ineffective, corrupt, powerless or non-existent. Politicians, policymakers and analysts should be brave enough to admit that, in some areas of life, Al Shabaab offers models that work for Somalia and Somalis, and to appreciate and learn from them.

Al Shabaab is everywhere in Somalia, and it is rarely clear who its members are at any particular time. This reduces trust, which is the very cornerstone of Somali society. Somalis have a powerful oral culture built up over centuries around a complex clan system; to this day it functions almost entirely on trust, and to have this shattered is traumatic for the whole society.

For hundreds of thousands, if not millions, of Somalis, living with Al Shabaab is not a matter of choice. They happen to reside in areas it controls. Some are too poor to leave, while some are prevented from doing so. Others do not see much point in going because the alternative is a tent city in a Somali town or neighbouring country. Others still are born and brought up under its rule, and have never known another way of thinking or behaving.

As this book has shown, those living in so-called government- or AMISOM-controlled areas cannot escape Al Shabaab. Even Somalis who have fled abroad have been directly threatened by the Islamists or have had relatives at home killed or intimidated as a way of punishing them indirectly.

CONCLUSION

Those trying to fight Al Shabaab militarily or by other means face huge challenges. Members of the Somali government and security forces are prime targets for the Islamists. Many, including those who have chosen to leave safe and comfortable lives abroad to work in Somali administrations, have lost their lives. It is not surprising that my Somali friends in the diaspora are worried when their mothers, sisters, uncles and cousins become government ministers or MPs back home, or decide to go to Somalia to start a business or other venture.

How can the Somali government build functioning institutions and offer attractive health, educational and other services when its members risk their lives every time they leave their compounds? Indeed, they are even at risk inside their compounds; on several occasions, Al Shabaab has penetrated Villa Somalia, ministries and other government institutions.

There is a confusion of forces fighting Al Shabaab—local, regional and international. There are militias, regional troops and a national army. There are the AMISOM troops, Ethiopian soldiers, Western special forces and advisers, Turkish and Emirati trainers, private security companies, and US drones and missiles. What the country needs above all is a strong, well-trained and properly resourced army; and a police force that can earn the trust of the people. But there is no sign whatsoever of this becoming a reality anytime soon.

There are other battles going on in Somalia over land and clan issues. There are personal vendettas, business rivalries and political disputes. There is conflict between the regional states, and between the regional states and the federal government. Some are solved using brute force, others by traditional dispute-resolution systems that have existed for centuries. Functioning examples can be taken from the more stable Somali territories, like Somaliland and Puntland—and small pockets of stability in South Central Somalia—to try to build a system that works for the whole country.

Al Shabaab can take advantage of all of this; it has focus, it is determined and it is a fluid, nimble organisation. Of course it has its own internal problems, including ideological divisions, leadership crises and periodic manpower shortages. But it is yet to crumble or implode. A defectors' programme has had some success in wooing senior, mid-level and low-ranking militants, and a number of leaders have been killed in air strikes. But the movement survives. Perhaps one day Al Shabaab will come to the end of its natural life. Perhaps, as has happened with other groups in Somalia, it will split into so many factions that it disappears. But its longevity and ability to adapt swiftly to changing challenges and threats suggest that, in one form or another, it will be around for years to come.

There has been talk of negotiating with Al Shabaab and coming to some kind of agreement to end the insurgency. Al Shabaab insists it will not speak to the 'apostate' Somali government even though in reality there are no closed doors in Somalia. Conversations take place all the time between Al Shabaab and other Somalis, some connected with the government. The weight of history dictates that most wars end with peace deals. Although Somali political agreements are usually years in the making, there is at least a chance that some kind of accommodation will be made between the federal and regional authorities on one side, and Al Shabaab on the other. The ongoing problems with Somalia's regional states are likely to delay even the chance of any kind of sensible, joined-up approach to possible peace talks, as the country is fragmented, and continues to fracture, along so many other fault lines. Some would argue that the refusal to allow the former deputy leader of Al Shabaab, Mukhtar Robow, to run for the presidency of the South West region was a missed opportunity, as it represented a real chance of bringing some of the militants into the fold.

It is nearly impossible to keep secrets in Somalia. Everybody knows everybody else's business. Information flows are key to staying alive. Many people are willing to talk about how their nephew, cousin or uncle has joined Al Shabaab. It is, in all likelihood, these very channels of communication that offer the best chance for proper peace talks to start, especially because mutual trust is such an essential part of any meaningful negotiations.

Many Somalis who have worked at the very heart of the intelligence services and have a deep understanding and knowledge of Al Shabaab agree that the only solution is to negotiate with the Islamists, although on a selective basis. As one former senior security official said: 'Those who understand the grey side of Somali politics are on my side. We have to talk to Al Shabaab. All three of Somalia's most recent presidents, Sheikh Sharif Sheikh Ahmed, Hassan Sheikh Mohamud and Mohamed Abdullahi Mohamed Farmajo, agree in private that dialogue is the way forward, even if they do not speak about this openly. But many members of the diaspora, inexperienced local politicians and members of the security services see the group in black-and-white terms. They believe we should never, ever speak to Al Shabaab. They are completely wrong. We will be stuck in this situation forever if we choose to follow their advice.'

There have been times when Al Shabaab conducts such unspeakable acts of violence that public disgust and anger reach a high point. This occurred when a Danish Somali suicide bomber blew up medical graduates in the Shamo hotel in 2009; when dozens of Somali students were killed in 2011 as they queued up to find out if they had won scholarships to study in Turkey; and when hundreds were killed by an enormous truck bomb in 2017. All of these incidents occurred in Mogadishu. But the rage eventually gives way to resigned sadness, and disappointment with the government and its allies for their failure to end the violence.

One of the most serious challenges is that many people, Somali and non-Somali, are benefiting from the status quo.

There are lucrative contracts for foreign consultants and private security companies, hundreds of United Nations jobs with extra hardship pay, and opportunities for Somali businesspeople and politicians to make deals without regulation or oversight.

Until the situation tips, and enough powerful people discover that they will gain more from peace than war, it will be very difficult to fundamentally change the situation in Somalia. In the meantime, it is likely that Al Shabaab will remain active, continuing to provide useful services while destroying lives, spreading its tentacles further into East and Southern Africa, and moulding children's minds.

NOTES

INTRODUCTION

1. Maruf, Harun and Dan Joseph, *Inside Al-Shabaab: The Secret History of Al-Qaeda's Most Powerful Ally*, Bloomington: Indiana University Press, 2018, pp. 43–4.
2. Arman, Abukar, 'The Making of Another Iraq', Foreign Policy in Focus, 3 January 2007.
3. Bruton, Bronwyn and Paul Williams, 'Counterinsurgency in Somalia: Lessons Learned from the African Union Mission in Somalia, 2007–2013', Joint Special Operations University, September 2014; Maruf and Joseph, *Inside Al-Shabaab*, p. 136.
4. Fragile States Index (formerly Failed States Index), The Fund for Peace, http://fundforpeace.org/fsi/data/, last accessed 6 February 2019. Somalia topped the list for six years in a row from 2008 to 2013, and then came second after South Sudan from 2014 to 2018, except in 2016 when it came first on the list.
5. Sperber, Amanda, *New Internationalist*, 'The legacy of Mogadishu', 8 January 2019, https://newint.org/features/2018/12/17/somalia-shock-waves, last accessed 6 February 2019. Reuters, 'Death toll from Somalia truck bomb in October now at 512: probe committee', 30 November 2017, https://www.reuters.com/article/us-somalia-blast-toll/death-toll-from-somalia-truck-bomb-in-october-now-at-512-probe-committee-idUSKBN1DU2IC, last accessed 6 February 2019. UN officials have told me they believe more than 600 people were killed in the explosion. Thank you to Peggy Longlens for her advice.

6. Journalists for Justice, 'Black and White: Kenya's Criminal Racket in Somalia', November 2015.

7. Maruf and Joseph, *Inside Al-Shabaab*, p. 29.

1. WHO AM I?

1. Interview with Sheikh Ali Dheere, Dalsoor TV, January 2017.

2. Al Arabiya TV, 21 June 2007.

3. 'Somali Ex-Militant Leader Runs For Political Office', Voice of America, 4 October 2018, https://www.voanews.com/a/somalia-ex-militant-leader-runs-political-office/4600091.html, last accessed 6 February 2019.

4. Hiraal Institute, 'Evolution of Al-Shabab', 3 April 2018.

5. Maruf, Harun and Dan Joseph, *Inside Al-Shabaab: The Secret History of Al-Qaeda's Most Powerful Ally*, Bloomington: Indiana University Press, 2018, p. 83.

6. Testimony of Ken Menkhaus, Hearing before the Committee on Homeland Security and Governmental Affairs, United States Senate, 11 March 2009, https://www.hsgac.senate.gov/imo/media/doc/031109 Menkhaus031109.pdf, last accessed 6 February 2019.

7. African Union Mission in Somalia (AMISOM), Strategic Concept of Operations, 'Draft Concept of Operations 2018–2021 baseline document', November 2018. Horseed Media, 'Somalia Parliament Debates on Employment of Foreign Workers', 13 August 2015, https://horseedmedia.net/2015/08/31/somalia-parliament-debates-on-employment-of-foreign-workers/, last accessed 6 February 2019.

8. Marchal, Rowland, 'The Rise of a Jihadi Movement in a Country at War: Harakat al-Shabaab al Mujaheddin in Somalia', Centre de Recherches Internationales, Sciences Po, 2011.

9. Hansen, Stig J., *Al-Shabaab in Somalia: The History and Ideology of a Militant Islamist Group*, London: Hurst, 2013, p. 58.

10. United Nations Monitoring Group on Somalia and Eritrea (UNSEMG), 'Somalia Report of the Monitoring Group on Somalia and Eritrea', 31 October 2016.

11. Marchal, 'The Rise of a Jihadi Movement in a Country at War'.

12. Hansen, Stig J. and Linnea Gelot, 'Anatomy of Counter-Jihad,

Community Perspectives on Rehabilitation and Reconciliation', Report for the United Nations Special Representative for Somalia, 2017.

13. Bruton, Bronwyn and Paul Williams, 'Counterinsurgency in Somalia: Lessons Learned from the African Union Mission in Somalia, 2007–2013', Joint Special Operations University, September 2014.

14. Human Rights Watch, 'Somalia: Al-Shabaab Demanding Children', 14 January 2018. United Nations Assistance Mission in Somalia, 'Countering Al-Shabaab Propaganda and Recruitment Mechanisms in South Central Somalia', 14 August 2017.

15. Human Rights Watch, 'Somalia: Al-Shabaab Demanding Children', 14 January 2018.

16. UNSEMG, 'Somalia Report of the Monitoring Group on Somalia and Eritrea', 31 October 2016.

17. Ibid.

18. Maruf and Joseph, *Inside Al-Shabaab*, p. 25. 'Key facts on hunted Al-Qaeda militants in Somalia', Reuters, 1 May 2008, https://www.reuters.com/article/us-somalia-conflict-militants-idUSWAL1240 2320080501, last accessed 6 February 2019. Federal Bureau of Investigation Most Wanted Terrorists list, https://www.fbi.gov/wanted/wanted_terrorists.

19. Osama bin Laden, 'Fight on, Champions of Somalia', 19 March 2009, https://archive.org/details/Fight-On-Champions-Of-Somalia, last accessed 6 February 2019.

20. Hansen, *Al-Shabaab in Somalia*, pp. 134–5.

21. Bacon, Tricia and Daisy Muibu, 'Foreign Fighter Influence in Al-Shabaab: Limitations and Future Prospects' in Michael Keating and Matt Waldman (eds) *War and Peace in Somalia*, London: Hurst, 2018.

22. Ibid.

23. Ibid.

24. Institute for Strategic Studies, 'Is another Boko Haram or al-Shabaab erupting in Mozambique?', 14 June 2018.

25. Central Intelligence Agency World Factbook, https://www.cia.gov/library/publications/the-world-factbook/geos/ke.html, last accessed 6 February 2019.

26. Hansen, *Al-Shabaab in Somalia*, p. 126.

27. Ibid.

28. UN Office of the High Commissioner for Refugees (UNHCR), 'Somalia Situation 2017'.

29. Food and Agriculture Organization of the United Nations, Food Security and Nutrition Analysis Unit—Somalia, 'Family Ties: Remittances and Livelihoods Support in Puntland and Somaliland', June 2013.

30. Osman, Idil, *Media, Diaspora and the Somali Diaspora*, London: Palgrave Macmillan, 2017.

31. Committee to Protect Journalists.

32. *The Guardian*, 'Somali journalists are dying from corruption as much as conflict', October 2012, https://www.theguardian.com/comment-isfree/2012/oct/11/somali-journalists-dying-corruption-conflict, last accessed 6 February 2019.

33. Meservey, Joshua, 'Travelling for an Idea: The Appeal of Al-Shabaab to Diaspora in the West' in Michael Keating and Matt Waldman (eds) *War and Peace in Somalia*, London: Hurst, 2018.

34. Ibid.

35. Ibid.

36. Ibid.

37. Testimony of Ken Menkhaus, Hearing before the Committee on Homeland Security and Governmental Affairs, United States Senate, 11 March 2009, https://www.hsgac.senate.gov/imo/media/doc/0311 09Menkhaus031109.pdf, last accessed 6 February 2019.

38. United Kingdom: Upper Tribunal (Immigration and Asylum Chamber), 'MOJ & Ors (Return to Mogadishu) Somalia CG v. Secretary of State for the Home Department', [2014] UKUT 00442 (IAC), 3 October 2014, https://www.refworld.org/cases,GBR_UTIAC,543438014.html, last accessed 6 February 2019.

39. The Heritage Institute for Policy Studies, 'Durable Solutions for Somali Refugees', December 2017.

40. Miami Law Clinic, https://media.law.miami.edu/clinics/pdf/complaint-immigration-clinic.pdf, last accessed 6 February 2019.

41. World Health Organization, 'A Situation Analysis of Mental Health in Somalia', October 2010.

2. WOMEN AND CHILDREN

1. Life and Peace Institute, Peace Direct, Somali Women Solidarity Organisation, 'Women, Conflict and Peace: Learning from Kismayo', April 2018.

2. BBC Somali Service radio interview with Abdullahi Noor Hassan, October 2016.

3. 'Khadija' and Stephen Harley, 'Women in Al Shabaab' in Michael Keating and Matt Waldman (eds) *War and Peace in Somalia*, London: Hurst, 2018.

4. Human Rights Watch, 'No Place for Children: Child Recruitment, Forced Marriage and Attacks on Schools in Somalia', February 2012.

5. Human Rights Watch, '"The Power These Men Have Over US": Sexual Exploitation and Abuse by African Union Forces in Somalia', September 2014.

6. BBC, 'Somali woman who alleged rape given jail term', 5 February 2013, https://www.bbc.com/news/world-africa-21336599, last accessed 6 February 2019.

7. Hiraal Institute, 'The Fighters' Factory: Inside Al-Shabab's Education System', May 2018.

8. United Nations, 'Report of the Secretary-General on children and armed conflict in Somalia', December 2016.

9. United Nations Monitoring Group on Somalia and Eritrea (UNSEMG), 'Somalia Report of the Monitoring Group on Somalia and Eritrea', 31 October 2016.

10. Human Rights Watch, 'Somalia: Al-Shabaab Demanding Children: Residents Threated to Hand Over Boys, Girls', January 2018.

11. Hiraal Institute, 'The Fighters' Factory: Inside Al-Shabab's Education System', May 2018.

12. UNSEMG, 'Somalia report of the Monitoring Group on Somalia and Eritrea', 31 October 2016.

13. Ibid.

3. MODUS OPERANDI

1. UN Office of the High Commissioner for Refugees (UNHCR) and UN Assistance Mission in Somalia (UNSOM), 'Protection of Civilians:

Building the Foundation for Peace, Security and Human Rights in Somalia', December 2017.

2. Hiraal Institute, Security Incidents Analysis, July to September 2018.

3. Maruf, Harun and Dan Joseph, *Inside Al-Shabaab: The Secret History of Al-Qaeda's Most Powerful Ally*, Bloomington: Indiana University Press, 2018, p. 136.

4. BBC, 'Kenya attack: nine arrests over bloody DusitD2 hotel siege', 17 January 2019, https://www.bbc.co.uk/news/world-africa-46902564, last accessed 6 February 2019.

5. Muibu, Daisy and Benjamin P. Nickels, 'Foreign Technology or Local Expertise? Al-Shabaab's IED Capability', *CTC Sentinel*, vol. 10, issue 10 (November 2017).

6. African Union Mission in Somalia (AMISOM), Strategic Concept of Operations, 'Draft Concept of Operations 2018–2021 baseline document', November 2018.

7. Muibu and Nickels, 'Foreign Technology or Local Expertise'.

8. Interview with Sheikh Ali Dheere, Dalsoor TV, January 2017.

9. Marchal, Roland, 'Rivals in Governance—Civil Activities of Al Shabaab', Portfolio of Expert Briefing Papers on Peace and Reconciliation in Somalia, January 2018.

10. Transparency International, Corruption Perceptions Index, https://www.transparency.org/research/cpi/overview, last accessed 6 February 2019.

11. Bruton, Bronwyn and Paul Williams, 'Counterinsurgency in Somalia: Lessons Learned from the African Union Mission in Somalia, 2007–2013', Joint Special Operations University, September 2014.

12. Hansen, Stig J., *Al-Shabaab in Somalia: The History and Ideology of a Militant Islamist Group*, London: Hurst, 2013, p. 84.

13. Ali, Hussein Y., 'Youth Radicalisation: Causes, Consequences and Potential Solutions' in Michael Keating and Matt Waldman (eds) *War and Peace in Somalia*, London: Hurst, 2018.

14. Marchal, 'Rivals in Governance—Civil Activities of Al Shabaab'.

15. Ali, 'Youth Radicalisation'.

16. Maruf and Joseph, *Inside Al-Shabaab*, p. 87.

17. Hansen, *Al-Shabaab in Somalia*, p. 85.

18. Ibid., p. 115.
19. The New Arab, 'UAE still supports al-Shabaab through Somalia's illicit charcoal trade', 5 March 2018, https://www.alaraby.co.uk/english/comment/2018/3/5/uae-still-supports-al-shabaab-through-somalias-illicit-charcoal-trade, last accessed 6 February 2019; United Nations Monitoring Group on Somalia and Eritrea (UNSEMG).
20. Hiraal Institute, 'The AS Finance System', July 2018.
21. UNSEMG, October 2018.
22. Journalists for Justice, 'Black and White: Kenya's Criminal Racket in Somalia,' November 2015.
23. UNSEMG, 'Somalia Report of the Monitoring Group on Somalia and Eritrea', 31 October 2016.
24. Hansen, *Al-Shabaab in Somalia*, p. 114.
25. Radio Dalsan, 'Al Shabaab Claims To Have Carried Out A Zakakat Distribution Near Mogadishu', 7 October 2018, https://www.radio-dalsan.com/en/2018/10/07/al-shabaab-claims-to-have-carried-out-a-zakakat-distribution-exercise-near-mogadishu/, last accessed 6 February 2019.
26. Hiraal Institute, 'The AS Finance System', July 2018.
27. UNSEMG, 'Somalia Report of the Monitoring Group on Somalia and Eritrea', 31 October 2016; BBC World Service radio report, 'Locals Fight Al Shabaab', 1 October 2018.
28. Fox News, 'Somali Extremist Group Bans Samosas in Country', 26 July 2011, http://www.foxnews.com/world/2011/07/26/somali-extremist-group-bans-samosas-in-country.html, last accessed 6 February 2019.
29. Reuters, 'Somali Islamists whip women for wearing bras', 16 October 2009, https://www.reuters.com/article/oukoe-uk-somalia-conflict-bras-idAFTRE59F1K420091016, last accessed 6 February 2019.
30. BBC, 'Somalia's al-Shabaab bans "Christian" church bells', 15 April 2010, http://news.bbc.co.uk/1/hi/world/africa/8623240.stm, last accessed 6 February 2019.
31. Al Jazeera, 'Al Shabaab's "halal" football a different game', 31 July 2014, https://www.aljazeera.com/blogs/africa/2014/06/99086.html, last accessed 6 February 2019.
32. Besteman, Catherine and Daniel Van Lehman, 'Somalia's Southern

War: The Fight Over Land and Labour' in Michael Keating and Matt Waldman (eds) *War and Peace in Somalia*, London: Hurst, 2018.

33. Ibid.

34. Ibid.

35. Hiraal Institute, 'Taming the Clans: Al Shabaab's Clan Politics', June 2018.

36. The Global Strategy Network and Hiraal Institute, 'The Islamic State in East Africa', 31 July 2018.

37. African Union Mission in Somalia (AMISOM), Strategic Concept of Operations, 'Draft Concept of Operations 2018–2021 baseline document', November 2018.

38. The Global Strategy Network and Hiraal Institute, 'The Islamic State in East Africa', 31 July 2018.

39. Ibid.

40. Hiraal Institute, Security Incidents Analysis, July to September 2018.

4. RESISTANCE

1. *New York Times*, 'Trump Team's Queries About Africa Point to Skepticism About Aid', https://www.nytimes.com/2017/01/13/world/africa/africa-donald-trump.html, last accessed 6 February 2019.

2. Hiraal Institute, 'Evolution of Al-Shabab', 3 April 2018.

3. African Union Mission in Somalia (AMISOM), Strategic Concept of Operations, 'Draft Concept of Operations 2018–2021 baseline document', November 2018.

4. Foundation for Defense of Democracies, The Long War Journal, https://www.longwarjournal.org/archives/2018/06/shabaab-northern.php, last accessed 6 February 2019.

5. Muibu, Daisy and Benjamin P. Nickels, 'Foreign Technology or Local Expertise? Al-Shabaab's IED Capability', *CTC Sentinel*, vol. 10, issue 10 (November 2017).

6. Hiraal Institute, Security Incidents Analysis, July to September 2018.

7. Williams, Paul, 'Joining AMISOM: Why six African states contributed troops to the African Union Mission in Somalia', *Journal of Eastern African Studies*, vol. 12, no. 1, (2018), pp. 172–92.

8. Williams, Paul D., *Fighting for Peace in Somalia: A History and Analysis of the African Union Mission (AMISOM), 2007–2017*, Oxford: Oxford University Press, 2018.

9. AMISOM website, http://amisom-au.org, last accessed 6 February 2019.

10. Williams, Paul, 'To Withdraw or Not to Withdraw? Reflections on Kenya's military operations in Somalia', The Elephant, 18 January 2018, https://www.theelephant.info/features/2018/01/18/to-withdraw-or-not-to-withdraw-reflections-on-kenyas-military-operations-in-somalia/, last accessed 6 February 2019.

11. Human Rights Watch, '"The Power These Men Have Over US": Sexual Exploitation and Abuse by African Union Forces in Somalia', September 2014.

12. BBC, 'African Union troops in Somalia arrested for selling military supplies', 6 June 2016, https://www.bbc.co.uk/news/world-africa-36459005, last accessed 6 February 2019.

13. United Nations Monitoring Group on Somalia and Eritrea (UNSEMG), 'Somalia Report of the Monitoring Group on Somalia and Eritrea', October 2014.

14. Williams, Paul, 'UN Support to Regional Peace Operations: Lessons from UNSOA', International Peace Institute, February 2017.

15. AMISOM, 'AMISOM develops document to guide transition and exit plan', 4 November 2018.

16. *New York Times*, 'Somalia Doesn't Need Tears: Help Us Fight Terrorism', 26 October 2017, https://www.nytimes.com/2017/10/26/opinion/somalia-united-states-terrorism.html, last accessed 6 February 2019.

17. Hiraal Institute, 'Evolution of Al-Shabab', 3 April 2018.

18. Al Jazeera, 'Somali MPs elect new president', 31 January 2009, https://www.aljazeera.com/news/africa/2009/01/2009130215552814717.html, last accessed 6 February 2019.

19. *Foreign Policy*, 'The Tears of Somalia', 10 October 2011, https://foreignpolicy.com/2011/10/10/the-tears-of-somalia/, last accessed 6 February 2019.

20. The Heritage Institute for Policy Studies, 'Turkey's Assistance Model in Somalia: Achieving Much with Little', February 2016.

21. Ethiopia Government Portal, http://www.ethiopia.gov.et/somali-regional-state last accessed 6 February 2019.

22. Sheik-Abdi, Abdi, *Divine Madness*, London: Zed Books, 1993.

23. International Crisis Group, 'Al-Shabaab Five Years after Westgate: Still a Menace in East Africa', 21 September 2018.

24. Rawlence, Ben, *City of Thorns: Nine Lives in the World's Largest Refugee Camp*, London: Portobello, 2016.

25. Saferworld, 'Inside Kenya's war on terror: breaking the cycle of violence in Garissa', July 2017.

26. Ibid.

27. Ibid.

28. International Crisis Group, 'Al-Shabaab Five Years after Westgate: Still a Menace in East Africa', 21 September 2018.

29. Ibid.

30. Ibid.

31. BBC, 'Aleppo dentist brings "Hollywood smiles" to Somalis after fleeing Syria', 8 January 2017, https://www.bbc.com/news/world-africa-38449941, last accessed 6 February 2019.

32. *The Guardian*, 'We should talk to al-Shabaab now—we owe it to the Mogadishu bomb victims', 14 October 2018, https://www.theguardian.com/commentisfree/2018/oct/14/al-shabaab-mogadishu-bomb-anniversary-somalia, last accessed 6 February 2019.

5. THE PROPAGANDA WAR

1. See, for example, SomaliMemo.

2. Menkhaus, Ken, 'Al Shabaab and Social Media: A Double-Edged Sword', *The Brown Journal of World Affairs*, vol. 20, issue 11 (Spring/Summer 2014).

3. Chonka, Peter, 'New Media, Performative Violence, and State Reconstruction in Mogadishu', *African Affairs*, vol. 117, issue 468 (2018), p. 404.

4. Williams, Paul, 'Strategic Communications for Peace Operations: The African Union's Information War Against al-Shabaab', *Stability*, vol. 7, issue 1 (2018), p. 3.

5. United States Agency for International Development (USAID), 'Somali Perceptions Survey', February 2017.

6. Committee to Protect Journalists, Global Impunity Index, https://cpj. org/reports/2018/10/impunity-index-getting-away-with-murder-killed-justice.php, last accessed 6 February 2019.
7. Osman, Idil, *Media, Diaspora and the Somali Diaspora*, London: Palgrave Macmillan, 2017.
8. *The Guardian*, 'Somali journalists are dying from corruption as much as conflict', https://www.theguardian.com/commentisfree/2012/oct/11/ somali-journalists-dying-corruption-conflict, last accessed 6 February 2019.

6. THE INDUSTRY

1. De Waal, Alex, *The Real Politics of the Horn of Africa: Money, War and the Business of Power*, Cambridge: Polity, 2015, p. 118.
2. Menkhaus, Ken, 'Non-State Security Providers and Political Formation in Somalia', Centre for Security Governance, April 2016.
3. Saferworld, 'Mogadishu rising? Conflict and governance dynamics in the Somali capital', August 2012.
4. Menkhaus, 'Non-State Security Providers and Political Formation in Somalia'.
5. *New York Times*, 'Blackwater Founder Said to Back Mercenaries', 21 January 2011, https://www.nytimes.com/2011/01/21/world/africa/ 21intel.html, last accessed 6 February 2019.
6. United Nations Monitoring Group on Somalia and Eritrea (UNSEMG), 'Somalia Report of the Monitoring Group on Somalia and Eritrea', 31 October 2016.
7. Reuters, 'Somalia plane bomber was meant to board Turkish flight: airline executive', 8 February 2016, https://www.reuters.com/article/ us-somalia-blast-turkish-airlines/somalia-plane-bomber-was-meant-to-board-turkish-flight-airline-executive-idUSKCN0VH0QA, last accessed 6 February 2019.
8. Chelsea Village website, http://thechelseavillage.com, last accessed 6 February 2019.
9. Bancroft Global website, http://www.bancroftglobal.org/about-bancroft-global/project-profile-somalia/, last accessed 6 February 2019.
10. United Nations Risk Review, Bancroft Global Development, 18 April 2013.

11. Ibid.
12. United Nations Preliminary Risk Report, Bancroft Global Development, July 2010.
13. Communications by phone and email with US military.
14. Reuters, 'U.S. airstrike in Somalia killed local militia, not al-Shabaab', https://www.reuters.com/article/us-usa-somalia-idUSKBN13526O, last accessed 6 February 2019.
15. Journalists for Justice, 'Black and White: Kenya's Criminal Racket in Somalia,' November 2015.